THE NEW
CONTEXT FOR
MINISTRY

The New Context for Ministry

The Impact of the New Economy
on Your Church

Lyle E. Schaller

Nashville
Abingdon Press

THE NEW CONTEXT FOR MINISTRY: THE IMPACT OF THE NEW ECONOMY
ON YOUR CHURCH

Copyright © 2002 by Abingdon Press

All rights reserved.

This book is printed on recycled, acid-free, elemental-chlorine free paper.

Library of Congress Cataloging-in-Publication Data

Schaller, Lyle E.
The new context for ministry : the impact of the new economy on your church
/ Lyle E,. Schaller.
  p. cm.
Includes bibliographical references.
ISBN 0-687-06580-1 (alk. paper)
1. Church fund raising—United Stats. I. Title.

BV772.5 .S33 2002
254'8—dc21

2002016343

Scripture quotations, unless otherwise indicated, are from the New Revised Standard Version Bible, copyright 1989, by the Division of Christian Education of the National Council of the Churches of Christ in the United States of America.

02 03 04 05 06 07 08 09 10 11 — 10 9 8 7 6 5 4 3 2 1

To Susan Davey

Contents

Introduction 13

Chapter One: From Black Tuesday to Black Tuesday ... 21

From Radio to Television 23
The Expanded Role of Government 26
Create Your Own Future! 30
Predators and Innocent Victims 34
Tribes, Nations, Empires, and Movements 38
One Book or Two? 47

Chapter Two: When? 63

Chapter Three: The Great Debate 67

Who Should Control It? 68
The Ecclesiastical Version 72
What's the Issue Here? 73
Three Questions 76
What Is the Future of the Middlemen? 77
What Is Your Institutional Relationship? 78

Chapter Four: Values, Rules, and Denial 83

Whom Do You Trust? 85
The New Lines of Demarcation 86

How Large Is the Circle? 87
Liberal or Conservative? 88
Culture or Politics? 89
Is It Either/Or? 90
Sending Money or People? 94
Shepherds or Entrepreneurs? 94
Renew the Old or Create the New? 95
Defining Success 97
What Is the Problem? 99
Where Else Do We Encounter Denial? 101

Chapter Five: What Happened to the Dollar? 105

What Did the Tooth Fairies Teach Us? 113
How Much? 118
What Will the Dollar Buy? 121
Before or After Taxes? 123
"I Can Remember . . . " 123

Chapter Six: Two New Economies 127

How Do We Isolate People? 130
Two Questions 134
Designing Tomorrow's Church 135
What Are the Options? 137
What Is the Fourth Alternative? 144
How Do We Renew Downtown? 144
What About Old First Church? 146
Children's Ministries 149
The New Fifth Economy 150
Who Will ManageYour Money? 152

Chapter Seven: The New Face of Philanthropy 155

Why? 157
What's Number Two? 158
Buildings or Causes? 159

What Have They Learned? 160
What Does This Mean? 161
The Power of Performance 161
The Power of Relationships 163
The Power of Language 164
How Large Is the Pie? 164
The Birth of the Big Gorilla 166
How Many Pies Are on the Counter? 170
Why Is That Third Pie So Small? 171
Three BIG Public Policy Questions 172
How Much Is $200 Billion? 174

Chapter Eight: How Many Income Streams? 177

The Old Ecclesiastical Economy 178
The Arrival of the Unified Budget 179
The Rise and Fall of Subsidies 182
That Big New Income Stream! 185
The User Fee Stream 186
How Many Streams? 187
How Many Streams for Your Church? 188
The Big Benefactor 189
Seven Questions 190

Chapter Nine: How Competitive Is This New
Ecclesiastical Marketplace? 193

A New Level of Competition 195
Consumerism and Higher Expectations 196
The Impact of Ecumenism 196
When Did People Stop Walking? 197
What Happened to Woolworths? 198
The Big Cutback 199
From Generalist to Specialist 200
From Teaching to Learning 202
The Impact of Marriage 202
The Competition for Time and Attention 203

Oppose or Endorse Change? 204
The Power of Tenure 205
Customer Service 207
Other Arenas of Competition 207

Chapter Ten: The Impact on Congregations 213

What Are Your Assumptions? 213
Taxes to Pew Rents to Chickens to Tithes to an
    Endowment Fund? 215
High Cost or Low Cost? 226
How Costly Is Diversity? 228
How Do You Define Missions? 234
Why Give? 243
Who Is Looking After Grandma? 254
A Learning Center? 256
The Economy of Scale Myth 257
Another Fork in the Road 262
Stewardship Education or Raising Money? 264
What Is the Best System? 266

Chapter Eleven: The Impact on
Denominational Systems 273

The Regional Judicatories 273
A National Perspective 282
Has That Time Arrived? 296
What Have We Learned? 302
What Are the Guidelines? 306

Chapter Twelve: The Impact on Parachurch
Organizations 313

Five Advantages 313
The Deregulated Marketplace 315
What Are the Consequences? 316
Good News or Bad News? 318

Chapter Thirteen: What Are the Consequences? 321

A Transfer of Influence 323
The Bar Has Been Raised! 324
Disappointment + Affluence = Litigation 326
The Fourth Economy 327
Federalism or Centralization? 327
What Will Tomorrow Bring? 330

Notes 335

Introduction

The seventy-two years between the crash of the American stock market in October 1929 and the hijacking of four commercial airliners on September 11, 2001, brought unprecedented changes in the context for ministry in America. These changes also came at an unprecedented rate. A total of 267 years elapsed between 1381, when John Wycliffe began to translate the Bible into English, and the Peace of Westphalia in 1648, which marked the beginning of the end of the Reformation in western Europe.

The combination of applied research, competition, and consumerism has transformed the American economy in only three-quarters of a century. The number of farms in the United States required to produce surplus quantities of food and fiber increased from 2.7 million in 1870 to 6.8 million in 1935 and, thanks to applied research and competition, plunged to 1.8 million in 2001. Between 1929 and 2001 the automobile and the airplane largely replaced the passenger train in long-distance transportation.

These revolutions in agriculture and transportation have wiped out the original reason for the existence of at least 150,000 rural Protestant churches.

In the delivery of health-care services, applied research eliminated several deadly diseases between 1929 and 2001.[1] Maternal deaths in America plunged from 67 per 10,000 live births in 1930 to 0.7 in 2001—a drop of 99 percent! Life expectancy at birth increased from 47 years in 1900 to 60 years in 1930 to 77 years in 2000. The population of the United States increased by 135 percent between 1930 and 2000, but the number age 65 and over grew by 440 percent.

Americans have been growing older, but they also have been growing more affluent. In new single-family detached homes, the three-vehicle garage is more common than the old two-car garage.

The adults of today who were born in the United States after that Black Tuesday in October 1929 have lived through an inflationary era unprecedented in American economic history. Between 1776 and 1933 the Consumer Price Index (1982–84=100) fluctuated between a low of 9 and a high of 21. Between 1940 and 2001 that index increased from 14 to 178 (see chap. 5). After adjusting for inflation per capita personal income in the United States doubled between 1929 and 1965 and doubled again between 1965 and 2001.

Americans also are better educated today than ever before in American history. The proportion of Americans, age 25 and over, who have completed four years of college doubled between 1929 and 1960 and more than tripled between 1960 and 2000.

Competition, consumerism, and affluence have transformed the sale of groceries, housing for college and university undergraduates, the size and shape of privately owned motor vehicles, the publishing industry, the economic base of large central cities, hospital management, and the size of new single-family homes.

Affluence, applied research, technological advances, and an open society have transformed the world of entertainment, the channels of communication, the tools of terrorism, the retail sales of books, the attainable goals of environmentalists, and the design of the space for people to gather together for the corporate worship of God.

While women and ethnic minorities continue to be confronted with more barriers than white men in the American labor force, the population of the United States doubled between 1900 and 1950 and nearly doubled again between

1950 and 2000. The number of women in the paid civilian labor force, however, tripled between 1900 and 1950 and quadrupled between 1950 and 2000.

That combination of competition, consumerism, affluence, the rewards of applied research, greater egalitarianism, an operational affirmation of the right of self-determination, and individual freedom have transformed the American economy and also the role of the United States in international relations. That combination also supplied grist for the mills of the terrorists who are convinced that the United States is the Great Satan. For better or for worse, the exports of the United States since 1929 have included food, money, democracy, technology, a free enterprise economic system, entertainment, a distinctive culture, human rights, weapons of war, images of emancipated women, the ideological concept of the separation of religion and state, education, American military strength, and freedom of the press. Among the imports have been students, clothing, food, physicians, terrorists, television sets, low-cost labor, scientists, refugees, tourists, and cell phones.

When invited to speak to a group of younger people, old men usually choose one of three themes: (1) my grandchildren, (2) my personal health history, or (3) how the world has changed since I was a boy.

This book takes off from that third theme and focuses on how the new American economy has transformed the context for ministry in America in the twenty-first century. The changes in America between those two Black Tuesdays have transformed the ecclesiastical culture of the United States.

This new ecclesiastical culture is organized around a premium on competence. As Jim Collins has pointed out, "Good is the enemy of the great."[2] Competition has replaced cooperation. Small institutions are being replaced by big institutions. Inherited institutional loyalty has been replaced by customer satisfaction. The old "one size fits all" prescription has been replaced by customization. (This is at the heart of the big and divisive debate in public schooling.) Communication now comes packaged in entertainment. The discontinuity of life has created a new demand for points of continuity, stability, and predictability.[3] As regional institutions replace the old neighborhood gathering places, the demand for community grows stronger and louder.

Three of the most interesting symbols of this new American economy appeared in late 2001. One was when millions of people watched in horror as television showed, in real time, the second aircraft hitting one of the two World Trade towers and an hour later the physical collapse of the two tallest buildings in the largest city in the United States. Never before have so many Americans been engaged in a memorable, meaningful, and unifying shared experience.

A second came a month later when it was announced that the United States Postal Service was delivering letters containing anthrax spores. What can a frightened American do when faced with that threat? Thanks to modern technology, most Americans had a back-up, germ-free system in place. It is called e-mail.

One consequence was that the Postal Service, already faced with a huge operating deficit, had to undertake expensive preventative measures. That was accompanied by a decrease in first-class letters, the milk cow on the revenue side of the ledger.

The third symbol of this new American economy came with the appeals for money to aid the victims of the terrorist attacks. Recent history suggested that $250 to $350 million might be raised from individuals and from charitable institutions such as the churches, foundations, and corporations. The actual total in cash and pledges by Thanksgiving was four times that estimate.

Television, the Internet, and the emergence of a new era in American philanthropy are among the factors that have transformed the context for ministry in America. Those and related influences help to explain why two-thirds of the pages in this book are devoted to the impact of this new American economy on financing ministry in the United States in the twenty-first century.

That theme can be summarized in a brief formula: More people plus more individual freedom plus far more dollars plus more inflation plus more choices equal far greater competition for the charitable dollar as well as for people's discretionary time.

Before elaborating on that theme, however, it may be helpful to look briefly at a half dozen other changes in the context for ministry that occurred between those two Black Tuesdays. Those six changes are discussed in the first chapter. The second chapter describes how the beginnings of a new American economy and the emergence of a new ecclesiastical culture in American Protestantism trace back to the mid-1960s.

One consequence of those and related changes was the debate over who is best qualified to choose the final destination of benevolent dollars. That continuing and highly divisive debate is reviewed in the third chapter.

The increasing competition for the charitable dollar has lifted up the values and rules that distinguish one competitor from another. That is the theme of the fourth chapter.

The fifth chapter is a light-hearted review of the impact of the longest inflationary era in American history, including the heavier burden placed on tooth fairies.

One slice of this new American economy is a growing demand for meaningful and memorable experiences. That may be having a greater impact on congregational life in general, on worship, on youth ministries, on learning, and on church finances than any other single force. That is the subject of the sixth chapter.

Instead of focusing on stewardship in discussing church finances, it may be more helpful to look at the larger picture of contemporary American philanthropy, the theme of the seventh chapter.

The heart of this book can be found in chapters 8, 9, and 10. They contain suggestions for congregational leaders who are convinced the new century, the new American economy, and the new ecclesiastical culture require a new strategy for financing congregational ministries.

For example, who will provide the dollars to pay the minister? Three hundred years ago, the Congregational minister in New England usually was paid from a tax levied on local property owners. Over the years that was replaced by pew rents, tithes, chicken dinners, and other sources. That story is a part of the tenth chapter.

A persuasive argument can be made that the greatest challenge rests with those responsible for designing a plan for the financing of denominational systems. The old patterns are being replaced with a variety of more lucrative sources, and that is the theme of the eleventh chapter.

The twelfth chapter focuses on the religious organizations facing the fewest adjustments due to the new American economy. These are the parachurch and para-denominational organizations. Most have either made the adjustment already or recognize that they are facing a crisis requiring major changes.

Every revolution brings unanticipated consequences, and a few of these are discussed in the last chapter.

This book is the successor, not the sequel, to an earlier volume, *44 Ways to Expand the Financial Base of Your Congregation*, published in 1991. The writing of this one took much longer and was interrupted by such agendas as the call for a "lockbox on Social Security taxes," debates over how to spend state and federal budget supluses, an "economic correction" that turned into a recession, the use of commercial aircraft as guided missiles on Black Tuesday 2001, and reflections on the generosity of the American people in responding to pleas for money to aid the victims of that attack.

One consequence is that I am deeply indebted to the editors at Abingdon Press for their flexibility on deadlines and revisions.

Finally, the lives of tens of millions of people on this planet are brightened every day by the ministries of millions of Christians who take Matthew 25:35-36 literally. They do not hesitate to put aside their personal agenda to help a stranger in need.

This book is dedicated to a stranger who modeled that passage of Scripture.

LYLE E. SCHALLER
November 2001
Naperville, Illinois

CHAPTER ONE

From Black Tuesday
to Black Tuesday

An American legend that has inspired hundreds of cartoons describes how wealthy Americans committed suicide by jumping out of skyscrapers following the crash of the stock market that began on Tuesday, October 29, 1929.

On Tuesday, September 11, 2001, an unknown number of Americans intentionally jumped to certain death from the top floors of buildings in New York City.

Those two Black Tuesdays can be used as bookends to describe an unprecedented series of changes on the world scene. Those two Tuesdays also illustrate several of the changes in the context for ministry. Taken together, these changes have transformed the rules for religious organizations in the United States.

A simple analogy is the young golfer of 1929 who has a grandchild who enjoys playing tennis today. Both games are played with a small round ball. Both require the player to hit that ball with a handheld device. Both require considerable stamina and a high level of skill. Both promise that practice will improve performance. Both count points to keep score. Both produce winners and losers. Both are highly competitive games. Both evoke feelings of frustration and even anger. Both sports assume that honesty, integrity, and courtesy are central components of good sportsmanship. Today both sports are enjoyed by women as well as by men. Once upon a time players in both sports wore distinctive clothing. Both have shoes that carry the name of that sport. Both can be viewed on television. Until recently, most of the championship professionals in both sports came from Great Britain or North America.

Despite these and many other similarities, golf and tennis are radically different sports. The players use different rulebooks. With a few exceptions, such as "Practice, practice, practice!" "Keep your eye on the ball!" and "Exercise, exercise, exercise!" the advice of the golfer of 1929 to today's tennis-playing grandchild has little relevance. These are two different games played with two different rulebooks.

Likewise the role and responsibilities of the parish pastor or the congregational leader or the denominational official of today are similar in several respects, but radically different in other ways, from their counterparts of the 1920s. The book is the same, but the channels for proclaiming the message of that book have multiplied. The message is the same, but the listeners of the 1920s have been replaced by new generations. The equipment for doing ministry today is far superior to what was available in 1929. In golf the balls are still round, but their composition has changed, as have tennis rackets and golf clubs. The level of performance has been raised. The best golfers and tennis players of 1929 would have difficulty if they were competing against the cream of today's players in those two sports.

The central thesis of this book is that the new American economy, which was interrupted but not derailed by the events of 9-11-01, and the new American Protestant ecclesiastical culture, which began to be visible in the 1960s, have transformed the roles and responsibilities of parish pastors, congregational leaders, denominational officials, and the staff of parachurch organizations. This new American economy and the new American religious culture have created a need to replace the old playbook on "How to do church" with a new playbook. This book is intended to offer suggestions on how to write a customized playbook for your congregation or your denomination or your parachurch organization. (The leaders of these parachurch organizations have become the third player in that foursome playing golf together. They are replacing the professional educators as influential voices in this new game. The other players, of course, are parish pastors, congregational leaders—who formerly were the fourth member of that foursome and now are second—and denominational officials.)

Neither the church nor the economy exists in a vacuum, however; therefore, it may be helpful to back off and look at the larger context. What happened between that Black Tuesday in 1929 and that Black Tuesday in 2001? One answer is, Those seven decades changed the role and responsibilities of the United States Secretary of State. In December 1941, Secretary of State Cordell Hull's responsibilities focused on declarations of war with three nations—Japan, Germany, and Italy. Secretary of State Colin Powell in the fall of 2001 focused on building an international coalition against faceless terrorism that is not confined by national boundaries.

In broader terms a half dozen changes stand out for this discussion. Each of these changes also has made an impact on the American ecclesiastical culture.

From Radio to Television

The stock market crash of October 29, 1929, had a direct and immediate impact on that relatively small number of Americans who owned stocks and bonds. Others heard about it over the radio or read about it in a newspaper. It was not until 1930 and 1931, however, that the impact began to be felt by large numbers. The economic recession for farmers had begun back in 1922, but for most Americans the impact of that Black Tuesday came gradually. National income dropped from $81 billion in 1929 to $68 billion in

1930 and to $53 billion in 1931 before bottoming out at $41 billion in 1932. It was March 1930 before Milwaukee opened its first municipal soup kitchen. The Empire State Building was completed in 1931. The number of house-holds with an annual income over one million dollars dropped from 75 in 1931 to 20 in 1932. The first door-to-door federal census of unemployment in April 1930 reported only three million out of the 48 million employ-able residents were out of work. It took another nine months for the number of unemployed to double to six million. By late 1932 that economic indicator had grown to 15 million jobless Americans.

By contrast, before noon on Black Tuesday 2001 scores of relatives had received telephone calls from among the approximately 3,000 innocent victims who were doomed to die that morning. Before sunset hundreds of millions of tele-vision viewers around the world had vicariously experi-enced that destruction of the two trade towers and one section of the Pentagon.

President Franklin D. Roosevelt relied on radio to chal-lenge Americans to remember that "day that will live in infamy." President George W. Bush used both radio and tel-evision to rally the people to support a war on terrorism.

During the last half of the twentieth century television transformed both the American economy and the American ecclesiastical culture. Television has taught people that the responsibility for grabbing someone's attention rests with the sender of the message, not the recipient. Television has revolutionized preaching. The old sequential introduction, point one, point two, point three, and conclusion style is being replaced by two concurrent story lines. Television has taught people that moving visual images on a screen are more powerful than the spoken word. Television has replaced Old First Church Downtown as the standard for defining what is a high-quality worship service. Television enables people to "be there" without leaving home. Television enables people at home to enjoy a better view of a professional fooball game than is available to fans who pay to watch from the stands. Television dictates the schedule and beginning times for the playoffs and World Series in professional baseball. Television has multiplied the costs of state and national political campaigns. Television guarantees that we never again will have an obese or physically unattractive person elected to serve as President of the United States. Those moving visual images on television on September 11, 2001, and later were powerful motivators in raising hundreds of millions of dollars for families of the victims. Television has taught people that the ability to read is not a requirement to understand the world in which we live. Television has taught people that relevant information comes wrapped, not in paper, but in entertainment. Cable television has taught viewers that they are entitled to a huge array of choices. MTV has taught people that music should be seen and experienced, not simply heard. An offspring of television, called videotape, has enabled a small but growing number of ministers to deliver the same message to different constituencies in different venues at the same hour. Television is destroying the market for what once was described as acceptable quality preaching. Videotapes are enabling small lay-led Christian worshiping communities to enjoy both the intimacy and interaction of the small fellowship and superb preaching.

Television also both symbolizes and leads the emergence of a new segment of the American culture called the experience economy.[1] The American economy of the 1920s and 1930s was built on (1) the production and gathering of commodities, (2) the transformation of commodities into goods (lumber into furniture, wheat into flour, petroleum into gasoline, etc.), and (3) the marketing of services (education, entertainment, health care, financial services, government, etc.). This new fourth economy has been created to provide meaningful and memorable experiences.

Watching the destruction of the World Trade towers on television on that Black Tuesday in September 2001 was a memorable and life-changing experience! (See chap. 6 for a more extensive discussion of the fourth economy.) Working in ministry with fellow Christians as a short-term missionary with a sister church in a different culture on another continent is more likely to be a life-changing experience than reading a book on missions.[2]

Television is not simply radio with pictures. Television enables people to experience reality vicariously. That experience changes people's worldview. A survey of residents of a rural area in Africa in the 1960s was designed to measure people's contentment with their lot in life. It revealed that the vast majority were content. They compared their lot in life with their kinfolk and their neighbors and concluded that they were reasonably well off. Three decades later the survey was repeated. It revealed a very high level of discontent. The residents now compared their lot in life with the people they saw on television and in motion pictures.

Television has transformed all of American life from formulating foreign policy to socializing two-year-olds into our culture to raising money for benevolent causes to designing meaningful worship experiences for teenagers.

The Expanded Role of Government

What is the most remarkable pair of statistics in this book? A persuasive case can be made for this pair. First, the number of miles driven annually on this nation's streets and highways increased from 200 billion in 1929 to 3,000 billion in 2001—a fifteenfold increase. The number of traffic deaths per 100 million vehicle miles driven dropped from 17.4 in 1929 to 1.4 in 2001. That was a 92 percent decrease in the highway death rate since this pilgrim enrolled in first grade! The death rate of 1929 would have produced nearly 600,000 traffic fatalities in 2001.

The actual number was close to 42,000, down 35 percent from the total of only thirty years earlier.

Most of the credit for this amazing decrease in the rate of highway fatalities goes to government. Federal, state, and local governments have constructed safer streets and highways; they have raised the standards for obtaining and keeping a license to drive; they have required teenagers to complete driver's education training; they have forced manufacturers to design safer vehicles; and they have enforced safety rules and laws.

Among the many consequences of these actions by governments are these: (1) somewhere between eight and ten million Americans are now alive who would be dead if the highway death rate of 1929—or even 1940—still prevailed; (2) regional institutions (motion picture theaters, retail stores, physicians'offices, churches, prisons, hospitals, and public high schools) are replacing neighborhood institutions; (3) the Social Security Administration sends out more checks every month to elderly Americans; (4) cemeteries still have vacant lots; (5) retirement centers are flourishing; (6) several denominations have a surplus of clergy; and (7) the journey from home to work, to shopping, to church, to the doctor, to school, and to entertainment keeps getting longer and longer.

The United States government subsidized the construction of the Transcontinental Railroad, it built the Panama Canal, it brought electricity to rural America, it created ARPANET—the parent of the Internet—and the federal government has financed most of the research that increased the life expectancy from birth for the average American by seventeen years between those two Black Tuesdays. Thanks largely, but not entirely, to civil rights legislation adopted by the federal government, racial discrimination has been reduced. Thanks to Social Security, the most common synonym for "poor" no longer is "elderly."

Government has enabled record numbers of teenagers to enroll in an institution of higher education.

In the months and years after that Black Tuesday in 1929, millions of Americans asked themselves, "What will we do?" In the hours and days after that Black Tuesday of 2001, tens of millions wondered, "What will the government do?"

For better or for worse, government already was playing a far more influential role in American life in the years before 9-11-01 than it was before 10-29-29. Increases in home ownership, cleaner air and purer water, subsidies for agriculture, expanded public welfare programs, a woman's right to abortion, Medicare, subsidies for housing for the elderly and the poor, a long list of decisions by the United States Supreme Court, export subsidies, lowering the voting age to eighteen, and accepting the role of the United States as the number-one player in international relations in Europe, Asia, and Africa represent a few of the ways the role of government has expanded since that Black Tuesday in October 1929.

One more way, which deserves a separate chapter, is the change in the rulebook for that game called charitable giving. Up through 1930 individuals, religious organizations, and other private nonprofit agencies, including private schools and hospitals, collected and disbursed most of the dollars for charitable causes. Chapter 7 discusses the role of government as the big gorilla in this new era of philanthropy. Who will contribute the charitable dollars required to compensate the victims, including the businesses, destroyed by the attack on the World Trade Center in New York on Black Tuesday? An early estimate is that federal, state, and local governments will contribute at least ninety to one hundred dollars for every benevolent dollar contributed by individuals, religious and charitable organizations, and foundations. Government now is expected to finance the cost of the safety net that formerly was the responsibility of individuals, families, and benevolent organizations.

Two years before that Black Tuesday of 1929, the Mississippi River flooded. The American Red Cross compensated victims for approximately 7 percent of the losses, twice the amount contributed by the federal government. In 1993 the federal government covered more than one-half of the losses produced by another flooding of the Mississippi, a hundred times what the Red Cross spent.[3]

Perhaps the most provocative statement on the role of government in the modern world has come from the Peruvian economist Hernando de Soto.[4] The best single approach to reducing poverty around the world requires rewarding hard work and thrift by enabling workers to acquire a clear and legally enforceable title to their real estate. This enables the poor to accumulate capital and to transmit capital to their heirs. That is possible only if the government is honest, reasonably efficient, and both able and willing to enforce property rights. That process also requires continuity in government. Revolutions and civil wars often produce the discontinuity that undermines property rights and creates an environment that fosters poverty.

That is an oversimplified summary of de Soto's argument, but it does point out the importance of effective civil government if the goal is to reduce poverty. Likewise corrupt, inept, and dictatorial central governments also create a hospitable climate for piracy and terrorism.

One of the reasons why a variety of institutional expressions of organized religions continues to exist and to grow in the United States is that government now protects all religions, not only the one approved by the central or regional government. That protection has made possible the emergence of a new American Protestant ecclesiastical culture concurrently with the growth of non-Christian religions.

Government also has encouraged the expansion of our democratic society and a free enterprise economy.

One consequence is that Americans today have an unprecedented degree of freedom to shape their own future. That generalization applies to most individuals, churches, denominations, parachurch organizations, non-profit organizations, and profit-driven corporations as well as to entrepreneurs in general and a new generation of pastors who believe they serve in an ecclesiastical culture without ceilings.

Create Your Own Future!

In the seven decades between those two Black Tuesdays, the walls came tumbling down. My favorite guru, Peter Drucker, has concluded that when the historians of 2200 or 2500 look back to describe this era, they will not lift up the advances in technology or the Internet or similar developments. Instead, Drucker contends, they will point out that for the first time in human history a substantial and rapidly growing proportion of people have choices. People now can manage themselves.

Drucker goes on to add, "And we are totally unprepared for it."[5]

For most of American history the boy born on the farm followed in his father's footsteps and grew up to be a farmer. His sister followed in her mother's career path and became a farmer's wife and homemaker. When the time came, most found a spouse from within that or an adjacent county. The choice of one's parents shaped the career of the child.

Today the farmer's son goes off to the state university to become an engineer or lawyer while his sister joins the Peace Corps after graduation from college, and their mother goes back to school for a degree in business administration.

Even more remarkable has been the opening of new doors to women since that Black Tuesday in 1929. American women are now exercising their Second Amendment Constitutional right to bare arms when they gather to worship God. That also is but one of many reasons why millions of adult males around the world feel threatened.

In 1952 congregational leaders asked themselves, "What is the future of our church? What is our role? Who constitutues our primary constituency?" A typical response was, "That was decided by our grandparents back in 1902 when they purchased this site and built this church to serve the people living in this neighborhood." The husband of a third-generation member who had been born and reared in another state commented, "But most of the adults who lived in this neighborhod fifty years ago are dead, and three-fourths of today's members don't live around here."

"That's an irrelevant point! This church was located here by our grandparents to serve the people who live around here, and therefore the residents of this neighborhood constitute our number-one constituency. We have to be faithful to the goals of the planning committee of 1902. The fact that the people who now live around here prefer to pioneer their own church rather than to come and fill our empty pews has nothing to do with it. We are obligated to implement the plans of our grandparents."

The contemporary counterpart to that discussion of 1952 resembles this one: "The folks who organized this as a new mission back in 1952, and my parents were among them, were thinking in terms of a neighborhood church. That explains why they were content with a one-acre site and a two-story building. Twenty years later, after the automobile had changed the habits of churchgoers, we sold that property and purchased this seven-acre parcel three miles to the west of the old location. We've now finished paying off the mortgage on our third and final building program," explained the fifty-six-year-old, life-long member of

Westminster Church. "I believe that all of those who objected to our relocation twenty-seven years ago, and are still around, agree that was a wise decision."

"That clearly was a wise decision at the time," agreed a thirty-five-year-old who was the newest member of the newly created Long Range Planning Committee. "We now have a combined average attendance of slightly over 600 at our three weekend worship services, but we've been on a plateau in size for at least three years. We have a limited outdoor recreation ministry. That ministry plus our building, the required setbacks, landscaping, and 235 offstreet parking spaces cover every inch of our land. I'm not challenging the wisdom of that decision of nearly thirty years ago. If I had been here at that time, I expect I would have agreed seven acres was a generous size for a church site. Before my wife and I moved here five years ago, however, we were members of a congregation about four times the size of this one. We were located on a thirty-one-acre site. All our buildings, with one exception, were only one story in height. The weekend schedule included nine worship services in three different venues. One is the worship center, one is a theater, and one is a big box with all movable fixtures and chairs. It can be arranged so it feels full with 150 people, but it also can be set up to accommodate 600. We had a huge outdoor recreation ministry and a prekindergarten weekday school with 600 three- and four-year-old children enrolled in it. We also needed nearly ten acres for interior streets and parking. I suggest the question is not whether or not the decision to relocate twenty-seven years ago was wise. I believe it was a wise decision. The question for this committee, however, is if we were forced to move from here, would we choose another seven-acre site, and would we construct two-story buildings with only one venue for worship? This real estate places a ceiling on our future."

Eighteen months later that committee recommended purchasing a sixty-two-acre parcel of land as one component of a larger strategy to become a two-site church.

One of the most interesting examples of this freedom of congregational leaders to create their own future, rather than live under a ceiling inherited from the past, is the number of Protestant congregations organized after 1950 that are now worshiping at their second or third congregationally owned meeting place.

A growing number of Americans, as well as people on other continents, are now prepared to manage their own future. That freedom to shape one's own future is the primary reason why tens of millions of people now living on other continents want to migrate to the United States or Canada.

On Black Friday 1929 there were fewer than seventy autonomous and self-governing nations on this planet. During the five decades from 1943 to 1993, 125 additional nations gained their independence beginning with Lebanon (1943), Syria (1944), and Iceland (1945).

To a significant degree that was a product of President Woodrow Wilson's famous Fourteen Points for world peace, which he announced on January 8, 1918. Subsequently Wilson elaborated on his goals by emphasizing that governments should exist only with the consent of the governed and that nations should live with one another in a climate of egalitarianism.

Only eleven of what are now nearly two hundred nations have a population of one hundred million or more, but they account for two-thirds of the six billion human beings on this planet. Another forty have a population under one million. The list of semi-autonomous dependencies, such as Greenland, Guam, and Gibraltar, exceeds sixty.

Together these new nations represent a growing worldwide demand for self-expression and self-determination. The people want to control their own future.

The counterpart on the American Protestant landscape has been the emergence of a huge and growing number of nondenominational or independent congregations. They represent that same demand for local control and self-determination. While exact numbers are not available, a reasonable estimate is that in 1929 at least 95 percent of all Protestant congregations in the United States were affiliated with a denomination or similar organized religious institution. By 2001 that proportion probably was well under 80 percent. For contemporary Protestant megachurches that proportion probably is under 60 percent. In addition, many of the denominationally affiliated megachurches faithfully pay their annual "franchise tax" to the denominational treasury, but otherwise act like completely autonomous, self-expressing, self-governing, self-propagating, and self-financing churches.

One consequence is that the leaders in scores of smaller denominationally affiliated congregations see these megachurches as predators and view themselves as victims—but that introduces the fourth of these six changes.

Predators and Innocent Victims

Up until 1940 the basic pattern in warfare was that military personnel killed other military personnel. Three of several major exceptions were the British attack on Washington, D.C., in 1814, Sherman's march to the sea in the American Civil War, and the rape of Nanking in the 1930s. Most of the casualties in war, however, were men in uniform. That changed in September 1940, when the Germans bombed London nearly every night. The war on civilians received another boost in August 1942 when Hitler decided to attack Stalingrad. An estimated 18 million civilians died during the subsequent battles.[6]

Military operations killed tens of millions of civilians during World War II. The next half century brought a continuation of that new pattern in which civilian deaths greatly outnumbered military deaths in modern warfare.

September 11, 2001, brought home to Americans the newest dimension of modern warfare. This called for nineteen suicidal civilians to kill 3,000 innocent civilians in a few hours.

The old formula for warfare called for nations to go to war against other nations. Civilian casualties were described as collateral damage. The new formula calls for networks to attack crowds of civilians and for civilian terrorists to kill soldiers and sailors. Palestinian civilians kill Israeli soldiers and civilians. Israeli police and soldiers kill Palestinian civilians.

This escalation of violence in international relations is reflected in American society. Teenagers used to settle grudges with their fists. The 1990s found teenagers "getting even" by shooting other teenagers. When they miss, young children may become the victims. Those are the most violent American expressions of civilian predators killing civilian victims.

The past half century has brought an increase in the number and variety of predators in both the new American economy and the new ecclesiastical culture. Predators are preying on elderly widows with a variety of home repair and home equity schemes. Predators have forced many parents to walk with their children to and from school. Predators control many prisons. The drug culture is owned and operated by predators. Predators can be found in the public schools, on the Internet, in the real estate business, and on cable television.

What the victims describe as predators has transformed Main Street. Home Depot has replaced the owner-operated hardward store. That 200,000-square-foot combination supermarket and discount store with fifteen acres of parking has replaced the Woolworth five and dime and the corner grocery. The new university schools of education and the state legislatures have called for the replacement of the old four-year public high school with an enrollment of 200 to 500 with large institutions filled with anonymity, alienation, under achievement, boredom, and anti-social behavior.[7] The new regional megachurches have undermined the future of the old neighborhood church.

The forest fire destroys the old to make way for the new. Biologists point out that predators thin out the herd of deer to ensure the survival of the fittest.

The predators have killed or swallowed up thousands of businesses, both on the Internet and of the brick and mortar type. Corporate farmers are buying out the family farmers—often thanks to the dollars sent from Washington to the big farmers. Is that good or bad? What is both bad and foolish is to believe that predators no longer exist. That assumption cost approximately 3,000 lives on Black Tuesday 9-11-01.

Many of the innocent victims have had their lives transformed by trends rather than by individuals or institutions. The shift from a labor intensive occupation to a capital intensive industry has eliminated most of the traditional family farms in rural America. The Internet has wiped out the jobs for thousands of bank tellers and travel agents. Workers in the entertainment, travel, and hospitality industries were among the victims of the predators who made 9-11-01 a Black Tuesday.

The response of the American people to the pleas for funds to aid the victims of Black Tuesday 2001 has undermined the financial base of other charitable institutions. Technology has sharply reduced the number of jobs for coal miners, file clerks, typists, and telephone switchboard operators. The economic recession that began in 2000 has threatened the welfare-to-work program. The growth of the commercial airlines wiped out the user-fee-financed interstate passenger train.

Among the many consequences of the arrival of the new American economy are (1) an increase in the number of both predators and victims, (2) a challenging business climate for creative enterpreneurs, (3) an increased demand for financial subsidies, (4) an increase in the level of competition, (5) creation of a safety net for the business cycle, (6) an enhancement of the power of the consumer, and (7) an expansion of the role of government.

On the ecclesiastical scene the predators were highly visible during the last six decades of the twentieth century in denominational mergers. Twenty or thirty years after that call for unity in the name of Christ produced the merger, it appeared that message really came from a hungry predator hunting for new victims. Who were the predators and who were the victims in those series of mergers that produced the United Church of Christ, the United Methodist Church, the Presbyterian Church (U.S.A.), and the Evangelical Lutheran Church in America?

How can the self-identified victims respond to the arrival of a new predator? One way is for the leaders of these two small Presbyterian churches meeting in buildings seven miles apart to appear at presbytery to protest the plans of a Presbyterian megachurch to locate its new second site halfway between those two churches. Another is for the local merchants, their employees, and their customers to oppose the proposed rezoning of a thirty-acre site on the west edge of town to accommodate a new WalMart store. A third is for the opponents of a proposed increase in the municipal tax rate to band together and defeat the referendum authorizing that tax increase. A fourth is for the opponents of that proposal to merge two denominations into one to withdraw and come together to create a new denomination.

A common response to the arrival of a new predator on the scene is to flee. That was a powerful motivating force behind the earlier migration of western Europeans to North

America. It is an even more obvious motivating force behind more recent waves of new immigrants to the United States from Cuba, China, North Korea, Russia, and a hundred other countries. For millions the name of that predator was starvation or Communism or dictatorship or pestilence or oppression or fear.

The response that transformed America on that Black Tuesday in 2001 is for the self-identified victims to demonize that powerful predator. That legitimates the use of violent terrorist tactics as the only response available to those comparatively weak victims. Terrorism has long been an acceptable response to predators. That has coined the explanation, "Your definition of a terrorist is my definition of a freedom fighter." That sentence also explains many episodes in American history, including the Boston Tea Party, John Brown's raid, Quantrill's guerrillas in Kansas in the 1860s, the labor strike of the 1930s, and the violence that accompanied the civil rights movement of the 1960s. The big contemporary example of this response is the teaching of terrorist tactics as the appropriate response to the predator. This response is being taught to young males in thousands of schools operated by the extremist wing of contemporary Islam, but that is a subject for the final pages of this chapter.

Who will turn out to be predators and who will turn out to be the self-identified victims in the war on terrorism that began on 9-11-01? Who will decide who were the victims and who were the predators? What tactics will the self-identified victims choose as their response? When someone surveys the ecclesiastical landscape in 2025, who will be identified as the victims and who will be described as the predators?

Tribes, Nations, Empires, and Movements

"The world will never be the same again." This was a frequently articulated response to the events of that Black

Tuesday of 9-11-01. One explanation for that comment was attacking the military forces of Japan after Pearl Harbor was a relatively easy-to-describe response, but how does one respond to the suicidal attacks by nineteen terrorists, all of whom also died on that Black Tuesday?

A more useful beginning point is to ask how human beings organize themselves into groups. For most of human history the answer has been in families, clans, and tribes. The family was and is a small gathering of individuals. The clan was an alliance of families. The tribe usually was a collection of clans.

More recently, about 2,500 to 3,000 years ago, a new institution called the city-state emerged. Athens and Rome were two of the newly famous city-states in Europe. The next stage brought nations and empires. The Holy Roman Empire, the Ottoman Empire, and the British Empire were early examples.

The reasons behind the growth of colonial empires controlled by western European nations during the seventeenth, eighteenth, and nineteenth centuries include trade, greed, new sources of raw materials, the lure of adventure and discovery, the natural desire of sinful human beings to control other sinful human beings, military advantages, and the ego-driven attractions of empire building.

A new reason became more influential in the nineteenth century with the emergence of a new class of predators called pirates. Many robbed at sea while others raided land-based caravans. This response was based on the ancient Roman law definition of pirates as "enemies of the human race."[8] One of the first organized national responses to piracy came in 1805 when American marines forced the pasha of Tripoli to sue for peace and release captive Americans. During the next hundred years Great Britain, France, Spain, Italy, the Netherlands, Germany, Portugal, Belgium, and the United States concluded that the most effective way to combat terrorism on land and sea was to take control of the lands where the terrorists were based. Does that sound familiar?

The second half of the twentieth century brought (1) the political independence of what formerly had been colonies—in 1960 alone fourteen former French colonies in Africa became independent nations—(2) a rise in the level of terrorism around the world, and (3) the hope that the United Nations could bring peace to this world.

It is difficult to believe, however, in a world heavily influenced by nationalism and the demands for self-determination, that the United Nations will be able to mobilize the financial resources, the expertise, the patience, the military forces, and the goodwill required for creating and governing a worldwide network of "mandated" colonies.

Back at the beginning of the twentieth century most of the residents on planet earth allegedly were citizens of a nation and/or a colonial empire. In the real world, however, tens of millions continued to act on the conviction that their primary loyalty was not to the British Empire or to a nation such as France or the Netherlands or the United States or Germany. Their primary loyalty was to their family, clan, or tribe. For many that was reinforced by a loyalty to their religion and their culture. In a normal, natural, and predictable manner the western powers often sought to impose their culture, ideology, and religion on the native-born residents of their colonies. One predictable consequence was tension, conflict, protest movements, and even rebellion.

The next stage began in the early years of the twentieth century, and especially after 1918, when the western world devoted huge quantities of resources to nation-building. The goal was to compress an evolutionary process that had required three or four centuries in western Europe into one or two generations. The model, of course, was naturally the one they knew best, the western European and North American models of self-governing nations. In mid-August

1947, for example, the Dominion of Pakistan and the Dominion of India were created. More than 106 million citizens of India voted in their first general election of 1951–52. Pandit Jawaharlal Nehru became the first Prime Minister of the Republic of India. Three years later four French colonies became part of the new nation of India.

Pakistan changed its status in 1956 from a dominion of the British Empire to that of an independent nation. The partition of April 4, 1972, created the new nation of Bangladesh out of what had been East Pakistan. Religion, cultural identity, and nationalism were three of the most powerful driving forces behind those divisions. Today the three nations of India, Pakistan, and Bangladesh are among the eight most populous nations on earth. Their combined population of approximately 1.4 billion in 2000 exceeds the combined population of the 160 smallest nations on this planet.

While each one is counted as an independent nation in the world political system, each one is too large and the population too diverse to create a cohesive, self-sufficient, and unified nation in two or three generations.

One normal, natural, and predicable consequence is the emergence of factions, political parties, protest movements, tribal warlords, dictatorial governments, and civil wars. The political history of Africa since 1960 also illustrates all of those responses to an undefined future. A recent count revealed a total of twenty-five civil wars being waged on this one planet.

How can a loose collection of individuals, clans, tribes, factions, interest groups, and protest movements be transformed into a closely knit and cohesive nation-state?

Throughout human history the most effective single strategy has been to identify a common enemy, demonize that enemy, and organize the people to fight that enemy.

One example of that organizing principle is captured in the title of a popular history of American Methodism,

Organizing to Beat the Devil.[9] A second was the decision by a variety of Protestant bodies in the 1820–1960 era to organize against Roman Catholicism. A third was the reaction of a nation badly divided on foreign policy on December 6, 1941, to organize to defeat Japan and Germany. A fourth was the use of that central principle by community organizers in the 1960s and 1970s.[10]

This basic organizing principle has several highly attractive features. It calls for a simplistic single-factor explanation of what usually is a highly complex issue. It is easy to articulate. This means it usually is easy to summarize the issue in a brief and memorable slogan. It places all the responsibility for the current state of affairs on the enemy The victims are innocent and blameless parties to the dispute. It divides the population into parties—us and them. Since the enemy created the problem, that means the enemy has to resource the solution. This central organizing principle tends to win the early support of those who seek a world filled with immediate satisfactions and quick victories and marginalizes those who are convinced that deferred gratification is one of the pricetags for changing the system.

More recently, factions of contemporary Islam have used this central organizing principle by identifying the United States as the Great Satan. One consequence was Black Tuesday, 9-11-01.

One moral of that story is that it is easier to rally people against a common enemy (a colonial power, the devil, another nation, the Vatican, terrorists, the employer, city hall, slavery, faceless corporations, bureaucrats, alcoholic beverages, etc.) than it is to rally them in support of the general good. A second lesson is that this is an easier strategy to implement if the enemy consists of strangers living in another place. A third lesson is that this places the Christian in a difficult position since Jesus instructed his followers to love their enemies.

What is the relevance of this discussion to the discussion of contemporary American Protestantism?

First, if one conceptualizes the contemporary American family as fewer than seven to ten people, that helps to explain why the ideal size for a small group is five to seven people. Second, if a clan is conceptualized as consisting of fifteen to sixty people, that helps to explain why the most common size for American Protestant congregations is an average worship attendance between fifteen and seventy. Third, if a tribe is conceptualized as consisting of between seventy-five and two hundred, that helps to explain why four out of five congregations in American Protestantism report an average worship attendance of two hundred or fewer. Unless the congregation benefits from a high degree of demographic and/or ideological homogeneity, an average worship attendance of three hundred is too large to build and maintain a cohesive tribal identity.

Fourth, this helps to explain why larger Protestant congregations usually follow one of these eight paths: (1) they conceptualize themselves as a collection of families, clans, and tribes (frequently described as classes, cells, choirs, circles, worship times, fellowships, organizations, task forces, committees, and groups) or (2) they are organized as followers of a magnetic and visionary personality or (3) they experience substantial shrinkage in numbers when that magnetic personality departs or (4) they are organized against a clearly defined common enemy or (5) they are exceptionally well organized in support of a common cause—usually missions and/or evangelism—or (6) the members represent an exceptionally homogeneous collection of individuals and families or (7) that congregation is a one-of-a-kind religious body in that larger community or (8) as the years roll by, the members grow older in age and fewer in number.

Finally, this analogy helps to explain the plight of many denominations in contemporary American Protestantism.

For this discussion, the nation-state is the equivalent of the denomination. Most of the Protestant denominations in America can be placed in one of these six categories: (1) they trace their origins back to before 1900, now include at least 5,000 congregations, and currently are disrupted by internal conflict among a variety of factions, caucuses, parties, causes, protest movements, and rebellious groups or (2) they were organized since 1900, currently include between 800 and 3,000 congregations, have not been diverted by one or more denominational mergers, are organized around evangelism and missions, and report a continued increase in the number of congregations and constituents or (3) they enjoy the leadership of an exceptionally gifted and attractive national chief executive officer who has been able to resist all efforts to place anything other than evangelism and missions at the top of the national denominational agenda or ecumenism has become the number-one item on the national denominational agenda and the shrinking numbers can be disregarded as simply one price tag on unity or (4) they have fewer than 200 affiliated congregations and resemble a clan rather than a nation-state or tribe or (5) they have identified an enemy, frequently the religious body they have left to create this new denomination, and their central organizing principle is to rally followers around the purity of their ideology or (6) they include a few hundred affiliated congregations who share a common ideological position.

My files contain data on 185 American denominations that can be placed under a broad definition of that category called "American Protestantism." It is not irrelevant to note that 49 percent report fewer than 200 congregations, 26 percent report 200 to 999 affiliated congregations, 13 percent claim 1,000 to 2,500 affiliated congregations, and only 12 percent include more than 2,500 congregations.

Over the past four decades, I have enjoyed firsthand contact with both congregational and denominational leaders from the largest 12 percent of these 185 denominations and with leaders from one-half of the other 88 percent. My observations suggest that those denominations with fewer than 200 affiliated congregations usually resemble a clan. Those with 200 to 1,000 congregations enjoy many of the benefits of a closely knit tribe that shares a common heritage and a clearly defined and widely supported culture. With but a few exceptions the affiliated congregations affirm their tribal relationship as the central component of their own identity.

Those American Protestant denominations that include somewhere between 1,000 and 2,500 affiliated congregations tend to fall into one of two categories. The minority continue to retain many of the characteristics of a very large tribe. Others resemble small nations. This distinction often surfaces when the time comes to choose a new chief executive officer. What is the number-one qualification of the ideal candidate? The individual who personifies the best of our tribal heritage? Or a leader who can earn the trust, loyalty, and support of opposing factions? Do we need a tribal chief? Or a president?

Finally, it is not irrelevant to note that the call to create a unified, self-governing, and self-expressing nation out of a collection of warring tribes in Afghanistan appears to be a huge challenge. The parallel in American Protestantism was the creation of scores of new denominations in the nineteenth century and early decades of the twentieth century. In recent years, however, that has been replaced by the emergence of a huge variety of movements, networks, and alliances. Many of these new creations either ignore or cross denominational boundaries. Several have been organized to counter the efforts of what is identified as a common enemy. Some clearly resemble an ad hoc coalition of tribes allied against the forces that now control the government of that nation (or denomination). Others have been created to respond to needs that have been ignored by those in power.

A fair number represent an ideological stance sharply different from the ideology of the officeholders.

When this distinction based on size and complexity is combined with the emergence of the consumer-driven economy, it raises a question about the role of denominations in the twenty-first century.

In the old American ecclesiastical culture denominations were expected to examine and approve candidates for ordination, regulate congregational life, enlist and raise the money to support missionaries to proclaim the gospel on other continents, and a variety of the responsibilities beyond the capabilities of congregations. That long list included planting new missions, organizing and funding institutions such as colleges, orphanages, seminaries, and retirement centers; creating and producing resources to be used by congregations; offering continuing education events for pastors and congregational leaders; operating camps and retreat centers; helping congregations utilize recent advances in technology; perpetuating a distinctive doctrinal position; serving as the building blocks for ecumenism, and organizing specialized ministries with women, men, and youth.

Denominations were evaluated by how well they fulfilled those responsibilities.

Today those and many other responsibilities are being carried out by congregations, parachurch organizations, and other Christian institutions.

In this new ecclesiastical economy denominational agencies are being evaluated on the basis of how they add value to the ministries of congregations rather than on what they do unilaterally.

In other words, the burdens and expectations placed on the chief executive and legislative body of a nation or a very large religious body are heavier and filled with more internal contradictions today than was true in 1925 or 1955.

In much of the Third World, the nations have office buildings, an e-mail address, a bank account, officials, staffs, and treasuries, but few loyal citizens. Several of the denominations in contemporary American Protestantism own or rent office space, receive mail, have an e-mail address, are led by an elected official who is assisted by paid staff, have a bank account, publish a magazine or newspaper, and schedule annual business meetings but are experiencing a shrinking number of loyal members. In both, the primary institutional loyalty is local, not national. In the first decade of the twenty-first century, does that generalization also apply to the United States of America?

One Book or Two?

During the middle third of the sixteenth century John Calvin, one of the great reformers of all time, rejected the notion of religious toleration. He equated that with opening the doors to the pollution of orthodox Christian doctrine. Calvin made it clear in his writings that rulers should defend the Christian worship of God and punish those who would "adulterate true doctrine" or disturb the peace of the church. Rulers should be guided by two books: the civil code and the Bible.

In 1541 Calvin persuaded the city government of Geneva to create a consistory as a standing committee of the civil government. The consistory was empowered to reprimand and punish those who violated a scripturally based moral code.[11]

Between 1639 and 1665 a similar arrangement prevailed in the New Haven colony. The governor and the most influential Puritan pastor, a Congregational minister, were the most respected leaders. The civil code and the Bible were the two reference books for controlling the behavior of sinful human beings.[12]

During the seventeenth and eighteenth centuries the Church of England was the established church in Virginia, North Carolina, South Carolina, and Georgia. The Congregational Church was the established religion in the three New England colonies. Over the years, however, the dissenters prevailed. Instead of establishing one specific religion, the reformers won the official approval of all Protestant churches. Discrimination against Roman Catholics and Jews continued.

In 1692 the General Court of Massachusetts required every town, except Boston, to levy a local property tax to pay the salary of an "able, learned and orthodox" minister. Only Congregationalists could meet those standards. The law also provided that buildings and schools also would be financed by the property tax. That meant Episcopalians, Quakers, Baptists, and others paid taxes to finance the ministries of the Congregational church. Another exception was in Swansea, Massachusetts, where the two Baptist churches and their ministers were supported by taxation.[13]

When Massachusetts became a state, the dissenters won one battle and lost another in drafting the state constitution of 1780. Article 2 of the Declaration of Rights guaranteed residents the right to worship God as they wished. It was an act of religious toleration. Article 3, however, endowed "the Legislature with power to authorize and require the several towns, parishes, precincts, and other bodies politic, or religious societies, to make suitable provision, at their expense, for the institution of the publick worship of God, and for the support and maintenance of publick Protestant Teachers of piety, religion and morality."[14] The voters in each community could choose any Protestant religion they preferred and would elect the person who would be the tax-supported minister of that community. Since four out of five residents were Congregationalists, however, this meant that in most communities property owners would be taxed to support the Congregational church. This aroused the opposition of the Baptists, who believed churches should be supported with voluntary contributions, not taxes. Since the First Amendment to the Constitution of the United States, adopted in 1791, applied to the United States Congress, not the states, the establishment of religion by a state government was a political issue, not a constitutional problem. (While the Bill of Rights to the United States Constitution was approved by the required majority of states in 1791, Massachusetts, Connecticut, and Georgia did not ratify those first ten amendments until 1939.)[15]

Article 3 also authorized the Legislature to make church attendance compulsory. It also allowed the voters to choose any Protestant religion, and over the next half century several communities implemented that option. But in the vast majority of places, outside Boston, the tax-supported church was Congregational. This concept of "nonpreferential" support was followed in several other states after the adoption of the United States Constitution of 1787.

The Religious Freedom Act of 1811 in Massachusetts allowed taxpayers to designate which congregation would receive their church tax as long as it had twenty or more members. Efforts to repeal Article 3 at the constitutional convention of 1820–21 failed, but in 1833 the eleventh amendment to the state constitution was ratified. Massachusetts became the last state to choose disestablishment. By that time fewer than one-third of the residents of the Bay State were Congregationalists, and revivalism had replaced orthodoxy.

That, however, did not mark the end of the Congregationalists' commitment to tax support for Christian institutions. One of the many Congregational ministers sent from the East to organize new churches and Christian schools on the western frontier was the Reverend George Atkinson. He and his wife were sent to Oregon in the middle of the nineteenth century. His strategy called for creating Protestant communities in which family, church, and a Christian school would reinforce one another by teaching the same value system. Atkinson also was the primary author of the legislation passed in September 1849 that created a system of tax-supported "common schools" in Oregon. Subsequently he was appointed to be the first public school commissioner for Clackamas County. By the time he died in 1889, Atkinson had earned accolades as the father of the common school in Oregon. During those four decades he was busy creating both public schools and private Christian academies. He urged educators to use the Bible as a textbook in public schools. When challenged about the possible conflict of interest, when he served as county Superintendent of Schools while also organizing and teaching in Congregational schools, Atkinson explained that there were only two kinds of schools in Oregon: Christian (meaning both public and Protestant) and Catholic. His goal was to expand the impact of the Christian schools.[16]

Congregationalism was no longer the established church in New England, but Congregational missionary dollars could still be used to strengthen the Protestant religion on the western frontier.

Finally, in 1947 the United States Supreme Court in *Everson v. Board of Education* ruled that the First Amendment to the United States Constitution does apply to the states as well as to Congress. Christianity can be ruled by its book, but only one book, the Constitution, rules civil society.

For most of the first four centuries of American church history, it was widely accepted that Americans should be ruled by two books: the Bible and the civil code. Much of the support for separation of church and state in the nineteenth and twentieth centuries was primarily an expression of anti-Catholicism. This was especially true in regard to the use of taxes for the support of churches and elementary schools.[17]

A year before that first Black Tuesday, a Roman Catholic candidate for the presidency of the United States from the

East, Alfred E. Smith, was defeated. Thirty-two years later another Roman Catholic from the East, John F. Kennedy, was elected.

The "G. I. Bill of Rights" of 1944 provided that federal tax funds could be used to pay the tuition of veterans enrolled in Roman Catholic or Jewish or Protestant colleges, universities, and theological seminaries.

For one hundred fifty years from 1639 to 1789 it was widely assumed that the Bible was the number-one book to be used as a reference in writing the laws that governed Americans. For the next one hundred fifty years that assumption was qualified that this would be an evangelical Protestant interpretation of Scripture. Concurrently the defining words evolved from "distrust" to "discrimination" to "prejudice" to "nonpreferential" to "toleration." Between those two Black Tuesdays that evolutionary process added such words as "ecumenism," "respect," "acceptance," "affirmation," and "approval." One of the most powerful forces to accelerate that process between 1929 and 2001 was the growing number of interfaith marriages. In the 1930s and 1940s that term usually was a synonym for Protestant-Catholic marriages. By the 1950s Christian-Jewish marriages were added to the list. More recently Christian-Islamic and Christian-Hindu marriages have become more common.

Black Tuesday 2001 brought a new agenda to the table. What should be the stance of American Christians and Jews toward Muslims? Prejudice? Discrimination? Toleration? Suspicion? Nonpreferential treatment? Respect? Accommodation? Acceptance? Affirmation? Approval?

Black Tuesday 2001 also brought a gradual recognition by Americans that this is a two-way street. One direction calls for asking what is the appropriate attitude of American Christians toward Muslims. The other calls for examining how Muslims view Americans. That evoked the question, "Why do they hate us?" The immediate and natural defensive response was, "They shouldn't! Look at all we have done for Muslims in Kuwait, Saudi Arabia, Bosnia, Kosovo, and other parts of the world."

A more sophisticated response emphasizes that the majority of Muslims in the world choose love over hate, peace over war, and hospitality over violence.[18] Another perspective declares that culture, politics, and education have taught millions of young Muslim males to hate the culture, the foreign policies, the affluence, and the entertainment industry of America.[19] Why did fifteen-year-old boys volunteer to join the Taliban in Afghanistan? Because they had been taught to hate America and to look forward to dying as a martyr in defense of Islam.

Before examining that statement more closely, it should be noted that this is not a new concept. For most of the nineteenth century in America and the early years of the twentieth century, the public schools in the United States taught children the inferiority of Negroes, Catholics, recent immigrants, Jews, and other groups. Lutheran readers, for example, may recall it was not until 1923 that the United States Supreme Court declared unconstitutional state laws prohibiting the teaching of foreign languages to children. Nebraska had made it a criminal offense to teach German in private, denominational, or parochial schools to a child who had not yet completed eighth grade. In *Meyer v. Nebraska* the court ruled that while the goal of fostering homogeneity among the American people might be commendable, that law was a violation of the Fourteenth Amendment to the United States Constitution.

Seventeen years earlier a boy by the name of Sayyid Qutb was born in Egypt. Sixty years later he was hanged by the government of Gamal Abdel Nasser.[20]

After spending two years in the United States, Qutb concluded that a secular representative democracy is incompatible with a true interpretation of the Koran. In his highly influential books he declared that any system of government that placed man above God would create a social, political, educational, and economic climate that would be incompatible with Islam. Therefore Muslims not only had a right, but they were obligated to attack any political or economic system hostile to Islam. From his view Qutb was absolutely certain the world should be governed by only one book, the Koran.

Qutb was right! The values and lifestyle he cherished are **not** compatible with a secular representative democracy and a free enterprise economic system. What he identified as American decadence has provided a supportive climate for religious freedom, individual opportunity, academic freedom, egalitarianism, equal rights and equal opportunities for women, free elections, modernity, and, what many Muslims see as the worst of all, the rise of the modern American entertainment industry. The contemporary American system also is hostile to the concept that one cleric or group of clerics should have the final authoritative voice on all political decisions.

Qutb's books have not only influenced the emergence of the extremist expression of Islam in the Middle East, Asia, Africa, Europe, and North America, but they have also influenced the curriculum in tens of thousands of Islamic schools and universities for males. They have been and are being taught an extremist interpretation of the Koran. They are being taught they have a religious obligation to defend Islam against all predators that may undermine the true faith.

One indicator of the effectiveness of these schools and their teachers can be seen in the reaction to Black Tuesday 2001. Although the vast majority of the people killed in the attack on the World Trade Center towers were Christians or Jews, no one in America described this as an attack on the Judeo-Christian religious tradition. The October response of the United States and Great Britain, however, was widely identified in other lands as an attack on Islam.[21]

Were the terrorists who planned the attacks on that Black Tuesday in 2001 motivated by Third World poverty? Or by ideology? The consequences of poverty often include envy, jealousy, alienation, out-migration, and, in a few cases, revolutions. By contrast, the consequences of severe ideological differences may include hatred and terrorism. From an Arab perspective, the Christian crusades of the eleventh century were motivated by ideological differences and produced terrorism.

It is only a slight oversimplification of history to suggest that the last third of the twentieth century brought two trends that have been moving in opposite directions. One trend, which has been nurtured by the writings of Sayyid Qutb and thousands of other teachers from the extremist wing of Islam, has been intolerance. This has sparked the growth of protest movements such as the Muslim Brotherhood in Egypt and Iraq, the opposition to the government in Saudi Arabia, Hamas and other anti-Israeli groups, and various revolutionary movements, including the Taliban.

For more than four hundred years, from the days of the Puritans in seventeenth and eighteenth century New England through the presidential election of 1960, the focus in interfaith relationships in America was largely on the differences that distinguish one religious tradition from all others. One expression of this was the founding of scores of denominationally related colleges. One goal was to educate future clergy. Another was to increase the probabilities that Lutherans would marry Lutherans, Methodists would marry Methodists, Catholics would marry Catholics, and Presbyterians would marry Presbyterians.

During the four decades before that Black Tuesday in 2001, the agenda gradually changed. The ecumenical movement encouraged Christians to focus, not on the differences that separate, but rather on what we share in common. Tolerance has largely replaced intolerance. Today religious intolerance in America is more likely to surface in intradenominational battles rather than in interdenominational or interfaith relationships. The civil rights movement of the 1960s was both a cause and a consequence of greater tolerance in interfaith relationships.

One of the lasting consequences of ecumenism in America and one emphasizing what various religious traditions have in common has been an increase in interfaith marriages. A much larger consequence has encouraged the religious migration of millions of American Christians as they found it relatively easy to switch from one tradition to another. Lutherans joined nondenominational congregations. Presbyterians became Episcopalians. Catholics switched to a Protestant congregation, and Protestants converted to Catholicism.

A carefully prepared statement that sought to balance differences with points of commonality was published in *The New York Times* on September 10, 2000. This ten-paragraph statement had been prepared by four Jewish scholars and was signed by 150 rabbis and scholars. "Dabru Emet" stands out as a landmark contemporary statement designed to improve Jewish/Christian relationships. The third paragraph declares that both Jews and Christians worship the same God—the God of Abraham, Isaac, and Jacob. While identifying other points of commonality, that historic statement also affirms "the humanly irreconcilable difference between Jews and Christians."

Will interreligious relationships in the twenty-first century focus on points of commonality? Before responding to that question, it may be helpful to identify five of the many differences between several strands of contemporary Islam and contemporary American Protestant Christianity. A quick comparison reveals that the most obvious difference is in the doctrine of God. Mohammed and Jesus are **not** comparable! Mohammed was a prophet of Allah. John 3:16 defines a radically different person and role in Jesus, the Son of God. The teachers in several strands of contemporary Islam interpret the Koran to mean the God of their

55

religion is not the same God worshiped by Jews and Christians. This raises a First Commandment problem for those proposing interfaith worship services designed for Christians, Jews, and Muslims.

The most highly visible difference, of course, is in the role of women.[22] A third difference is that Christians believe human beings are sinners and can be converted. Islam teaches that everyone is born a Muslim, but some need to be brought back to the faith into which they had been born. Thus Christians focus on conversion while Muslims define this as reversion. Fourth, several strands of Islam have three facets: religious, political, and military. Contemporary American Christianity certainly has been active on the political front, but, with the exceptions of a few crackpots, it does not have a military presence advocating violence against an enemy. While most of the 10,000 Islamic schools in Pakistan not only teach the Koran, they also teach the young males to be prepared to enagage in a violent defense of the true faith and to kill the infidel.

That is consistent with the central organizing principle of several strands of contemporary Islam. This calls for identifying an enemy and organizing against that enemy. The Muslim Brotherhood that emerged in Egypt a couple of decades ago is one widely known example. Today the Middle East is notorious for other examples.

Fifth, and this is the point of this narrative, several strands of contemporary Islam teach that all of society should be governed by one book, the Koran. This is not foreign to western Christianity. The religious wars in medieval Europe, John Calvin in Geneva, the Congregationalists in New England, American missionaries to the second and third worlds, George Atkinson in Oregon, and many others believed one book, the Bible, should be the rulebook for governing the people. Others compromised and accepted two books, the Christian Bible and the constitution of that state or nation.

One of the most significant trends in America between those two Black Tuesdays has been a gradual affirmation that this country should be governed by only one book, the United States Constitution.

Concurrently, the past decade or two have seen the language of politics in a score or more of Muslim countries change from nationalism to religion. That list includes Afghanistan, Algeria, Egypt, Indonesia, Iran, Jordan, Malaysia, the Philippines, Pakistan, Saudi Arabia, Sudan, and Syria. The pendulum of religion/government relationships swung in one direction in the United States and in the opposite direction in the world of Islam. That suddenly became very clear on 9-11-01.

As the Muslim population of the United States continues to increase, will the advocates of religious pluralism conclude that American society should be governed by one book?

Two of the key variables in answering that question will be (a) the sources of that immigration of Muslims and (b) their motivations in coming to the United States. In December 2001 Freedom House in New York reported that three-fourths of the non-Muslim nations on this planet are democracies. By contrast, only one-fourth of the predominantly Muslim nations can be described as democracies. Will the new wave of Muslim immigrants come largely from democratic nations such as India? Or from dictatorships such as Iraq?

Nearly all the tens of millions of immigants to the United States from western Europe came after the Protestant Reformation. The Peace of Augsburg of 1555 and the Treaty of Westphalia of 1648 both affirmed a modest degree of religious pluralism. That was reinforced by those European immigrants seeking religious liberty.

Will the next wave of Muslim immigrants come because they want to live with a government organized as a representative democracy with a firmly established separation of church and state? Will they come wanting to be part of a culture governed by one book? Or by two? Or by three? If only one, should that be the Christian Bible? The United States Constitution? Or the Koran?

A reasonable guess is that while many would object, several million American women today would be comfortable if the Christian Bible served as the primary reference point in legislating the laws of this land. A larger number probably would be comfortable if legislators relied on two books, the Christian Bible and the appropriate state or national constitution as their primary references in legislation. A far, far larger number, however, probably would object if the Koran became the primary reference point for legislators and governmental officials in the United States.

What will be the most likely scenario for interfaith relationships in the twenty-first century? One scenario calls for Muslims to follow one book, the Koran, but with two radically different interpretations of that book. Those who are convinced that all civil governments should enforce the teachings of the Koran will perceive secular representative government—and all other political systems that place man above God such as Fascism and Communism—to be a predator to be opposed by terrorist tactics.

Those who are comfortable following the trail blazed by Mohammed Ali Jinnab, the founder of Pakistan, may come to America convinced that the religious freedom of the United States provides a climate supportive of both Islam and a full range of human rights.

That raises the most difficult question of all. Who speaks for Islam in America? No one person is accepted as the spokesperson for Christianity in America. No one person is accepted as the spokesperson for Judaism in America. Is it reasonable to expect one person will emerge to speak for all of Islam in America?

Probably not. A reasonable guess is one Islamic leader will explain that Muslims worship the same God as is worshiped by Christians and Jews while on that same day a prominent Christian will declare the God worshiped by Jews is not the same God worshiped by Christians, and another Muslim leader will proclaim the God of Islam is not the same God worshiped by Christians. That ambiguity will create many different scenarios for interfaith relationhips.

That introduces the most optimistic scenario. This assumes the overwhelming majority of Muslims coming to the United States will be motivated by a desire for greater individual freedom, the opportunity to create their own future, the dream of a better life for their children whom they plan to enroll in American public schools, a personal determination to "get along" peacefully with people unlike themselves, the goal of a more prosperous life, a belief in the values of the separation of religion and state, and the expectation they will be assimilated by that great American melting pot... and everyone will live happily ever after.

Another scenario can be found in England. The British government is far more protective of the civil liberties of self-identified victims of political oppression and refugees from the legal systems of other countries than is the United States or France or Germany. It is far, far, far more protective of the civil liberties of dissidents and political refugees than is Egypt or Libya or China or Pakistan or Iran or Iraq or Syria or scores of other countries.

One consequence is that in England three tents reflect one scenario for this subject. In that tiny tent over there are gathered those who are committed to the nonviolent overthrow of that secular system of representative government and replacing it with a government organized under the law of Islam. In a larger tent are gathered those who advocate the violent overthrow of the present government and replacing it with a government based on Islamic law. Gathered in a huge tent are the religious leaders in England who are convinced their religious tradition can thrive in a political climate protected by a secular form of representative government.

Black Tuesday 2001 brought four new perspectives to interreligious relationships. The first, which had been talked about for years, was the realization that globalism really has arrived. None of those nineteen suicidal terrorists were natives of the western hemisphere.

The second was that Islam must be added to the traditional list of Catholicism, Protestantism, and Judaism as the major religions in America.

A third was a growing demand for greater tolerance in matters related to religion.

A fourth was the opposite. This is the recognition that the most rapidly growing religious bodies in America during the second half of the twentieth century share three common characteristics. First, they proclaim a clearly stated, unambiguous, and precise statement of what they believe and what they teach. Second, they project high expectations in both belief and behavior of their adherents. Third, they excel in reaching, attracting, serving, and assimilating both recent immigrants and younger generations of American-born residents.

Unlike the three tents in contemporary England described earlier, interreligious leaders in America in the twenty-first century may be housed in two big tents. Above the entrance to one will be a sign declaring, "Religions follow different roads here on earth, but all of these roads lead to the same God in the same Heaven."

The sign above the entrance to that second tent will read, "We welcome everyone who agrees with John 14:6. ("I am the way, and the truth, and the life; no one comes to the Father, but by me.") At one end of this tent are gathered the Catholics and Protestants who share the common belief of the real presence of Jesus Christ in the elements of Holy Communion.[23] For many that is a deep line in the sand, but for the majority of those gathered in this tent, that is not an issue,[24] and they are scattered among dozens of clusters throughout the rest of this tent.

The big unknown is how many American-born residents in 2010 and how many recent immigrants to the United States will not feel welcome in either tent.

Another unknown is how many religious leaders in America in 2025 will be interested in visiting either tent. Many find that their agenda already is overflowing as a result of so many tents being erected under their own denominational umbrella. The intradenominational differences of today already come close to matching interfaith differences in both content and intensity.

Finally the question must be asked, Is this a big issue? The two best data bases suggest the Muslim population at the end of 2001 as somewhere between 1.2 and 1.8 million. A tiny proportion are Americans of European ancestry who have converted to Islam, a much larger proportion are American-born converts with an African ancestry, and the vast majority are immigrants or the children or grandchildren of Muslim immigrants.

How many is 1.6 million? That is equivalent to the membership of the Episcopal Church or one-third the membership of the Church of Jesus Christ of Latter-day Saints or one-tenth the membership of the Southern Baptist Convention.

How many tents do you believe should be ordered to house interfaith groups and organizations? Perhaps fewer than you need to house all the caucuses, factions, interest groups, political parties, and movements in your denomination?

CHAPTER TWO
When?

*"The American culture clearly and remarkably unrav-
eled from the mid-1960s onward."—Walter Dean
Burham,* Democracy, *Summer 1982.*

What is the subject we should discuss next? The design of
those Sunday morning services when people come together
for the corporate worship of God? The appropriate size for
a parcel of land for a new mission? America's role in international relations? How often you should plan to replace
the tires on your car? The role of women in higher education? Where you will live in retirement? The future of the
United States Postal Service? How to transmit the Christian
faith from one generation to the next? How many major
league baseball teams should be located west of Chicago?
In designing that new supermarket, how many square feet
of retail space should be under roof? Where do we look for
a successor to our senior minister who is about to retire?
How many cows are needed for a dairy farm to be economically viable? How many hours do I have to work to
pay for ten gallons of gasoline for my car? How many
screens will be needed for that new motion picture theater?
What is ahead for interfaith relationships? How many
young couples live together before marrying? What should
be done about the fact that your pulse rate varies between
thirty-six and forty beats per minute? Should the United

States send a human being into outer space? How old must an American citizen be to vote in local, state, and national elections? Is it possible to transplant one person's heart into the body of another human being? What are the rights of American-born blacks? What do adults living on farms do to be able to pay their bills? What are the chances an adult American will die from tuberculosis? From polio?

One point of commonality for all of these, and for scores of similar questions, is that the answer today is not the same as it was forty years ago. About halfway between that Black Tuesday of 1929 and that Black Tuesday of 2001 the American culture, the American economy, and the American ecclesiastical landscape all began to change in the mid-1960s. By the mid-1960s most of the mainline Protestant denominations had cut back sharply on new church development. The resulting vacuum was filled by new religious movements, new nondenominational congregations, the Southern Baptist Convention, and new denominations. The civil rights movement blossomed in the 1960s. This nation experienced the longest inflationary cycle in its economic history as the Consumer Price Index, which had doubled between 1865 and 1960, multiplied sixfold between 1960 and 2002. The liberation of American women became a highly influential movement in the 1960s. The late 1950s and the 1960s brought a new wave of denominational mergers that have transformed the American ecclesiastical landscape. As described briefly at the end of the previous chapter, the Islamic extremists began to become a highly influential force on the world scene in the 1960s. In America, the 1960s conflict in Vietnam and the civil rights movement brought a new era of alienation between a large proportion of the citizens and the national government. The mid-1960s brought a new dimension and new life to the ecumenical movement. The enrollment in institutions of higher education more than doubled during the 1960s, and the number of doctoral degrees awarded each year tripled.

Between 1965 and 1972 a new community college campus opened at an average of once a week.

That seventy-two-year period between those two Black Tuesdays divides into two eras. The period from 1929 to the mid-1960s brought a shake-out among the old institutions of American society. Many, like the one-room, one-teacher elementary school, the small family farm, the owner-operated retail store on Main Street, several American automobile companies, and the physician who had his office in his home, began to disappear. Others, like the franchised fast food restaurants, the mainline Protestant denominations, the medical clinic with several physicians on the staff, the national chain of discount stores, very large state universities, a variety of parachurch organizations, and major league baseball prospered and expanded.

The second half of that seventy-two-year period extended from the mid-1960s to that second Black Tuesday. That era was dominated by the combination of the survivors from among those old institutions and the birth of thousands of new institutions. The new ones include those that brought a revolution in the delivery of health care, in the delivery of food, in the delivery of educational services (distance learning opportunities, community colleges, and multi-campus universities), in the delivery of the mail (United Parcel Service, Federal Express, the fax machine, and e-mail), in the delivery of entertainment, in the delivery of resources to congregations, in the delivery of financial services, in the delivery of political campaign messages, and in the delivery of airline tickets.

The dominant characteristics of this second post-1965 era can be summarized in eight words: *competition, competence, creativity, convenience, consumerism, choices, customization,* and *communication.*

One consequence is that the 1960s marked the beginning of what has been called the new American economy. The old American economy was organized around the perception that there is a scarcity of resources. This new American economy is organized around the perception that there is an abundance of resources. That distinction is illustrated by the response to the attack of December 7, 1941, and the attack of September 11, 2001. In 1941, the American people were called to sacrifice. In September 2001 the admonition was to shop and spend.

Those same eight words also summarize what has happened on the ecclesiastical landscape since the mid-1960s. The remaining chapters of this book represent an attempt to describe the impact of this new American economy and this new ecclesiastical culture on a means-to-an-end issue financing the ministries of congregations, denominations, and parachurch organizations.

The emergence of an economy organized on the assumption that there is an abundance of resources made it easy for the United States Congress in September 2001 to scrap the concept of a lock box for the Social Security surplus and focus on a huge financial bailout for a few commercial airlines, to expand unemployment compensation, and to spend the surplus.

On the other hand the great debate over who can be trusted to allocate that abundance of resources continues in both political and religious circles—but that requires another chapter.

CHAPTER THREE

The Great Debate

"Americans are more deeply divided and angry with each other today than at any time since the 1850s. Now, as then, distrust of leaders and institutions is widespread, and charges of conspiracy by one group against the liberty, livelihood, or principles of another pour out in torrents of speeches and news stories."—Robert William Fogel, The Fourth Great Awakening and the Future of Egalitarianism

The new American economy has created a very large number of people with high incomes. Their annual income not only covers all of their desires for food, clothing, shelter, education, transportation, personal services, and entertainment, but it also leaves them with substantial amounts of discretionary income.

The new American economy also has created a huge number of people with substantial accumulated wealth. They have accumulated far more money than will be needed to enable them to maintain a comfortable standard of living until they die. They own a large amount of discretionary wealth.

A third and overlapping group have both discretionary income and discretionary wealth.

Who Should Control It?

From the mid-1960s the big contemporary public policy debate in the United States has been over who should decide how that discretionary income and wealth should be allocated.

One point of view contends that the people who earned the income and/or accumulated the wealth should be free to decide where it will go. One way to encourage them to give it to charitable, religious, educational, and other benevolent causes is to exempt most or all of the money given to charity from the income tax. Another is to encourage holders of that accumulated wealth to donate real estate or stocks or bonds that have appreciated in value to a charitable institution and be able to deduct most or all of that appreciated value from their income in calculating their taxes.

A second and related perspective contends that parents who have accumulated this wealth should be able to transfer it, tax-free, to their children at the death of the parent. They oppose the estate tax or "death" tax as it is defined by its critics.

Both of these policy positions rest on the assumption that the people who earned that income and/or accumulated that wealth and who already have paid their fair share of income and property taxes should be able to control the disposal of their income and wealth.

They have earned that income as a result of their hard work, competence, creativity, education, persistence, ambition, productivity, and commitment to a dream. That accumulated wealth is a reward for hard work, long hours, frugality, the decision to place deferred gratification ahead of immediate satisfactions, sacrifice, education, creativity, problem-solving ability, and wise investments. (With many, it also is a product of being born to well-educated and/or wealthy parents.) They have earned (or inherited) the right to decide who will benefit from their discretionary income or discretionary wealth. That point of view has dominated the American political scene for most of the time since 1787.

A completely different public policy position is advocated by those who begin with a different assumption. The primary reason why so many Americans enjoy high incomes or have accumulated so much wealth is that they live in a democratic society with a free-enterprise economy. That is a benefit enjoyed by only a tiny fraction of this planet's population.

The primary reason why these people have so much money is not because they are creative, energetic, and productive workers. The key variable is that they enjoy the good fortune to live in the United States. Likewise frugality and wise investments are not the primary reasons behind all that accumulated wealth. That wealth is a product of a democratic society and a dynamic economy.

This is not a new issue! In 1820 Daniel Webster urged that tax-supported public schools represented "a wise and liberal system of police, by which property, and life, and the peace of society are secured."[1] The prosperous should be willing to pay taxes to support the common schools since that was a way to protect their wealth. The leading school reformer of that era, Horace Mann, argued that wealthy property owners were in fact only the "trustees" of the wealth of the total community. Nature, God, and earlier generations were the real creators of wealth. The current owners were only trustees who had earned only the right to oversee the property for the benefit of the community at large. These property owners have a moral, religious, and even a quasi-legal obligation to pay school taxes for the common good.[2]

The heart of that debate, however, was not over the authority of local governments to levy property taxes. The driving motivation was the anti-Irish and anti-Catholic sentiment among native-born Protestants who objected to tax funds being used to support Catholic schools for the children of Irish (and German) immigrants. Tax funds could be allocated to private schools, public schools, or English-language Protestant church schools, but not to parochial schools or Irish Catholics!

During the past century, however, a body of political support has emerged for a single public-policy position on this issue. The people who have created and maintained that democratic society and have contributed to the prosperous economy should decide how that discretionary income and that discretionary wealth should be used. The way to do that is to give the people's elected representatives in local, state, and national governments the authority to allocate those discretionary funds. The operational way to implement that position is to tax both income and wealth. Income can be taxed by income taxes, sales taxes, fees, licenses, etc. Wealth can be taxed by property taxes, capital gains taxes, estate taxes, and transfer taxes. For many the ratification of the Sixteenth Amendment to the United States Constitution on February 3, 1913, settled this issue. That amendment authorized Congress to levy an income tax. Not everyone, however, views this as a permanent agreement.

This difference of opinion over who should control the ultimate destination of discretionary income and accumulated wealth was a major issue in the presidential campaign of 2000. The Republican position held that the individuals and families who paid the taxes that produced the growing surplus in the federal budget should receive a reduction in their taxes so they could choose the final destination for those discretionary dollars. The Democratic response in 2000 was that federal income tax rates should not be reduced substantially and the elected representatives of the people should decide on the ultimate destination of those surplus dollars.

An interesting sidelight of that debate was offered by elected Republican officials at the state and local levels. They supported continuing high levels of federal taxation with the understanding that an increasing share of the federal surplus income would be returned to state and local governments in the form of undesignated block grants. "Let the president and the Congress take the blame for high taxes, and give us the authority to spend the surplus."

A similar debate continues in several denominational families. Should congregations or denominations determine the final recipients of discretionary dollars? Or should the individual donor decide?

A relatively new and growing fourth position begins with a different assumption. This perspective points out that the capability to earn money or accumulate wealth does not necessarily carry with it a high level of competence in giving away money. Thousands of wealthy people agree. They have learned it is easier to accumulate wealth than it is to be a good, wise, and responsible steward of that wealth.

One consequence is that large number of American adults who have concluded, "I know how to make money, and I'll continue to do that. I also know that I am not prepared to make wise decisions on how to give away my discretionary income or wealth, so you do that for me." One example of this position was the public statement signed by two hundred wealthy Americans in early 2000 who opposed elimination of the federal and state taxes on the estates left by the deceased.

The highly visible illustration is the twenty-five-year-old gifted professional athlete who is paid several million dollars annually and incorporates a foundation to give away part of that income. A second is the gifted thirty-six-year-old entrepreneur who enjoys creating the new in the world of electronic communication and incorporates a foundation to give away some of that accumulated wealth. A third was the generous financial response of millions of Americans in September and October 2001 to the disasters in New York and Washington, D.C.

More numerous and less visible are the tens of thousands of family foundations created since 1990.

The historic answer to this problem goes back to the organization of the Cleveland Foundation more than one hundred years ago. It was created so people could bequeath accumulated wealth to a responsible group of trustees who possessed the capability to make wise decisions on who should benefit from those gifts. Some donors indicated they preferred their gifts be used for health or education or similar causes.

That concept of a community foundation has been adopted by local leaders in more than six hundred cities all across the United States.

A potential counterpart is the community Christian foundation that would receive charitable contributions. The annual income from these invested funds could be used to undergird and expand the kingdom of God.

The Ecclesiastical Version

Trinity Church was founded in 1902. The original meeting place was destroyed by fire in 1913. A new masonry building was constructed on a larger site one block away. In 1958 the congregation voted to relocate since what originally had been a residential neighborhood was being transformed into commerical uses. That move was completed in 1959 to a three-acre site.

Trinity Church peaked in size with an average worship attendance of 483 in 1965. After several years of gradual decline, it has plateaued in attendance. The current pastor arrived in 1976 when worship attendance was slightly below 300. By 1985 the average worship attendance was back up to 355. For the past five years that number has fluctuated between 342 and 359. The most influential variable has been the weather. The second variable has been the ups and downs of the children's choir that sings at the first service on the second Sunday of every month.

In 1976 the median age of members ages fourteen and over was thirty-six years. Last year that indicator was forty-five years. That is not an uncommon pattern. The aging of the long-tenured pastor frequently is accompanied by an aging of the constituency.

Last year total receipts from member contributions totaled $549,000, of which 20 percent was allocated to benevolences. Back in 1999 a complete renovation of the forty-year-old building was undertaken. That project also included the purchase of two adjacent single-family residences, razing the structures and tripling the size of the parking lot. The total cost of $1.2 million was covered by a fifteen-month capital funds campaign that ran from May 1, 1998, to July 31, 1999. Total receipts from member contributions came to slightly over $1.3 million in 1998 and nearly $1 million in 1999.

This is not a congregation of poor people on public assistance! On the other hand, it is far from a church filled with wealthy families.

Recently several of the most well-informed leaders agreed, "If the needs were clearly presented and if our people were challenged, Trinity Church could raise well over a million dollars a year from our members." One of these leaders added, "I know of at least a dozen families who are major contributors here, but who give more money every year to other charitable causes than they give to Trinity."

What's the Issue Here?

For this discussion we will assume that the members at Trinity Church could contribute an additional $600,000 to $700,000 annually to religious causes. In this particular case that probably is a low estimate of the potential.

Should Trinity Church encourage those members with that discretionary wealth and income to give directly to the charitable needs of their choice? After all, they earned those dollars, so why shouldn't they decide who will benefit from those charitable gifts?

Or should Trinity Church provide a financial counseling service, on a fee basis, for those parishioners with accumulated wealth and children? The focus would be to help these parents design a customized fnancial plan that would maximize the number of dollars the children would receive following the death of the parents.

Or instead of adopting a budget of nearly $600,000 for next year with $120,000 allocated for benevolences, should Trinity Church challenge its members with a $1.1 million dollar budget with $600,000 for benevolences?

After all, Trinity Church is not simply a collection of church members. It really is a covenant community. We have agreed that we will make decisions together on how we will be responsible stewards of what the Lord has given us. Jesus warned that those to whom much has been given, from them much will be expected. Our whole budgeting process is based on that conviction. That also is a powerful factor in how we allocate the time and energy of our volunteers. Trinity Church has been richly blessed with a loving shepherd as a pastor, gifted volunteers, an attractive meeting place, a competent staff, and a solid financial base. Therefore as a worshiping community, we should act together, not unilaterally, on how to return to the Lord our combined tithes.

Another perspective is advocated by those who recall that the denominational board of home missions took the initiative in the founding of Trinity Church back in 1902. On that occasion plus again after the fire in 1913, that board provided financial grants, not loans, to Trinity. Three members of Trinity have responded to God's call to the parish ministry. All three were educated in denominational seminaries. At least three dozen members of Trinity have attended a denominationally related college or university. Two other members of Trinity have become full-time missionaries—one in Africa and one in Asia. Both were educated, trained, equipped, placed, and supported by this denomination. When they were much younger, four of those leaders who expressed such confidence in the financial potential at Trinity spent a week every summer in a church camp operated by the regional judicatory. One of them recalled that was when he first met the girl to whom he has been married for the past forty years.

Given all of that and much more, perhaps the best decision would be to challenge the members with that $1.1 million dollar budget with $500,000 for operating expenses, $100,000 for benevolences recommended by the missions committee, and $500,000 to be divided between the regional judicatory and the national denominational budgets. Let those who have the best overall view of needs and resources decide how those discretionary dollars should be allocated.

Finally, a fifth alternative has been suggested by several leaders who did not have any previous relationship with this denomination before coming to Trinity Church. Two are new Christians, three others were reared in Roman Catholic families, and five are refugees from other Protestant denominations.

This group of ten relatively young leaders displays zero loyalty toward Trinity's denomination. All ten are strong advocates of what sometimes is referred to as localism. They favor local control whenever feasible over centralized and distant bureaucracies.

When they first heard about it, all ten immediately became enthusiastic supporters of challenging the members of Trinity Church with a $1.1 million budget. Their plan, however, calls for $500,000 for the operating budget and $300,000 rather than $100,000 for the budget of the missions committee. They urge that a separate 501(c)3 corporation, The Trinity Foundation, be incorporated and the remaining $300,000 go to this new foundation. A couple of them insist, "If we can start it off with $300,000, aggressively encourage our people to give to it directly, and promote the idea of members including the foundation in their wills, in five years the foundation should have assets of at least $4 million. When that total reaches $5 million, all the income from investments can be allocated for missions. It will be easier to reach that $5 million goal if we keep the control here with trustees of the foundation who are elected from among the members of Trinity. Twenty years from now that foundation could be providing a million dollars a year for missional causes!"

As faithful stewards of the resources with which they have been entrusted, which of these alternatives should be chosen by the members at Trinity Church?

Perhaps the prior question is, Should the leaders at Trinity Church challenge the members with a $1.1 million budget for the coming year? That averages out to approximately $60 per worshiper per week. The total combined operating and benevolence expenditures in most American Protestant congregations average out to somewhere between $10 and $40 per worshiper per week. One reason for that, of course, is in most churches the challenge is not to tithe, but simply to underwrite the budget. If every household at Trinity Church tithed their annual income and returned only one-half of that tithe to the Lord via the Trinity Church treasury, the member contributions would average close to $60 per worshiper (not per member!) per week. That calculation does not include any contributions from accumulated wealth, only from current income. It also assumes two-thirds of the baptized members are in worship on the typical Sunday morning.

Three Questions

1. What are the criteria the leaders at Trinity Church should use in arriving at a recommended course of action?

2. Why even raise this question? Because this reflects one impact the new American economy has had on tens of thousands of American churches! Should we challenge our people to be more generous in their charitable giving?

3. If we do challenge them and they do respond generously, who should decide on the ultimate destination of
those charitable gifts? That is the great contemporary
debate and introduces another question for the policy-
maker at Trinity Church.

What Is the Future of the Middlemen?

In November 2001, Brian A. Gallagher of Ohio became
the new president of the United Way of America. Mr.
Gallagher described his definition of the issue before the
United Way in these words, "Ours is a world these days
hellbent on eliminating middlemen and we have been
fund-raising middlemen. With technology you can move
money from point A to point B at virtually no cost, so if you
are going to be an intermediary you had better add value to
dollars by being organized by issues like education, health,
safety and race relations. The question is, can you drive
down truancy rates, reduce violence and make other
improvements with those donations?"[3] Gallagher is right.
The new American economy has been eliminating middlemen. The victims include typists, telephone switchboard
operators, bank tellers, travel agents, retail sales personnel,
newspaper reporters, and insurance agents.

This new American economy also is challenging those
denominational systems that have served as intermediaries
between the donors of charitable dollars and the ultimate
recipients of those contributions. In the old ecclesiastical
economy Christians gave money to their congregation,
which sent a percentage to the regional judicatory, which
sent a fraction of those benevolent dollars to the national
denominational headquarters, which allocated some of
those dollars to its world missions board, which used some
of those dollars to provide the compensation for a missionary in Africa.

Today the adult children of those church members send
their tax deductable contributions directly to a parachurch

organization that provides the financial support for a missionary in Africa. The number of intermediaries has been reduced from four to one.

In the old ecclesiastical economy that national foreign missions board might declare, "We will add value to your contribution by matching it dollar for dollar with income from our investments." Or it might explain, "We will add value by supervising those missionaries."

That old ecclesiastical economy built the evaluation system on inputs, on how much money was raised and spent. The new ecclesiastical economy demands an evaluation system designed around outcomes. How did you use our contributions to proclaim the good news of Jesus Christ? How were lives transformed?

If the leaders at Trinity Church do decide to create that foundation to receive and distribute charitable gifts, should it be designed to add one more middleman to the list? Or should the trustees of that foundation channel benevolent dollars directly to the individuals and oganizations that are engaged in doing ministry? Or should it focus on funding new ministries designed to respond to unmet needs?

What Is Your Institutional Relationship?

One of the consequences of the emergence of the new American economy is a greater openness to terminating the existence of what earlier had been assumed to be an essential component of the larger economy. Examples include the disappearance of the Sears and Roebuck mail order catalog, the five-and-dime variety store on Main Street, the one-teacher elementary school, the manual typewriter, plow horses, the military draft, and the tuberculosis sanitorium. The endangered species list now includes the small family farm, the physician in solo practice, the single screen neighborhood motion picture theater, at least 20,000 small post offices, the corner drugstore, and interstate railroad passenger service.

A growing number of American Protestants are ready to add traditional denominational systems to that list of endangered species.[4] Parachurch organizations, publishing houses, megachurches, for-profit corporations, and entrepreneurial individuals have come forward to do what formerly was the responsibility of denominations.

Five major points of view dominate this discussion. The traditional perspective, which peaked in influence in the 1950s, declared that denominational systems, like congregations, are legitimate orders of God's creation. This perspective has its strongest supporters in Catholic, Anglican, and Reformed circles. This is an important component of the western European religious legacy to the United States —less in Canada or Latin America. One of the supporting arguments is the threat of heresy. A second is to affirm the interdependence of congregations. A third is the need for control and care of the clergy, and a fourth is distrust of local leadershiip.

A second perspective moves ecumenism ahead of denominationalism in planning for the institutional expression of the Christian faith. This view was turned into an action plan in June 1925 when three Protestant denominations plus 70 percent of the Presbyterian congregations in Canada came together to create the United Church of Canada. Subsequently additional denominations and congregations have joined that union.

A parallel response to denominationalism has been taken in various Asian countries.

A similar strategy is beginning to evolve in the United States with the creation of a new coalition including the Episcopal Church, the Evangelical Lutheran Church in America, the Presbyterian Church (U.S.A.), the Reformed Church in America, the United Church of Christ, and the Moravian Church in America. This could evolve into a south-of-the-border version of the United Church of Canada.

A third perspective distrusts denominationalism, but affirms the importance of the interdependence of congregations and the value of cooperation. A brief and lucid summary of this point of view was articulated by Robert T. Carlson, Chair of the Executive Committee of the National Association of Congregational Christian Churches, who recalled that the founders of the Congregational Way in the 1500s and 1600s were committed to the "purity of the Gospel to be experienced in the local church and the local church alone with Matthew 18:20 as the New Testament test." He followed that with the admonition, "We never know God's will if we are not able to come together" and explained that the vehicle for doing that is to come together as a voluntary association of congregations, not as a denomination.[5]

A fourth and largely overlooked point of view affirms the value of denominational systems. This perspective also recognizes that it is completely unrealistic to expect any one denomination to be able to respond effectively to all the needs of every congregation. Since in this increasingly competitive ecclesiastical culture many churches need all the help they can get, the best stewardship of resources requires that congregations that so choose may enjoy a full affiliation with two or more different religious traditions or movements concurrently. One consequence has been an increase in the number of dual affiliation churches.

The fifth perspective is represented by that rapidly growing number of independent or nondenominational congregations. Most of them devote slightly less energy to this issue than they do to whether or not the United States should return to the gold standard as the foundation for the nation's currency. This increase in the number of nondenominational churches is both an American trend and a worldwide phenomenon. In 2001 the independent Christian churches throughout the world reported a combined total of 400 million adherents. That is fifteen times the number of Methodists or twenty times the number of Lutherans on this planet.

The impact of this new American economy on Christian congregations will be influenced by whether they are a member of one denominational family or of an association of congregations or are competely independent or are part of a new uniting church or choose to relate to a variety of denominations, movements, and fellowships.

That choice also will influence the final destination for that charitable dollar. In recent decades the American response has been that the majority of dollars contributed by individuals for what historically have been described as acts of Christian mercy should be funneled through governmental organizations rather than through religious organizations (see chap. 7). In dollar terms that is the largest and most divisive component of this great debate, but it received very little attention in the weeks following Black Tuesday 2001. It was widely assumed that most of the dollars required to respond to that disaster would be raised by taxes and distributed by governmental agencies while secular charitable organizations would distribute the other benevolent dollars. Those assumptions introduce a discussion on the values and rules that determine how religious organizations collect and allocate charitable contributions.

CHAPTER FOUR

Values, Rules, and Denial

"We want a market economy, not a market society."
—French Prime Minister Lionel Jospin in 2000

Like the old American economy, the new American economy is the source of bitter ideological debates. That same generalization also applies to the new ecclesiastical economy. Jesus told us that the poor in spirit will inherit the kingdom of God, but that does not mean the poor in wealth will be the winners in either the economic or the ecclesiastical marketplace in the twenty-first century.

The new American economy is not the best road to social justice. It is not supportive of participatory democracy. The wealth being distributed in America by the contemporary generation of Christian philanthropists does not automatically go to the most worthy of causes!

As I attempted to point out in an earlier book, the recipients of today's charitable and religious giving tend to display six characteristics.

1. They take the initiative. They ask for money. They are active players, not passive spectators.

2. They articulate their plea for money in terms of an attractive cause, not simply the budgetary needs of an institution. (Taxes are levied or services are sold to fund governmental budgets.)

3. They rely on skilled and persuasive messengers to present that attractive cause to potential donors.

4. They understand the need for credibility with potential donors. Credibility is more important than the merits of the cause in moving on to the next step.

5. They recognize the value of continuing relationships with prospective donors. The second gift often will be larger than the first.

6. Whenever possible, they offer the prospective donor a choice among several attractive needs and encourage the donor to choose from among those needs with a gift designated for a specific need.[1]

Some experts in the field insist this should be a seven-point strategy, and the seventh is a BIG thank you to the donor. In a few cases that expression of gratitude is naming a building or a room for the donor. In others, it may be a plaque or a name among a list of donors. At a minimum it is a letter of gratitude.

Nowhere in that list, however, is any suggestion that the most worthy causes will receive the most money. The current rulebook for philanthropy in America rewards initiative, creativity, persuasiveness, relationships, trust, persistence, public reinforcement, superb skills in communication, credibility, choices, expressions of gratitude, and the trading of favors.

A parallel is major league professional sports. The players who are the ideal adult role models for children and youth or the players who merit a grade of A+ on character or the players who are the most respected leaders in the clubhouse often are not among those receiving the highest salaries. The marketplace for professional athletes places character below athletic ability and the competence of agents in defining the reward system.

The reward system of the free market does not always reward such cherished American values as loyalty, perseverance, hard work, character, generosity, thrift, honesty, participatory democracy, neighbor-centered love, or a forgiving spirit. The free market is as likely to reward one for a wise choice of parents or good health or a natural gift or the place of one's birth or for a choice of friends as it is to reward hard work or generosity or good character. The free market is not a synonym for fair play!

This introduces the most divisive of the value questions generated by the new economy.

Whom Do You Trust?

The shortcomings of the free marketplace have generated pleas for regulation. One expression of the response is governmental regulation. The extreme form of this is communism in which government controls not only both the means of production and distribution of goods and services, but also speech, political activity, employment, and consumption. Communism is based on the assumption that the individual cannot be trusted.

At the other end of the political spectrum are those who place unreserved trust in the individual functioning in a completely unregulated free marketplace.

The political compromise in the United States has been to enact two sets of governmental regulations. One set is designed to protect public health, safety, welfare, and the environment. These include compulsory school attendance, inspections of restaurants, traffic regulations, land use controls, and the criminal justice system. The second set represents attempts to control the economic workings of the marketplace. These include tariffs, farm price supports, the regulation of public utilities, licenses, marketing agreements, patents, copyrights, subsidies, anti-trust laws, and taxation policies.

On the American ecclesiasical scene, several of the Christian religious bodies that trace their origin back to a western European religious heritage have created a powerful top-down or command-and-control regulatory system. These include the Roman Catholic Church in America, the

United Methodist Church, the Episcopal Church, and the Presbyterian Church (U.S.A.).

The New Lines of Demarcation

For most of American history the widely used lines of demarcation in classifying the population were skin color, gender, place of birth, nationality, language, wealth, education, occupation, military service, religious affiliation, place of residence, age, marital status, income, political affiliation, citizenship, and criminal record.

Today several of those have been blurred and others lowered to minor importance. For every line of demarcation that has been removed from that list, however, at least two have been added. Chapter 3 described a relatively new one: Who should control the expenditures of discretionary wealth and income? The creator of that income or the first recipient of charitable gifts?

Another is simply how to evaluate the arrival of the new American economy. Is that good or bad? For many this evaluation process produces a favorable response to the market economy but a negative response to a market society.[2]

Likewise, many leaders on the ecclesiastical landscape welcome the impact of the market economy but have severe problems with the emerging free market in the ecclesiastical culture. Those who are convinced that they were chosen by God to be regulators naturally are skeptical of the free market on the school playground, in the economy, in society, or on the religious scene.

For collectors of trivia, one of the interesting coincidences is that the increase in the number of unregulated plants for generating electricity has overlapped the rapid increase in the number of large independent or unregulated Protestant congregations. These twin trends are most highly visible in the Southwest and the West. The old regulated providers of service are facing the competition of the new unregulated providers of services.

How Large Is the Circle?

A persuasive argument can be made that the most influential change in the ecclesiastical marketplace is a product of the erosion of two values plus the increase in the ownership of private motor vehicles. One value that is still strongly supported by many political and religious leaders is the concept of the geographically defined neighborhood. People should support neighborhood institutions such as the local public school, the corner drugstore, the owner-managed hardware store, the neighborhood one-screen motion picture theater, the neighborhood church, and others.

A second old value was to create an internal institutional identity and unity by defining the enemy. For fourteen or fifteen decades several American Protestant denominations reinforced their distinctive religious identity by defining Roman Catholicism as the enemy. That value was replaced in the 1960s by the power of ecumenism. "Instead of focusing on the differences that separate us, let's lift up what we have in common." This encouraged an increase in both interfaith and interdenominational church switching by younger generations as well as to interfaith marriages.

Thus by 1980 it often was easier and quicker for a family to travel by car to the church of their choice seven miles from their home than it was for their grandparents to walk a mile to church in 1925.

The congregation that serves a constituency scattered over a seven-mile radius from the meeting place serves an area twelve times the size of the church with members living within a two-mile radius. That not only means that the larger circle may include twelve times as many "competing" congregations, but also that the success of the ecumenical movement plus the impact of denominational mergers since 1950 may mean the proportion of congregations that church shoppers will place on their shopping list of "acceptable" alternatives has at least tripled. In simple

terms that could mean the congregation with a constituency drawn from a two-mile radius was competing
with only one or two other congregations in that neighborhood in the 1950s. Today it may be competing with two to
three dozen other churches within a seven-mile radius. The
old admonition, "Patronize your neighborhood grocery or
neighborhood hardware store or neighborhood school or
neighborhood church" has been replaced by a new value in
this consumer-driven American economy. "I drive four
miles to a supermarket because they offer more choices
and lower prices. I drive seven miles to Home Depot
because of the prices, choices, and service. Our nine-year-
old takes the bus to a magnet school rather than walk to
our third-rate neighborhood school. We also drive eight
miles each way to church two or three times a week
because it offers what we want for ourselves and for our
children."

Which value should religious leaders aggressively support? Recreating the geographically defined neighborhoods
of 1950? Or the individual's right to a larger array of attractive choices?

Liberal or Conservative?

One of the victims of the new American economy and
culture is the value of the old liberal/conservative
dichotomy. One example is in the rights of parents. Does a
pregnant mother of two have a right to abort that unwanted
pregnancy? Does she also have a right to choose the tax-
funded elementary school that is prepared to provide the
appropriate ecological and pedagogical environment for
her seven-year-old son and nine-year-old daughter?

The current political liberal answer is yes to the first and
no to the second. (In hundreds of communities she has a
right to choose the appropriate tax-funded pre-kinder-
garten experience for her four-year-old but not for that
older child.)

The conservative response is no to the first and yes to the second.

For many years politically conservative leaders in Congress advocated a balanced federal budget, a reduction in the number of adults receiving some form of public welfare, and a lowering of the economic barriers to international trade. Liberal Democrats opposed all three. By the end of his eight years as president, William J. Clinton could boast that a balanced federal budget, welfare reform, and free trade were three of the most important legacies of his leadership. What is the liberal position? What is the conservative view?

On the local church scene the theologically conservative congregations are more likely to create innovative new ministries than are the theologically liberal churches.

Culture or Politics?

One of the most useful insights on the liberal/conservative line of demarcation originated with Daniel Patrick Moynihan, the former senator from New York. "The central conservative truth is that it is culture, not politics, that determines the success of a society. The central liberal truth is that politics can change a culture and save it from itself."[3]

That distinction provides a useful context for understanding the intradenominational quarreling now occurring in several religious traditions in the United States. One group walks the path that believes that affirming and reinforcing the distinctive culture of that religious tradition is the only correct road to the future. Another group chooses the path that is based on the conviction that the culture must be changed and politics is the way to do it.

This debate becomes even more confused when both groups identify themselves as conservatives or when theological liberals (or conservatives) are both numerous and influential in both groups.

Is It Either/Or?

One of the new lines of demarcation places on one side those who believe it is possible to enjoy the benefits of a free-market economy, but not to have to put up with the consequences of a free-market society. That is a widely shared hope in Europe and Japan as well as in America.

On the other side are those who argue that the costs go along with the benefits. The United States really is one giant culture, and it is unrealistic to expect people who enjoy the benefits of a free market in travel, entertainment, vocational opportunities, the purchase of groceries, the location and design of their place of residence, telecommunications, restaurants, trucking, women's reproductive health care, and marriage will not also want a free market in education, the purchase of energy, health care, and religion.

Between those two views is a third that declares it can be a both/and world. Tax-funded and parent-controlled charter schools can exist in the same political environment with the professionally controlled public schools.

One of the best known students of the American culture argues in an award-winning book that the free-market economy can co-exist with a culture that meets the hunger for an enhanced quality of life, affirms and undergirds the value of community, nurtures those on a personal spiritual pilgrimage, and enriches a civil society.[4]

The eighty-year-old Bethany Church peaked in size with an average worship attendance of nearly 400 in 1953. During the next forty years it gradually decreased to an average of 260. A new pastor arrived in 1994. Last year the combined attendance for the three weekend worship services was nearly 700. The most pressing problem is the shortage of off-street parking. The second is the functional obsolescence of the original building completed in 1926 and expanded in 1954.

Approximately one-third of the members favor relocating the meeting place to a fifteen-acre site and constructing new physical facilities. Another third, consisting largely of long-time members who also contribute slightly over one-half of the annual receipts from members, oppose abandoning this sacred site. The remaining one-third either do not perceive the existence of a problem or have no opinion.

Instead of choosing up sides over the relocation issue, the leaders at Bethany decide the best answer is, "Yes." A $2.7 million capital funds campaign is launched with $1.8 million to be allocated to the purchase of that fifteen-acre site and the construction of what will be a heavily mortgaged first unit. Three mission projects will divide $270,000, and $630,000 will be used for overdue renovation of that old building. The younger generations, most of whom favor relocation, come out as winners, as do the older members, most of whom have close ties to that old location.

With a circulation of nearly 21 million in early 2001, the largest consumer-driven magazine in America confronted the generational divide. How will *Modern Maturity*, the flagship of the AARP, reach the older of the two baby boomer generations? Can one publication speak to the agendas of adults born in 1925 and also those born in 1950? Rather than choose an either/or response, AARP concluded it had two different constituencies with two different sets of expectations. The decision was to create a new magazine, *My Generation*, for a new aging constituency and redesign the cover of *Modern Maturity*. The anticipated outcome is a circulation of 10 million for *My Generation* by 2006 with a circulation of perhaps 15 million for *Modern Maturity*.

Less can be more.

On the local church scene the frustrated leaders of the numerically shrinking and aging congregation know they cannot change that 10:30 Sunday morning service. It is organized in a presentation-type style with a pipe organ, a robed choir in a divided chancel, and "classical" Christian music with the worshipers confined to pews in a room with a sloping floor and large clear windows on both sides. On the typical Sunday morning that room is half empty.

Rather than lose what is sure to be a highly divisive battle, the leaders decide on a both/and strategy. That first-floor fellowship hall with a high ceiling is remodeled, dark screens are placed on the windows, comfortable stackable chairs are purchased, a large moveable high stage is constructed in four sections. That room becomes the venue for a fast-paced, high-energy, and participatory-type worship experience following a meal on Saturday evening.

The design includes projected visual images on one very large screen, contemporary Christian music, cordless portable microphones for the five-person worship team, a nine-piece band, and a lapel microphone for the minister, who walks around while delivering the message in a one-to-one conversational style.

These illustrations introduce several questions about values. They also illustrate the importance of internal consistency between values and goals.

Which is the higher value? To become a multigenerational congregation or to perpetuate local traditions in a half empty room on Sunday morning?

Which is the higher value? To publish one magazine that is intended to meet the needs of a growing constituency, and thus become a unifying force as well as symbolize the role of that organization? Or to recognize that the old American economy still has a large constituency, but the new American economy is driven by a constituency with a different value system and a different agenda?

In the old ecclesiastical culture a congregation's identity was defined largely by its denominational affiliation, its real estate, and its constituency. That called for numerically growing congregations to solve their space problem by planting what would become self-governing, self-expressing, self-financing, and self-propagating new churches.

The new public definition of a religious congregation places a high value on what that church is doing and what is happening in the lives of its constituents. Thus the dominant value is on making that ministry available to more people, not on maintaining only one meeting place.

How large in numbers can an American Protestant congregation become before the sense of community and the spontaneous "caring for one another" begin to erode?

One answer is an average worship attendance in the 15-40 range depending on the frequency of attendance among those worshipers. (At least one-third of all the Protestant congregations in the United States report an average worship attendance of 48 or fewer.) If 90 percent of all worshipers are present on the typical Sunday morning, the answer may be as high as 60. The lower the frequency of attendance among those worshipers, the lower that number.

How large must a congregation be in the new American economy and today's ecclesiastical culture to both afford and justify a full-time and fully credentialed resident pastor?

In the absence of a long-term financial subsidy from an endowment fund or the denominational treasury, the answer is an average worship attendance of 120 to 160—between double and triple the answer in 1900.

Which is the higher value? A size that makes it relatively easy to create and nurture the feeling that this is truly a caring Christian community? Or a size that makes possible ten- to twenty-year pastorates for full-time and fully credentialed resident ministers?

In the new ecclesiasical economy, should a congregation focus on one slice of the population? Or seek to become more inclusive?

The both/and response, if the goal also includes a high degree of demographic diversity in the constituency, is the carefully designed congregation of congregations with each a collection of caring communities. This typically requires three to seven different worship experiences every weekend with a combined average attendance of at least 800, three different venues for the corporate worship of God, at least two full-time highly skilled preachers, a parish nurse, an effective staff specialist in building and nurturing the group life of that church, two or three leaders of worship teams, an executive pastor, plus a half dozen or more part-time specialists in ministry.

Sending Money or People?

What is the number-one criterion in the evaluation of the ministry of the missions committee? The old American economy and the old ecclesiastical culture often placed a high value on the number of dollars allocated to missions. A typical goal was (a) that number should be higher than it was a year earlier, (b) that number should represent at least 20 percent of the total congregational expenditures, and (c) that proportion should be increasing by at least one or two percentage points every year.

The new American economy and the new ecclesiastical culture place a high value on experiences and the transformation of lives. Therefore the new number-one criterion for the annual evaluation of the missions committee may be stated in these terms: "This past year fifteen of our people plus three from other congregations spent two weeks in teams of six each working in ministry with Christians in three sister churches, one in Africa, one in Peru, and one in Mexico. A year earlier we sent two teams of seven each to two sister churches. How many teams will we send this year?"[5]

Which is the higher value? Sending money? Or sending people with resources to share? Which is the point of greater loyalty? To the denomination? Or to those sister churches?

Shepherds or Entrepreneurs?

For most of American Protestant church history in congregations choosing a new pastor, a high value was placed on such qualities as character, Christian commitment, education, communication skills, knowledge of the holy scriptures, competence as a loving shepherd, an orthodox Christian faith, parenthood, and relevant experience.

The 1960s introduced a new era in American society, and the responsibilities of a pastor became both more numerous and far more difficult. An unprecedented number of congregations were approaching or had passed their one hundredth birthday. A higher level of competence as an initiating leader is required to revitalize or renew the forty- or eighty- or one-hundred-year-old congregation than is required to plant a new mission or to shepherd a relatively homogeneous constituency that is comfortable remaining on a plateau in size.

One result has been a growing demand for pastors who possess the gifts, skills, personality, and vision required to be transformational leaders. This shortage of transformational leaders has raised a highly divisive question. Is it fair to expect a theological school designed to train scholars and theologically informed shepherds to meet that demand for transformational leaders? The ensuing debate has produced a clash of values and expectations that has yet to be resolved. The compromise is to begin to implement plans to shift theological education for pastors from the old German university campus-based model to a congregation-based model.

One facet of that process has raised another value question: Should the student come to the professor? Or should the professor go to the student? One part of that debate is taking place in academic circles. The decisive debate, however, is occuring in the marketplace. The potential of distance learning leads some to suggest that a win-win response is possible, but the issue may not be settled before the arrival of the broadband for the World Wide Web.

Renew the Old or Create the New?

While that debate continues, another new issue has surfaced. An increase of 35 million in the nation's population between 1870 and 1900, plus the impact of the emancipation of the Negro slaves, led to the greatest church planting boom in American history. An average of more than 3,000 new Protestant congregations were organized annually back in that thirty-year period from 1870 to 1900.

Between 1950 and 1980 the population of the United States increased by 76 million. (Between 1980 and 2000 the official population increased by another 55 million.) This led to a call to plant tens of thousands of new missions to reach the new generations of American-born residents and recent immigrants. The early response was to launch a new big wave of new missions. By the late 1950s, however, a new debate over values surfaced. Which deserved to be the higher priority in the allocation of scarce denominational resources? The renewal of aging and numerically shrinking congregations or the planting of new missions? Since at denominational meetings the members of those aging congregations could outvote the members of the new missions that were yet to be started, the outcome was clear. The top priority should be given to renewing the old rather than creating the new.

Another vote, however, was held out in that free ecclesiastical marketplace. Those who favored planting new missions to reach new generations and recent immigrants received a big majority from those younger generations and recent immigrants. Thus the ecclesiastical marketplace of the 1950–80 era was the birthplace of thousands of what today are referred to as independent churches.

While they have received far, far less attention, two other important debates over values were held in the last third of the twentieth century. Both were decided in that increasingly competitive ecclesiastical marketplace. Both produced celebrated winners and frustrated losers.

The first debate was over who would be best qualified to lead in the renewal of those aging and numerically shrinking congregations: The minister who has received a solid theological education along with training and an apprenticeship as a loving shepherd? Or the person who may not have attended seminary, but is a self-taught learner who possesses the gifts and skills required to be an effective agent of planned change initiated from within an organization?

The seminary-trained shepherd often was chosen in the tradition-driven ministerial placement process, while the skilled change agent prevailed in that competitive ecclesiastical marketplace.

Was that fair? The answer, of course, is that the marketplace in the new American economy is not noted for its fairness.

A parallel debate took place in selecting a new generation of church planters. Who should be chosen? The seminary graduate with several years' experience as a loving shepherd? Or the entrepreneurial person with a passion for evangelism who is convinced that every new venture has a natural ceiling over it that can be raised?

That debate also was resolved in the ecclesiastical marketplace. It also motivated at least a few among the clergy to suggest that entrepreneurial personalities should not be licensed to proclaim the gospel of Jesus Christ. That, however, is not a new complaint in North America. It was widely heard in earlier centuries.

Defining Success

The increase in the number of charitable dollars waiting to be given away and the increase in the level of competition for those dollars has created an interesting question: How do you define success? This can be illustrated by three different approaches to capital funds campaigns.

The traditional systems were designed to produce victories. The professional fundraiser arrived and installed a system designed to produce results that exceeded the goal. "This is the seventy-third consecutive capital funds campaign we have conducted for congregations in which the cash and pledges exceeded the goal." The price tag on that success story may have included a few individuals who felt they had been the victims of a high pressure campaign, but a year or two later those hurts and bruises were largely forgiven and forgotten.

More recently professional fundraisers have designed sytems that emphasize Christian stewardship. "The secondary goal is to reach the target, but our primary goal is when we leave, your congregation will have advanced to a higher level of stewardship. That's the legacy we want to leave with you." A year or two later the pastor comments, "We collected 96 percent of what was pledged, which I guess is better than average, but more important in the long run, there has been a substantial increase in the level of stewardship here."

The arrival of the new American economy with that new emphasis on the transformation of the lives of people (see chap. 6) has created a third approach to capital fund campaigns. "We can help you raise the money you need for your capital expenditures; that's the easy part of the assignment in an economy based on abundance rather than scarcity. Our focus, however, is to make that a transformational experience for many of your people. A year or two after we have left, we want you to have the money you need to expand your ministry. That's important, but that's not what we're about. We sincerely believe Christianity is a transformational religion. We believe the gospel of Jesus Christ does transform lives! Two or three years from now we want you to evaluate what we did here by asking one simple question. Did this shared experience help a lot of your people move to the next stage of their personal spiritual journey? We believe we are called to be in the business of helping churches like yours transform lives."

When the time comes for your congregation to seek the help of a professional in a capital funds campaign, what are the criteria you will use to choose the right firm? Two years after the conclusion of that capital funds campaign, what will be the number-one criterion in evaluating that experience?

What Is the Problem?

The natural, normal, and predictable human response to unwelcome change initiated by others is denial. The first child, who is now three, looked forward eagerly to the arrival of that "new baby brother." No one, however, had been able to prepare that three-year-old for a new role. Instead of being the only child in the family, he now has to share the spotlight with an intruder.

After a series of diagnostic tests and invasive procedures, the physician explains to the patient, "You have two choices. One option is surgery, and we believe you have a 90 percent probability of surviving that and enjoying good health for several years to come. The alternative is no surgery, and you'll probably be dead within six months."

The patient offers the natural, normal, and predictable response: "I prefer good health without surgery."

The new forty-five-year-old pastor arrives to serve this eighty-year-old congregation averaging 135 at worship. Three years later attendance has doubled to 275. Four years after that, worship attendance has climbed to a combined total of 425 on the average Sunday at three services. The pastor reluctantly agrees that the time has come to add a second full-time minister to the staff. That newcomer turns out to be a superb communicator who delivers memorable and inspiring sermons. The schedule is redesigned to provide two "peak hours" on Sunday morning with Sunday school classes for all ages at both of those ninety-minute periods plus two concurrent, but substantially different, worship experiences at each period. Twelve years after arrival, the senior minister preaches to an average of 160 worshipers at the first service in the sanctuary and 180 at the second. The associate minister is the "teacher" in that new room resembling a theater with a combined average attendance of 450 for those two services.

Shortly thereafter, a third ordained minister is added to the staff. This "new" minister fills in for the other two when one is gone and also carries the primary responsibility for organizing and leading a new Saturday evening worship service. After four years, it now averages nearly 250 in the theater.

Eghteen years ago the staff configuration called for one ordained minister. Seven years later it was expanded to include a senior pastor and one associate minister. Six years ago it was reconfigured to include a senior pastor, one senior associate minister, and one associate minister plus other program and administrative specialists.

Has the time come to reconfigure it as an egalitarian five-person team of three excellent preachers plus a program director and an executive pastor? Or should that issue be postponed for two years until the senior minister retires? What are the tradeoffs in doing it now versus postponing that change? Which is the higher value? To perpetuate that traditional hierarchical arrangement for a couple more years? Or to take advantage of this senior pastor's experience, political clout, and leadership skills to transform the staff configuration into a five-person team before retirement? Or more immediately to promote the senior associate pastor to be the new team leader and look for a new associate pastor when the present senior pastor retires? Or should everyone agree that the old system is still valid and deny that most younger clergy persons prefer to work as a member of a team rather than as solo performers?

The arrival of the new American economy has brought many reactions. Perhaps the most widely shared is denial. One version is simply, "That is not true! Life today is a linear projection of the 1950s."

A second form of denial recognizes that conditions have changed, but denies the consequences. "Yes, things are different, but if we continue to play the game by the old rule-book, we can perpetuate the past."

In late 1998, for example, a survey completed by the National Opinion Research Center at the University of Chicago, one of the most highly respected social science research operations in the world, reported that among all American households including two adults of opposite genders, 32 percent were unmarried couples without children under age fifteen at home, 30 percent were married couples without children under age fifteen, 26 percent were married couples with children under age fifteen at home, and 12 percent were unmarried couples with children under age fifteen at home.

What was the reaction to those proportions among congregational leaders designing a ministry for the next five years? "I doubt the accuracy of that report, but if that is true nationally, that certainly is not the pattern in our community!" A second widespread response was, "If that's true, that's too bad. But our number-one priority is to reach, attract, serve, and assimilate married couples with young children." Those are both expressions of denial.

Where Else Do We Encounter Denial?

As an incurable list builder, I found the easiest section in the writing of this book came with the decision to offer several examples of operational denial in contemporary American Christianity.

1. "Four out of five of our last pastors have been loving shepherds. Our most recent pastor never should have entered the parish ministry. We all agree that what we need is another loving shepherd to replace him. It's true that our worship attendance is only half what it was back in the 1950s, but we are convinced that if we can find the right shepherd, it will go back up."

2. "You remember the movie that taught us that if you build it, they will come? We have decided to relocate our

meeting place closer to where our people live. We're convinced if we build a big new sanctuary, it soon will be filled."

3. "Our goal is to build a large congregation that projects high expectations of every member and to combine that with a congregational system of governance in which the vote of every member carries the same weight as the vote of any other member."

4. "We want to continue to have a low threshold into full membership so we can attract as many newcomers as possible, but we want to transform this into a high-commitment congregation."

5. "Our goal is to organize a new mission that will grow into a very large congregation that will include a very high degree of demographic diversity in the membership as well as welcome a wide range of theological pluralism."

6. "We welcome the marketplace economy, but we insist on perpetuating a highly centralized command and control system of governance for our denomination."

7. "We are asking the congregations in this regional judicatory to increase their contributions to our annual budget by 3 percent every year for the next ten years and to make those payments the top priority in their financial plan."

8. "Our goal is to persuade every clergyperson in this community to become an active member of our local ministerium. Our central organizing principle will be to speak with one voice on all issues of social justice."

9. "Rather than spend a lot of money to plant new missions, our top denominational priority will be to revitalize our numerically shrinking congregations with an aging membership. One reason for that is we are short of pastors who have the gifts and skills to be successful church planters."

10. "Our current plans call for (a) expanding the demographic diversity of our membership and (b) building a 1,500-seat worship center so our whole congregation can come together for a common worship service every Sunday

morning. When the new building is ready for occupancy, we will be able to cut back to one big worship service every Sunday morning."

11. "From a denominational perspective we are convinced the best career path for a seminary graduate is to spend the first three to five years after school serving a two- or three-church parish. That should be followed by four or five years as the pastor of a small-town congregation averaging somewhere between 100 and 150 at worship. Those two pastorates should prepare that minister to relate to and serve a wide variety of people. The third pastorate should be in a congregation averaging 150 to 250 at worship with a staff that includes a couple of part-time specialists in music, youth, pastoral care, or evangelism. After seven to ten years in that pastorate, the minister should be ready to move on to become the senior pastor of a large church with a multiple staff."

12. "Everyone knows you begin the budget building process by calculating anticipated income. After that has been done, the next step is to make sure the budgeted expenditures do not exceed the anticipated income. How can you begin that process by projecting desired outcomes when you won't be able to measure those outcomes until after two or three or four or five years have passed?"

13. 'The financial plan for our regional judicatory calls for asking our most successful congregations to minimize expanding their ministry and to help subsidize our failing congregations. It also calls for asking those congregations with a high level of stewardship to subsidize those with a poor level of stewardship. Finally it calls for our numerically growing congregations to subsidize our numerically shrinking churches. We believe the fortunate should share their material blessings with the less fortunate."

14. "Our members are growing older and fewer in numbers. Therefore we need an attractive young minister who can encourge young adults to come to our church. We know that is the best way to keep our older members happy."

15. "Money is money, and our people don't like to hear us talking about money all the time. Therefore we have scheduled one big, but brief, financial campaign for next November. At that time we will ask our members to make one pledge to underwrite our operating budget, a second pledge to fund our next building program, and a third pledge for designated second-mile gifts to missions." (See chap. 10 for why this represents either denial or a failure to understand the differences between contributions for operational costs and capital expenditures.)

The most disruptive incidents over denial during the second half of the twentieth century, however, were experienced by the Tooth Fairies. That story requires a new chapter.

CHAPTER FIVE

What Happened to the Dollar?

The best introduction to this chapter may be to review the events that led up to the general strike of May 2000. While it has been overshadowed in the memories of Americans by what happened on 9-11-01, the general strike turned out to be the most widespread and disruptive labor dispute in American history.

In the old American economy of the late 1930s and the 1940s, children knew that when a baby tooth came out, they should place that tooth under their pillow as they went to bed. Sometime during the night the Tooth Fairy would come, take the tooth, and leave a silver dime in its place. As the years rolled by, this custom placed an increasingly heavy burden on the tooth fairies. The number of six-year-olds in the American population in 1967, for example, was 30 percent higher than in 1937.

The tooth fairies were advised by their Fairy Godmother that they would have to increase their work load from 300 to 400 stops per night. This was accomplished by changing their routes from the old north-south pattern to east-west routes. This gave each tooth fairy an extra hour of darkness every night. The change was implemented in January 1961 in order to take advantage of the longer night as the tooth fairies had to master new wind currents as well as to learn new routes.

The big inflationary wave of 1973–82 required a long overdue change in the reward system. A quarter replaced the dime as the reward for surrendering that baby tooth. This meant a heavier load for each Tooth Fairy since quarters are far heavier than dimes. Fortunately that trend was offset by a decrease in the number of toothless children. The number of six-year-olds in 1980, thanks to the birth dearth of the early and mid-1970s, was down to 3.2 million from that 4.2 million in 1967. This reduction plus an increase in the number of tooth fairies in the late 1960s allowed the Fairy Godmother to reduce the number of stops per night from 400 back to the old standard of 300.

Unfortunately what appeared to the Fairy Godmother to be a surplus in her work force persuaded her to reduce the number by attrition. During the 1980s fewer than one thousand new tooth fairies were enlisted and trained. That did not begin to match the number of retirements and was a factor that led to the general strike of May 2000.

A second big factor was the new baby boom in 1986–2002. For only the second era in American history, the first being 1954–64, the number of live births exceeded four million annually. The aftershock was a sharp increase in the number of five-, six-, and seven-year-olds during the 1990s and later.

The third change was inflation. By 1979 two quarters were required to equal the consumer purchasing power of a dime in 1940. A couple of years later a new generation of six- and seven-year-olds began to protest the decreased buying power of a lost tooth. Finally, in 1987 another cost-of-candy-and-ice-cream adjustment was made, and the tooth fairies were instructed to exchange three quarters for every tooth they found under a pillow.

The impact of this order can be understood only if you realize the weight of three American twenty-five cent pieces is equal to the weight of thirty-nine dimes!

It also is necessary to point out that the median age of the tooth fairies was rising, retirements exceeded the number of new recruits, their loads were getting heavier, and their routes were getting longer.

The result was that for the first time in their history, the American tooth fairies voted to organize, and their union officials were authorized to call a strike.

Three days before that deadline, a wealthy benefactor who had made a huge fortune manufacturing high-calorie candies intervened. He declared, "This is ridiculous! Our tooth fairies deserve an easier life. Instead of reacting to inflation, let's get ahead of the game. My foundation will make annual grants to the Fairy Godmother to enable her to replace this order for three quarters for each tooth with a dollar bill. In fact, my grant will cover the difference between two quarters and a dollar bill. That's a fifty cent subsidy for every lost tooth, but it's worth it to make life easier for our loyal and faithful tooth fairies." That, indeed, was a generous offer! That annual subsidy soon climbed to over $40 million a year. (The other $40 million came from income from investments in the Tooth Fairy Endowment Fund.) This was not as generous as it first appeared, since in 1998 the Consumer Price Index was ten times the 1942 average when a dime was worth a dime.

The tooth fairies breathed a sigh of relief and canceled their plans for a strike. To start out in the evening with a purse filled with 300 dollar bills is a far lighter load than a purse containing 900 quarters. Most of them simply shrugged in 1992 when the Fairy Godmother announced that because of the recent increases in the number of five-, six-, and seven-year-olds, the new work quota would be 350 stops per night. An extra fifty one dollar bills adds only a little to the weight of that purse.

The devastating blow came in February 2000 when the United States Treasury Department, as part of its $40 million advertising campaign to increase the circulation of the new gold Sacagawea dollar coin, urged Americans to use the new coin as a birthday present or to replace that tooth under the pillow. The tooth fairies ignored that suggestion and continued to use dollar bills. Apparently, however, parents were beginning to interfere as they replaced the dollar bill left by the tooth fairy with that shiny new dollar coin. At this point, a couple of trial lawers approached the officers of the Tooth Fairy Union and offered to file a class action suit on a contingency fee basis. The tooth fairies, however, explained that would violate their religious belief system and rejected the offer.

A few weeks later the Fairy Godmother announced, "We are patriots, and we are obligated to support our government. Therefore beginning on April 1, 2000, you will leave the new gold coin, not a dollar bill, for each tooth you pick up."

This galvanized the tooth fairies to action! This new gold coin weighed about the same as a quarter but was far heavier than a dollar bill. The vast majority decided to ignore the order and continued to swap dollar bills for teeth. Most of the younger ones, however, felt obligated to obey their Fairy Godmother and switched to the new gold coins. "After all, for years we exchanged two quarters for every tooth, so this is only half the load we used to carry," was one explanation.

What first appeared to be a minor dispute over working conditions in one small segment of the new American economy began to escalate. What no one had considered was that the six-year-olds of 2000 were not carbon copies of the six-year-olds of 1940. This new generation of six-year-olds brings far higher expectations of the world than was true of their parents and grandparents. Furthermore peer pressure is far more powerful today than in earlier years.

"Mom, all my friends find a gold dollar coin under their pillow when the Tooth Fairy comes. All I get is a wrinkled old dollar bill. Why can't we switch to a better brand of tooth fairies?"

Two weeks after the ban on dollar bills was announced, the Fairy Godmother suggested a compromise. For the first tooth a child lost, the Tooth Fairy would leave a gold Sacagawea dollar coin. For each lost tooth thereafter, however, the Tooth Fairy would leave a dollar bill.

This announcement moved the issue to the top of the political agenda in that presidential election year. Several members of Congress running for re-election responded by pointing out that since millions of senior citizens also were losing their teeth, Medicare should be expanded to finance a lost tooth payment to seniors. Seventy-year-olds vote, but six-year-olds don't!

Another bill was introduced in Congress to subsidize a full dollar reward for the children of single-parent mothers who had been finding only a dime or a quarter under the pillow.

Children complained, "Mom, when David lost his last baby tooth last year, he got a gold dollar. You mean I will only get a paper dollar for each tooth I lose after the first one? Why can't I get a gold dollar for every tooth?"

A frequent response by harried mothers was, "Go ask your father. He'll explain it to you."

One group of fathers replied, "I'll wash the dishes; you explain it."

Many others began to fulfill their paternal responsibility by suggesting, "This is a very complicated subject. First of all, your mother and I were born into the end of the old American economy, and we have had to adjust to this new American economy. That's part of the story, and we'll talk more about that later; but you will have to learn to adjust to this new economy just as we have had to adjust.

"A second factor is inflation. You've heard your grandfather recall time after time that when he was a boy, a candy bar cost a nickel. A double dip ice cream cone was a dime, and he could go to the movies for a dime or fifteen cents. Those days are long gone, and they won't return.

"A third part of the explanation is that the United States Treasury Department used to finance itself largely from taxes, but several years ago they recognized the Postal Service was making millions of dollars every year from commemorative stamps that were sold, but never used for postage. So the Treasury decided it would go into the business of producing and selling collectibles. They expect to make a profit of over $6 billion dollars on this new series of commemorative quarters that honor each of the fifty states.

"The Sacagawea golden dollar costs the Treasury approximately twelve cents to produce, but they sell them to banks for a dollar. So far they've minted a billion of these coins for a net profit of over $800 million. One reason they want the tooth fairies to use these coins, rather than a dollar bill, is that would place another 80 million in circulation every year. One reason the tooth fairies object is that in another year or two they will be expected to leave a gold dollar and a silver quarter for each tooth. That would be necessary to equal the purchasing of a dime back in 1940, which is the base year used to calculate the value of a lost baby tooth. Now, do you have any questions?"

"Yes, would you help me build an airline terminal with my Lego set?"

On April 28, 2000, the tooth fairies announced that they were fed up with the whole mess. They drew a line in the sand. Either they would be given lighter purses or they would go on strike! The deadline was set for noon on May 1, 2000. Henceforth, when youngsters who had lost a tooth placed it under their pillow at night, they would awaken in the morning to find that tooth would still be there. Neither a paper dollar nor a gold dollar would be there to replace it.

Within days millions of young mothers of children who were losing their baby teeth began to realize the implications. On Monday, May 8, 2000, many of those mothers who were employed outside the home began to walk off the job to witness to their sympathy for the tooth fairies. Others persuaded their union leaders to call sympathy strikes.

Airlines had to cancel half their flights. Surgeons postponed all but the most urgent surgical procedures because of the shortage of nurses. Banks had half hour lines of customers waiting for a teller or a personal banker. Public schools, medical clinics, law offices, post offices, hotels, real esate offices, municipal buildings, museums, retail stores, and manufacturing plants closed as mothers walked out in solidarity with the tooth fairies. The nation's economy slowly was moving toward a standstill.

During that second week in May, millions of fathers and grandfathers were confronted by angry six- and seven-year-olds. "Which side are you on, Dad? Are you for or against the tooth fairies?" "Grandpa, are you supporting the Treasury Department or the tooth fairies?" "Uncle Dave, when are you going to walk off the job to support the tooth fairies?"

Television stations scheduled reruns for most of their air time. The New York Stock Exchange closed. The construction industry shut down.

On May 9, President Clinton met with several hundred tooth fairies. He assured them he felt their pain. He also recalled that when he was a boy in Hope, Arkansas, the Tooth Fairy left him only a nickel under his pillow when he lost his first baby tooth. Governor Bush of Texas sent a note explaining that as a compassionate conservative, he believed the federal government did not have a role in this dispute, but that the tooth fairies had a constitutional right to choose between either dollar bills or dollar coins. Both are legal tender. He also added it should be up to each state, not the federal government, to decide whether senior citizens should receive visits from a volunteer cadre of retired tooth fairies.

On May 11, when the economy was approaching a total collapse, the general strike was settled. The compromise called for tooth fairies to leave one of those gold colored Sacagawea dollars for the first tooth a child lost. Thereafter the Tooth Fairy would leave a small gold colored plastic chip for each additional lost tooth. These chips could be exchanged at any bank, discount store, or supermarket for one of those Sacagawea coins. That compromise greatly reduced the weight of the purse each Tooth Fairy carried.

When both the Fairy Godmother and the Secretary of the Treasury signed the agreement, the general strike of May 2000 was over! Most agreed this was a win-win solution. The children were happy. Those gold colored plastic chips became collector's items, and their price hovered around $1.20. Mothers, fathers, uncles, aunts, and grandparents returned to work, and the economy quickly recovered. Everyone lived happily ever after.

One reason why everyone lived happily ever after is that in February 2001 the United States Treasury announced tooth fairies no longer would be expected to deliver gold dollars. The Treasury had entered into an agreement with Safeway, Inc., to distribute 1.6 million of those gold dollars via Safeway's 1,500 supermarkets.

Those who believe the Fairy Godmother has too much authority should do the arithmetic. During the 1990s an average of slightly over 80 million baby teeth came out each year. That is an average of approximately 220,000 each day! Most of them came out between noon and eight in the evening. Since each tooth fairy makes 350 stops every night, that means the Fairy Godmother has to prepare 6,300 different customized schedules every evening during a two-hour period. No two are alike, and none are duplicates of the previous evening. The larger group is for the Eastern-Central time zone trip, and the smaller number for the Mountain and Pacific time crews.

For the first time in their history, the new contract gives the tooth fairies a night off. On a rotating basis, each works seventy-one consecutive nights and has the seventy-second night free.

The typical tooth fairy comes to the warehouse about two hours before dark, receives and memorizes the customized schedule for that night, loads the purse with twenty to twenty-five Sacagawea dollar coins plus 340 of those gold plastic chips, eats a light snack, and prepares for what usually is a ten-hour tour plus the return flight. The average purse is slightly heavier than it was with 350 dimes back in 1940. In addition, the new contract requires every rooth fairy to carry a pager. On the average, each tooth fairy receives, while in flight, two to three additions and one or two deletions to that night's schedule.

With that pager, today's Tooth Fairy is carrying a heavier load than was required in 1940, makes more stops, covers a larger territory, and puts up with more hassles. In return each tooth fairy now has five free nights every year.

The Fairy Godmother needs adequate authority to manage that crew of more than 6,300 workers and to create that many different schedules every day! She has to run a tight ship!

What Did the Tooth Fairies Teach Us?

What is the moral of this long story?

First, that decision by the tooth fairies to organize and vote to strike is one more recent illustration of the conflict between obedience and participation discussed in the previous chapter. The training program for tooth fairies had always placed a high value on unquestioned obedience to their Fairy Godmother. That training was based on values of the old economy. These included institutional loyalty, sacrifice, obedience to authority, and hard work. That decision to organize and, if necessary, to go out on strike is consistent with the value system of those who insist anyone affected by a decision should have a right to participate in making that decision.

Second, this story illustrates the fact that the new American economy has had an impact on every facet of American society, including benevolent organizations such as the tooth fairies. This new economy encourages tooth fairies and others to draw a line in the sand and use that line for choosing up sides. The new economy affirms individual initiative and courage.

Third, it helps to explain why that arthritic old man will stoop over to pick up a stray penny on the sidewalk, but the nimble nine-year-old won't bother. That old man thinks a penny is money. The nine-year-old knows the only thing a penny will buy is a one-cent postage stamp, and who wants those?

Fourth, the tooth fairies born back before World War I and earlier have had to adjust to a radical change in the American economic system. These long-tenured tooth fairies had been taught that a dime in 1940 had the same buying power as a dime in 1778 or 1816 or 1869 or 1932. Inflationary waves were offset by periods of deflation. Give or take a nickel, the buying power of a dime continued to be approximately the same decade after decade and generation after generation. The big difference was that for a sailor or a farmer or a laborer to earn a dime required slightly less time in 1940 than was required back in 1900.

"Sound as a dollar" was a compliment, not a diagnosis of a terminal illness.

Fifth, for most of American history, adjustments in the economy were made by periods of inflation or deflation. Wars brought inflation and eventually were followed by periods of deflation. That has changed! High inflation is now followed by low inflation, which is followed by another wave of high inflation.

Conventional wisdom persuaded a twenty-two-year-old in 1960 to invest $100 in a tax-deferred fund that guaranteed an annual interest rate of 4 percent compounded yearly. Thanks to compound interest, forty years later, in 2000, this investor, now sixty-two, was able to withdraw nearly $500. The capital gains tax on the increased value meant that the $100 investment of 1960 had grown to approximately $400 after taxes. In 2000, $400 had approximately the same consumer purchasing power as $62 back in 1960. Saving money was not the road to wealth!

CONSUMER PRICE INDEXES*

(1982-84=100)

1725	8	1948	24
1745	5	1950	25
1770	8	1961	30
1778	14	1967	33.4
1800	17	1970	39
1808	16	1974	43
1814	21	1976	57
1817	16	1977	61
1828	11	1978	65
1836	11	1980	82
1846	9	1981	91
1865	15	1983	100
1884	9	1988	118
1903	9	1990	131
1913	10	1991	136
1920	20	1992	140
1925	18	1997	160
1933	13	1998	163
1936	14	2000	172
1940	14	2001 Est.	178
1942	17		

*Sources: The numbers for 1814 through 2000 are from the several Historical Series on U.S. Consumer Price Indexes published by the United States Bureau of labor Statistics. The numbers for 1725 through 1808 are derived from the tables in John J. McCusker, How Much Is That in Real Money? (Worcester: American Antiquarian Society, 1992.)

Sixth, inflation has appealed to elected public officials who appreciate an increase in income from taxes without raising tax rates. School districts, counties, cities, states, and the federal government have seen that the same tax rate on real estate, sales, or personal income produce greater revenues every year as inflation increased the market value of what was taxed. Additional revenue could be secured by increasing the tax rates "to offset the impact of inflation." From an elected political leader's perspective, inflation is a more comfortable trend than deflation. The same reaction comes from homeowners and borrowers.

Seventh, inflation plus the rising cost of providing labor intensive personal services helps to explain why the costs of health care, education, and legal services keep rising.

Those two factors also help to explain why the ministerial marketplace has a surplus of seminary educated clergy and a shortage of congregations that are convinced that they can afford fair compensation for a full-time and fully credentialed resident pastor. How large does a congregation have to be to afford a full-time and fully credentialed resident pastor with no other sources for family income?

About twice the size required in 1940. That explains the current campaign for every parish pastor to be entitled to two spouses, one or both of whom will be employed full-time in the secular labor force. How else will those 150,000 small American Protestant congregations be able to have their own full-time pastor?

For the benefit of the dozen or so readers who do not believe in tooth fairies, another slice of American economic history may be enlightening.

The Erie Canal, which linked the Atlantic Ocean to the Great Lakes, cost $7.2 million to construct and opened to boat traffic in 1825. During the next 57 years $121.5 million in tolls was collected.

For decades the canal provided "steady jobs at good pay for unskilled laborers," so applicants exceeded the demand

In 1830 a common laborer was paid $ .75 a day. From 1852 through 1862 the daily wage of a common laborer on the canal was a dollar for a twelve-hour day. In 1860 a carpenter was paid $1.75 a day, a mason $2.00, and a man with a team of horses received $3.00 a day.

The consumer purchasing power of a dollar in 1898 was the same as back in 1860, but by 1922 $2 was needed to purchase what a dollar had bought in 1860 or 1898. By 1967 $4 was required to match the consumer purchasing power of that earlier dollar. By 1972 inflation had pushed that up to $5, to $10 by 1980, to $15 by 1989, to $20 by 1998, and to $21 by 2000.

Eighth, inflation produces winners and losers.

The farmer who paid $20,000 for an 80-acre dairy farm in 1922 and was forced into bankruptcy by the combination of the droughts and economic depression of the 1930s was forced to sell that farm for $12,000. He was a loser. The purchaser who borrowed $9,500 to buy it and sold it for $50,000 in 1952 was a winner. The twenty-five-year-old buyer who paid that $50,000 in 1952 and sold it fifty years later for $1.4 million for commercial and residential development also was a winner.

In order to finance their relocation and the construction of new physical facilities, Salem Church in 1971 sold twenty-year bonds, paying 7 percent annual interest, to members. In 1991 the church paid off all those bonds. The bondholder with a $10,000 bond had collected $700 each year in interest. That came to a total of $14,000 in taxable income. If we assume federal and state income taxes totaled $3,000 on that taxable $14,000, it leaves a net interest income of $11,000. The $10,000 received for the bond was a tax-free return of capital, but it represented only $3,200 in consumer purchasing power in 1991 when compared to what $10,000 would have bought back in 1971. After allowing for the gradual year-by-year erosion of the buying power of those $700 annual interest payments, that bondholder received in after-tax interest income the equivalent of approximately $6,000. In terms of after-tax consumer purchasing power, the bondholder received approximately $9,000 in return for a $10,000 loan made two decades earlier.

The winner, of course, was Salem Church. In 1991 it paid back with cheap dollars those expensive dollars it had borrowed back in 1971. In effect, Salem Church paid thirty cents for every dollar it had borrowed. Each year it used cheaper and cheaper dollars to meet those interest payments. In the twentieth year of those interest payments, that 7 percent interest rate of 1971 was the equivalent of slightly over 2 percent in 1991.

The total "subsidy" from inflation for that million dollar building program at Salem Church, which was paid by those bondholders, totaled approximately $920,000. (That represents the "write down" on the bonds plus the "subsidized" interest rates.)

Finally, the events leading up to that mythical general strike of May 2000 suggest an answer to the question, "How much should I drop in the offering plate on Sunday?"

How Much?

How much money should a respected, middle-class, generous, and regular churchgoer drop in the offering plate every Sunday morning?

First of all, the answer depends on what year it is. If this is 1790, a dollar a week is an extremely generous offering. One hundred years later, in 1890, an American dollar had almost exactly the same buying power in the consumer's marketplace as it had in 1790.

The second variable in this narrative is whether it is a dollar per person or a dollar per family. The answer to that question will vary greatly, depending on the size of the congregation, the region of the country, the difference between the rural church with a part-time lay pastor and the city congregation with a full-time seminary educated minister, and other variables. For this discussion, however, a somewhat oversimplified answer back in 1790 or 1890 was one dollar per worshiper age fourteen and over. The purchasing power of that dollar was approximately the same in both years.

Thanks to the inflationary period following World War I, that middle-class churchgoer in 1921 needed to contribute $2 a week to produce the equivalent buying power of one dollar in 1790 or 1890. For a husband/wife couple with two teenagers in worship every Sunday morning, that came to over $400 a year in contributions to their church. The majority of American churchgoers failed to meet that standard in 1921, but more generous donors made up the difference.

The deflationary impact of the Great Depression was more than offset by the inflation following World War II. "The next depression that will curl your hair" was predicted, but it never arrived. Thus nearly fifty years later, in 1969, four dollars were required to match the buying power of one dollar back in 1790 or of two dollars in 1921. That meant the husband/wife couple with two teenagers needed to drop $16 in the offering plate every Sunday they were in church if all the bills were to be paid from the offering plate.

At this point we are introducing a third variable. In addition to inflation and the size of the family, we are adding the frequency of worship. These calculations assume that these churchgoers are in church every weekend. Since financial contributions often correlate with the frequency of worship attendance, this often meant that the family of four in 1969 who never missed worship contributed approximately $800 a year, but the family who attended on an average of only twice a month contributed only $400 to $500 a year.

One of the biggest inflationary waves in American history arrived in the 1970s. The American dollar lost one-half of its buying power between 1969 and 1979. That meant that in 1979 our respectable, generous, and regular church-goer had to contribute $8 a week, or $32 a week for a family of four to keep the church treasurer happy.

This, however, requires introducing a fourth critical variable. Congregations tend to purchase those items in the marketplace on which the price tag has risen faster than the general pace of inflation. The costliest is the increase in the price for an hour of a person's time. That fact of life is reflected in the rising costs for health care, education, legal services, newspapers, and the judicial system.

The ministry of a worshiping community also is labor intensive. Much of this labor is contributed by volunteers, but congregations also puchase other items that are labor intensive to produce, such as printed resources, fresh sermons, a new roof, custodial services, sending children to summer camp, or health insurance for the staff.

A rough estimate is that the costs incurred by congregations, like other organizations that provide person-centered and labor intensive services, increased twice as fast as the consumer price index during the twentieth century.

When this is factored into the discussion, what does it cost a congregation to pay all its bills in 2002? The broad range is from $900 a year times the average worship attendance to $2,000 a year times the average worship attendance. Below the low end of that scale is the small church with a lay pastor who makes a living at a full-time secular job. Total annual expenditures may average out to only a few dollars per week per worshiper including rent for that small meeting place.

Beyond the $2,000 per year per average worship attendance are a modest proportion of Christian congregations that are big contributors to missions and various local and national benevolences and/or investing in the future via an expensive building program. In these congregations the total annual expenditures may average out to $3,000 or more times the average worship attendance.

That figure of $900 a year times the average worship attendance comes to slightly over $17 a week per worshiper. An average of $17 per week in 2002 would be required to keep up with the rise in the consumer price index. In other words, $17 in 2002 is approximately the equivalent of $1 in 1790 or 1890 or $2 in 1921 or $6 in 1976 or $10 in 1981. What was a generous contribution in 1986 is now a below-average donation!

When the increase in congregational costs beyond inflation (for electric lights, indoor plumbing, central heating, telephone service, air conditioning, specialized staff, continuing education for the laity, etc.) is factored in, the successor to that respected, middle-class, generous, and regular churchgoer of 1790 or 1890 who contributed a dollar a week to the church contributed $35 a week in 2002. For the husband/wife couple who never miss Sunday morning, that adds up to approximately $3,600 a year, or 5 percent of a family income of $72,000.

What Will the Dollar Buy?

If the focus of this discussion is shifted from income to expenditures, a significant trend surfaces.

In September 1940, for example, the total expenditures for the academic year of the eighteen-year-old enrolling in the tax-supported state university amounted to from $250 to $400. That total included fees, a room in a university dormitory, three meals a day, transportation, books, tickets to an occasional movie, a coupon book to attend all theuniversity's athletic events, and personal expenses such as toothpaste, paper, pens, milk shakes, and perhaps one meal a week at a restaurant. That averaged out to one dollar to two dollars for every day the student spent on campus.

For that previous year in the local public high school, the school district spent an average of approximately fifty cents to a dollar a day per student to operate that school.

Today the presidents of various private universities boast that their schools are a bargain at $100 to $150 a day for students. Fees, a dorm room, meals, a laptop computer, a printer, a cell phone, the cost of purchasing and owning a good used car, and other personal expenses may average out to $60 to $100 per day for the student attending the state university.

A member of the American labor force today works far fewer minutes than was required in 1950 to earn the after-tax income required to purchase a loaf of bread or a radio or an electric stove or a wrist watch or an automobile or a television set or a pound of salt or a can of soup or a ballpoint pen or a calculating machine. In addition, the quality often is far superior to what was available in 1950.

In 1940 the sixteen-year-old babysitter was paid $ .30 an hour (well over the cost of a gallon of gasoline) plus a snack and was delighted to receive a dollar bill for three hours. Today's parents often expect to pay $7 or $8 an hour, but cannot find a reliable babysitter.

In 1950 the mother of a new baby spent six days in the hospital. The cost was $50 plus $ .50 a per day for the baby plus $10 for the delivery room. Her granddaughter today spends only 48 hours in the hospital for the birth of her baby, but the hospital bill is $1,600.

What happened? The costs of providing person-centered services such as health care, education, legal counsel, and parish ministries have increased at a more rapid pace than the rate of increase in personal income. By contrast, increases in productivity in the manufacture of many goods have sharply reduced per unit costs. A common bonus is that rise in quality.

What has happened to the costs of financing the ministries of a worshiping community? That is a subject to be discussed later in chapter 10, but those expenditures reflect the increase in the cost of providing person-centered services.

Before or After Taxes?

Does the concept of the biblical tithe apply to income before or after deductions from the paycheck for taxes and other items?

Obviously, there is no unequivocal biblical answer to that question. One widely used response begins with the assumption that governments now accept responsibility for financing charitable concerns formerly carried out by the churches. That long list includes sheltering the homeless, feeding the hungry (free meals for children from low-income families in the public schools and food stamps are two expensive examples), caring for the poor, operating hospitals, and elementary schools, helping the elderly, etc. For millions of taxpayers, 5 percent or more of their annual income goes to taxes that pay for these charitable services formerly provided by Christian churches.

Therefore this response declares that the tithe applies to income, including capital gains, after taxes, but before deductions for Social Security, health insurance, and other benefits.

Another response is unequivocal. The tithe applies to all the Christian's income. Furthermore, the tithe should not be seen as a charitable contribution. Tithing is simply returning to the Lord what was his to begin with, and the Christian's charitable and religious contributions begin with what is given after returning that tithe.

The good news on this issue is that far, far fewer than a million Americans are now drawing some form of public assistance because they contributed excessive amounts of their income to charitable causes.

"I Can Remember..."

Finally, this whole discussion is influenced by the increased life expectancy of adult Americans.

As they drove home together from the annual meeting at First Church, the sixty-seven-year-old Mrs. Brown released her pent-up hostility on her husband. "I didn't feel free to say anything because I believe Pastor DeVries is a committed Christian, a good preacher, and a caring shepherd, but when the chair of the finance committee recommended a cash salary of $32,000 for next year plus nearly $30,000 in fringe benefits including housing allowance, utilities, pension, book allowance, health insurance, continuing education, and car allowance, I almost choked. My dad served for over forty years as a pastor, and when he retired in 1961, he was being paid a cash salary of $4,400, and he and Mother lived in a hundred-year-old parsonage that badly needed remodeling. They paid their own utilities and never complained. When they retired, they didn't have a nickel in equity in a home. If he stays here until he retires, Pastor DeVries will have his home all paid for. They can sell it, take the money, and buy themselves a nice home in Arizona and not have a mortgage. My folks still had seven years of mortgage payments left when Dad died. It seems to me that in Dad's time, men went into the ministry because they loved the Lord. Today a lot of them apparently see it as a job, not a calling."

It might have helped if, before making that recommendation on Pastor DeVries' compensation, the chair of the finance committee had introduced the subject by explaining, "Per capita personal income in the United States is thirteen times what it was forty years ago and up 50 percent since 1991. Our recommendation for Pastor DeVries' compensation for 2001 is slightly more than 50 percent higher than what we paid his predecessor back in 1991. The reason for that is the cost of health insurance has more than doubled since 1991."

This is one of the most persuasive arguments for nominating only people born after 1960 for membership on the finance committee. The ideal candidate may not be that elderly and deeply committed Christian who recalls, "We paid

$9,800 for our first house, and it was brand new! The next year we bought our first new car, and we paid only $1,400 for it."

The new ecclesiastical culture still has difficulty accepting that inflation has become a continuing component of the new American economy.

CHAPTER SIX

Two New Economies

One reaction to 9-11-01 was, "Life will never be the same again." That is true. The central theme of this book, however, is that life in America began to change in the mid-1960s, and the 1950s are gone forever. That means September 11, 2001, made obsolete the old playbook for fighting wars. A hint of that came in 1990 when Iraq invaded Kuwait and the first priority in the American response was to create a new alliance. By contrast, on December 7, 1941, the alliance already was in place.

The new American economy has made obsolete the 1950s rulebook on how to do church in general and has created a new playbook on church finances in particular.

A persuasive case can be made that from a larger perspective the most significant change in the American economy is the addition of two new tiers. This also has tremendous implications for educators, the entertainment industry, consumer-driven businesses, the clergy, journalists, publishers, politicians, airlines, military planners, worship teams, financial institutions, travel agents, church architects, restaurants, and those responsible for the renewal of the central business district of a large city.

A brief analysis of this five-tiered economy provides a larger context for looking not only at church finances, but also for other facets of contemporary life.

In their book, Pine and Gilmore describe this as the experience economy.[1] They explain that for most of human history the economy was organized around the gathering of commodities (wood, water, berries, flint stones, salt, meat, leather, gold, corn, iron ore, wool, etc.) provided by nature. Centuries later a second tier was added as a small number of people transformed commodities into goods (candles, flour, knives, shoes, canoes, jewelry, bread, clothing, kerosene, etc.). More recently the third tier was added as entrepreneurs invented services that could be traded for commodities and goods. Services include shoe repair, education, health care, printing, carpentry, restaurants, hotels, financial services, pastoral care, transportation, communication, and a safe and dependable supply of water.

The big expansion in the American economy during the past few decades has been in the fourth tier—what Pine and Gilmore describe as the experience economy. One example they offer is the farm wife who gathered home-grown commodities (eggs, wheat that had been ground into flour, milk, butter, etc.) and baked a birthday cake in the wood-fired kichen stove. Her daughter purchased a cake mix at the store, added a few ingredients such as eggs, water, and oil, and baked a bithday cake in the oven of her electric stove. When the granddaughter became a mother, she purchased a service in the form of an already decorated birthday cake in the bakery section of the supermarket. Her younger sister pays a fee to Chuck E. Cheese or the Discovery Zone to provide an exciting and memorable experience for her eight-year-old. They throw in a birthday cake as part of the package fee.

In the old ecclesiastical culture an adult Sunday school class spent an hour every Sunday morning for several months studying maps of the Holy Land as they sought to gain a deeper understanding of the life and ministry of Jesus. A publishing house produced and sold those maps as part of its service to congregations.

In the experience-based economy today's adults spend ten days on a guided educational tour of the Holy Land.

Ten years later most of the members of the Sunday school class that studied those maps have only a vague recollection of the relationship of the Temple Mount to the rest of Jersalem or the relationship of the caves that held the Dead Sea Scrolls to the Sea of Galilee or of the walls and streets of the old city.

A decade later, however, those who took that tour of the Holy Land still carry in their heads vivid images of what they saw and experienced. They still remember that boat ride on the Sea of Galilee.

In the old ecclesiastical economy congregations performed a service for those who wanted to support foreign missions. Congregations received the financial contributions designated for missions. These dollars were sent to a regional judicatory, which forwarded them to the national denominational board of missions, which decided how those dollars should be spent. A service was performed, and a fee was charged for that service.

Today that same congregation challenges the laity to go and spend two weeks working with fellow Christians in a sister church on another continent.

When the sixty-six-year-old volunteer returns, a long-time friend inquires, "Well, how was the trip to Peru?" The friend replies, "I'm not the same person I was three weeks ago. That experience has transformed my life!"

Memorable and meaningful experiences do have the power to transform lives. The experience of Paul on the road to Damascus is but one of millions in the history of Christianity. Experiencial learning is a constant theme of the four Gospels as well as in the books of the Old Testament.

In the old ecclesiastical culture the missions committee and the Christian education committee usually were organized as components of a service economy. In today's congregations, in which the central focus is on the transformation of the lives of people on a spiritual pilgrimage, these two committees are more likely to fit on the fourth tier (experiences) of the economy rather than on the third (service) tier.

A more common example of this distinction is the congregation with two worship services every weekend. The one on Sunday morning is the hour-long presentation-type worship service that was widely perceived to be the norm in the 1950s. It continues to be the preferred format for most of those who have been regular churchgoers for at least forty years.

The Saturday evening schedule begins with a meal, fellowship, some sharing, and perhaps a time of prayer. It evolves into a high energy and faster paced worship experience that relies heavily on projected visual imagery. Two and one-half hours after the people gathered for the meal, most of them have left. For several, however, that whole experience has reinforced the feeling that this is not only a worship experience, but it is a gathering of the most meaningful community, or social network, in their current world. It is difficult to leave that community to go home to an empty apartment or house.

A similar pattern can be seen in that Tuesday morning or Thurday evening adult Bible study group that meets for 120 to 160 minutes every week. Instead of being organized as an educational (service) type class, it is designed to become a learning community. Three or four months later several members agree, "This has been the most meaningful experience I've enjoyed in all the years I've been coming to this church."

How Do We Isolate People?

Out in another part of the contemporary world are two different tax-funded efforts to isolate people from the rest of the work-a-day world. One is called the state prison system. It includes four or five different environments. One is the high security prison for the most dangerous felons. A second is the medium security for the less dangerous. A third is the low security campus, largely for felons who committed "white collar," rather than violent offenses. A fourth may be the contemporary version of the reform school for juvenile delinquents. The fifth may be the halfway house that enables parolees to hold a daytime job but return to confinement for the night.

The entire system also is designed to reward good behavior with an early release.

To use an old cliché, the assumption is, "Different strokes for different folks."

Also scattered across the country are nearly 6,000 tax-funded public high schools with an enrollment in excess of 1,000 students. Among the assumptions driving the design of these schools are (a) a desire to provide specialized employment opportunities for adults, (b) a need to have a large enrollment in order to provide these specialized jobs, and (c) a requirement to cover a large service area in order to provide that large enrollment.

One consequence is that instead of the faculty and students walking to school, the majority will come by bus or private automobile. This requires reserving a large area for parking school buses, faculty-owned vehicles, and student-driven cars. It also means that instead of the teenagers exercising by walking to and from school, time must be set aside during the school day for physical exercise. Typically that means one less period for study hall or classes.

If that bus system serves grades K-12, it also means the daily schedule is dictated by an efficient use of those school buses. This often means an early beginning for teenagers who tend to go to bed late in the evening and would prefer to sleep late in the morning.

That schedule is beneficial, however, for employers who hire teenagers to work after school.

This adult-driven influence also usually is reflected in the design of the physical facilities. A common practice is to design one wing or floor for the math and science departments, another for the department of communication arts, a third for the social studies department, and a fourth for the arts, health, and sports, with a fifth housing the smaller departments. The theater and the gym each may occupy a full wing.

For the students this often means a long and hurried walk from a math class to a history class and leaves no time to socialize with friends. Some overcome that by chatting on a cell phone with a friend who also is changing class-rooms, but in a different corridor. In schools where the student use of cell phones is prohibited, the laptop computer can be used as a channel of communication with friends in another wing during class.

More recently, the number-one driving force in designing new secondary school buildings is security and safety. That, of course, is the number-one driving force in designing high security prisons.

Since the students who will be confined to this building for three or four years are all guilty of the same crime—being born about fourteen to seventeen years earlier—the same pedagogical system should fit all of them. Instead of "Different strokes for different folks," the relevant slogan is, "One size fits all."

In summary, the physical design of most very large high schools is consistent with the producer-driven planning of the old American economy: real estate and schedules should reflect the agendas of the producers of services. In the very large public high school, that group includes bus drivers, administrators, security officers, department heads, and teachers.

The same dynamic drives the design of prisons. They are designed for the safety and convenience of the paid staff, not for the rehabilitation of felons.

Imagine for a moment a public high school designed partly for the convenience of the people responsible for the transportation of teenagers to that school, but largely for the enrichment of the lives of the students.

In the consumer-driven planning of this new American economy, the first big divisive debate would be over a choice between, for example, one very large school with an enrollment of perhaps 2,500 or five to eight schools each with an enrollment in the 300 to 500 range. Research completed over the past four decades suggests the smaller school is a superior ecological environment.[2]

Before that issue is resolved, however, a second issue must be raised. Should this high school be designed on the assumption that one pedagogical style fits all? Or on the assumption that the learning environments (note that word is plural) should be customized to match the needs of the students? Instead of designing the physical facilities and the staff configuration to accommodate an academic approach (chemistry, Spanish, history, English composition, physics, geography, math, et al.), the design would affirm that students should be able to choose the learning environment that matches their gifts, personality, career goals, and other attributes.

Perhaps one-fourth would choose the traditional academic-centered college preparatory learning environment. Perhaps one-half of today's teenagers would benefit from one of several varities of experiential approaches to learning by doing. Another 10 percent would benefit from one form of special education while another 5 percent require a more sophisticated and expensive special education experience. Another 5 to 10 percent can thrive in any learning environment.

The guiding slogan would be the same one used by judges in sentencing felons.

At this point in this consumer-driven planning process, the policymakers would choose between two alternatives. Should we (a) house these learning environments on five or six or seven different campuses or (b) in order to meet the needs for shared services house several different academies under one roof so one cafeteria, one theater, one bus system, one set of athletic facilities, and two or three parking lots can serve all of these academies? If a very large site is available, and if security is not a big factor, these academies could be housed in seven different buildings on one campus and surround a structure that houses the cafeteria, gymnasium, theater, and other common uses.

Two Questions

At this point, the reader may ask two questions. First, why discuss prisons and high schools in the same few pages? Second, what does this have to do with the impact of the new American economy on the churches?

That first question is the easier to answer. During the past quarter century I have placed a high priority on listening to high school students. I also have asked them several questions.[3] One of them is, "Tell me which of these most closely resembles your high school: An academic learning center like a college? A day camp where you spend the day in recreational and learning experiences, but eat two meals at home and sleep in your own bed at night? A warehouse where we store what we don't need now, but we know that eventually we will have a need, so we want to store it safely? A factory where workers put in their time and look forward to the bell at the end of the day and eventually a free weekend? Or a prison where people are confined for a specified period of time and their daily schedule is closely regulated by the adults in charge?"

After a few minutes, during which we discuss the students' questions to sharpen their common understanding of each analogy, we go around the circle and ask for individual responses. Typically somewhere between 50 and 95 percent of these teenagers reply, "Prison." "Academic center" usually is the fourth or fifth most common response.

Frequently a teenager will elaborate in responding to make sure this visitor fully understands the message. One fourteen-year-old, for example, after hearing seven out of eight earlier respondents say, "Prison," replied, "A low security prison," and explained in significant detail why he believed his high school was a superior environment, partly because it was much smaller than the four schools attended by the others in the room.

In another group, a sixteen-year-old girl responded, "Academic center." Three of her friends immediately interrupted to explain to me that she attended a small elite private high school.

On several occasions one or more of the boys explained, "The big difference between my high school and a prison is in prison you get time off for good behavior. In my high school, early release is the reward for bad behavior."

Another reason for this discussion is that every year billions of dollars are spent in the United States for construction of prisons, high schools, and churches designed by a producer-driven planning process.

Finally, it is only a tiny stretch to suggest that the rehabilitation of convicted felons, the education of teenagers, and the pilgrimage of low-commitment Christian believers to become fully devoted followers of Jesus Christ all fit under the common umbrella of the transformation of the individual. Another parallel is the design of that "home away from home" for each constituency should be guided by the old slogan, "Different strokes for different folks."

The closer the design of those physical facilities to the needs of the current constituents, the greater the probability this home away from home will be more comfortable and attractive than that person's real home.

Designing Tomorrow's Church

Readers with long memories can recall the holy trinity for the design of a church building. The common design of 1952 called for housing worship, Christian education, and fellowship. Offices, restrooms, corridors, and storage space were squeezed in among those three primary uses. The church kitchen was on the other side of one wall of the fellowship hall. This was a producer-of-services driven planning model and was based on the assumption that one basic design does fit all. The big exception came when the classrooms for children were designed for small people, including special restrooms serving two classrooms.

The process and the product were consistent with the old service-centered economy. The staff configuration was consistent with the design of the building. The minister should be comfortable and competent to serve as a worship leader, preacher, teacher, and administrator, and also enjoy the fellowship of being with a crowd in that big hall.

The room designed for the corporate worship of God frequently either was modeled after a western European cathedral or a large American lecture hall. Both designs called for the preacher to be a skilled orator. Both placed substantial distance between the preacher and the personal space of the people. The arrival of television in the 1950s marked the beginning of the obsolescence of those two designs. During the last half of the twentieth century the electronic era called for a new approach to communication. One-to-one conversation has replaced the old pattern of the orator addressing a crowd.[4]

Planning in this new American economy and the contemporary ecclesiastical culture is driven by a different set of forces. One, which is a repeated theme in this book and also a highly divisive issue, is the arrival of the consumer-driven society. A second is television. A third is that a large number of regular churchgoers are on a self-identified spiritual pilgrimage. A fourth is that the longer a congregation has been in existence and/or the larger the number of pastorates over the past three decades and/or the larger the proportion of constituents born after 1960 and/or the larger the proportion of the constituents who are relatively new to that congregation (this may be reflected in a high turnover rate or in rapid numerical growth) and/or the greater the degree of demographic diversity and/or the broader the range of theological pluralism, the greater the probability that today's constituents are scattered along a wide spectrum in terms of that pilgrimage. It is not unusual for one congregation to include searchers, seekers, inquirers, new believers, low-commitment believers, eager lifelong learners, disciples, and apostles.

One consequence of this increase in demographic diversity and consumer pluralism is the arrival of new criteria in designing church buildings. Perhaps the most highly visible illustration of this is the large amount of space devoted to recreation, both indoor and outdoor. More subtle and far more important, however, is the provision of two or three different rooms for worship. One may be a worship center, while the second is a big box, and the third is a theater.

For congregations averaging more than 300 at worship and also seeking to be or to become an intergenerational community, this usually means the meeting place should include at least two different rooms that serve as places for people to gather for the corporate worship of God. One or both may be multipurpose rooms.

The multigenerational congregation averaging more than 700 at worship may need three rooms for worship, although all three may not be on the same campus. At an absolute minimum any congregation seeking to reach and serve the generations born after 1950 should have one room that is designed for the kinesthetic speaker.[5] In simple terms this means that the speaker can walk to within three or four feet of the majority of the people within that room. The design of that room also should make it easy for the speaker to utilize projected moving visual images and/or change the pace by the use of proxies.

What Are the Options?

Multigenerational congregations are discovering that one impact of this new ecclesistical economy is a new set of choices. One alternative is to concentrate on creating a homogeneous congregation. The goal is to bring together people who reflect a minimal degree of diversity in terms of theology, culture, stage of their spiritual journey, marital status, nationality, social class, and the expectations they bring to church. Planning can be based on the assumption that one design does fit all.

A second alternative is to accept a high rate of turnover as the norm. The pastor of a fourteen-year-old independent church explained the dynamics of that congregation in these words.

"Since we're a nondenominational church, we receive zero new people each year as a result of intradenominational transfers. Last year we averaged a combined worship attendance of nearly 1,100 at our four weekend services. We don't have a membership roster, but about 1,200 people worship with us on a regular basis plus a few hundred others who attend here less frequently. Our core constituency, however, consists of those 1,200 who are here nearly every weekend. At least half of them are involved in something else going on here during one or more other occasions during the week. In the typical year about 300 of those 1,200 leave us, and we replace them with 300 to 350 newcomers.

"That's an unbelievably high turnover rate!" I observed.

"No, that goes with the territory," was the reply. "We're really not in the business of converting nonbelievers. We focus on two stages of a Christian's faith journey. One group of newcomers consists of committed, but bored, members of other churches who are looking for more than their congregation offers. The church growth people call them switchers, but that's really a superficial view. We identify these folks as people who are eager to progress from being a believer to becoming a learner. They want to learn more about what it means to be a believer in Jesus Christ. Our six o'clock Saturday evening teaching service, which is preceded by a meal at five and followed by several ninety-minute classes, is designed for people at this stage of their spiritual pilgrimage. We aim for people at that same stage of their journey on Sunday morning with adult classes at nine and the teaching service at eleven. The big differences between the two are on Saturday evening the study groups focus on the message they just heard, the format is more informal, the music is livelier, and the meal is at the beginning. I am the teacher for both services on forty-seven or forty-eight weekends every year. The Sunday morning study time focuses on the message from the previous week, and some of the people have met in Bible study groups to discuss that text. The service is a bit more formal, the music is slower, and the meal follows that service."

"Any significant differences between the two constituencies?" I ask.

"Yes, there are several," replied this thoughtful pastor. "That early Saturday evening crowd is the largest of our four services. That is one reason why we meet in the theater, but the big reason we meet there is in that service we place a heavier emphasis on drama and projected visual images. That early Saturday evening crowd also is younger, we have many more singles and young childless couples, and we have lots of people who come to that who are in their own home church on Sunday mornig. Some come to size us up and eventually become regulars. Others come for the teaching, but do not come for the meal or stay for the adult classes. On Sunday morning we have almost the identical crowd at nine and eleven, but at least a third don't stay for the meal. That eleven o'clock Sunday morning service is in our worship center."

"Earlier you told me you have two slices of the church-going population," I inquired."What's the second?"

"The second is designed for learners who are ready to be transformed into disciples. Our seven-thirty service on Saturday evening, which also is preceded by an optional meal and a time for intercessory prayer, and the early service on Sunday morning are designed for people at that stage of their faith journey. I speak at those two services once or twice a year, but my colleague and the two worship teams carry 95 percent of the responsibility for those two services."

"This is very interesting," I declared. "If I understand correctly, you focus on two stages of people's faith journeys. What happens to these learners who become disciples?"

"Most of them leave," was the flippant response. "I'm afraid I failed to describe our ministry fully. Most of our newcomers fit into one of five categories. The largest, as I explained earlier, consists of committed but bored Christians from other congregations who are looking for more than what their church offers. The second largest are people who came to accept Jesus Christ in what some people call the seeker-sensitive church. If that church doesn't fulfill their desire to become active learners, some of them come here. A much smaller third group includes nonbelievers and some weak believers who marry a deeply committed believer. The fourth group just wander in for no clearly defined reason other than they're looking for a new church home. Finally, every year we welcome a dozen or so burned-out refugees from a highly dysfunctional church. They find a nurturing home in one of our learning communities.

"Before I address your question on what happens to those new disciples, I need to review a bit of history. When we organized this new church a little over fourteen years ago, we decided God was calling us to build a learning community. We did that. About three years later we woke up to the fact that we had been successful and now we had to deal with success. After several months of prayer, reading, visiting a couple of dozen other churches, and study, we concluded that the time had come to add a second component to our ministry plan. That was and is to challenge learners to be transformed into fully devoted followers of Jesus Christ."

"As one who years ago was taught to think sequentially, I can affirm that, but you still haven't told me why an average of 300 of your constituents leave every year," I said.

"Well, I misspoke a minute ago," confessed this creative pastor. "Let me back up and first describe why we lose 300 of our constituents in the average year. First of all, we are a high expectation church. While I can't say for sure, since we don't do exit interviews, although maybe we should, my guess is that after a year or two here about a hundred people every year decide that while they want to be in a good church, our expectations exceed their level of commitment.

"Second, every two or three years we send out about 200 disciples plus a few dozen who are at the learner stage, but have special gifts such as music or teaching, plus three full-time paid staff and two part-time staff members to go out and plant a new mission that is designed to begin as a high expectation learning community. Last year we planted our fourth new mission in a community fourteen miles east of here.

"Third, every year a couple dozen of our disciples who are ready to become apostles leave us to help revitalize some other congregation.

"Fourth, we experience the natural annual exodus of a younger constituency as about 10 percent move their place of residence to some other part of the world. That means we have to replace them out of our pool of new disciples.

"Finally, a few continue to live near here and worship with us, but they devote their discretionary time and energy to serving as volunteers in some other ministry or parachurch agency or social service program.

"The ironic bit of our story is when we began we chose the name Crossroads Church. That was short and easy to remember with only three syllables. We intended it to mean that we minister with people at the crossroads where the Christian faith, family, work, and the search for meaning in life come together. Now we realize that our name symbolizes the fact that we minister with people at a crossroads where believers and learners come together to take the road that leads to discipleship. That also explains why we sometimes describe ourselves as a restaurant serving spiritual food for a passing parade of Christians on a variety of faith journeys. My colleagues and I work in the kitchen. Most of our volunteers wait on the customers while others venture out every once in a while to open a new restaurant at another crossroads of life or to help renew a restaurant that is not sure what the menu should be for a new generation of believers."

"Do you intentionally try to help your people understand that you focus on two different stages of a Christian's faith journey?" I asked.

"Certainly!" was the crisp reply. "That's why we offer two different pairs of worship experiences every weekend: two for believers who are eager to learn more and two for learners who are ready to be transformed into disciples. That's why we have two different worship centers. Each is designed to be the appropriate environment for that stage of one's faith journey. Each one has its own narthex and its own set of adult classrooms. The two groups do share restrooms and dining facilities, but most of the believers park near the entrance to their worship center on the east side, and most of the future and new disciples park near the entrance to their worship center on the west side. When that eager learner decides the time has come to move on to discover what it means to be a fully devoted follower of Jesus Christ, we want them to experience that transition in their lives by moving to a new physical environment. We describe it as a parallel to graduating from high school and going away to college. Our disciples find it easier to date that transformation in their lives by when they moved from one environment to another. Many people look back and refer to when they moved from Iowa to California as a personal watershed in their lives. We try to replicate that in their spiritual pilgrimage."

"You're describing an exceptionally narrow and precisely defined ministry plan," I interrupted. "Is this as intentional as you make it sound?"

"I sure hope so!" replied this patient pastor. "We know what we believe God has called us to do, and we also know what we don't know how to do. Many of our visiting firemen like you are dismayed when we admit we do not concentrate on converting nonbelievers into believers. Tens of thousands of other churches see that as their top priority, and many of them excel in that. We don't pretend to know how to do that. As I've tried to explain to you and to others, we believe God has gifted us to feed those believers who are eager learners and to help transform learners into disciples. That's all we try to do. We are confident the 350,000 other Christian churches in America have the resources to do what we don't know how to do."

"One last question," was my final observation. "Your design does not strike me as a low-cost venture. It sounds to me as if your goal is to house two congregations under one roof and accept a high turnover rate as one price tag. The other price tag is you that have an expensive physical facility here with two worship centers, two sets of adult classrooms, and two large parking areas. Most Christian congregations I'm acquainted with try to serve people at all stages of their faith journey. If you could do that, you might be able to reduce that high turnover rate."

"Forgive my lack of tact," began the reply, "But you sound like a really old, old man! You're talking about an evaluation process that focuses on the input of resources. That's a carryover from the old American economy. In the new American economy, the evaluation process focuses on outcomes. One of the most meaningful questions we ask each year is how many of those eager learners have graduated from that stage of their faith journey and moved on to accept the challenge to become disciples. One yardstick for measuring that is to count how many have moved out of one of those two teaching services into one of our two discipling services. Another is that we celebrate the departure of disciples who leave us to plant a new mission or to go and help revitalize a congregation that should move into the next chapter in its pilgrimage. The cost of constructing and maintaining duplicate physical facilities is not a problem. That is simply designing the building to house two different learning communities. We need two different venues for two different worship experiences and two different learning experiences."

What Is the Fourth Alternative?

Most multigenerational congregations must choose from among alternative ministry plans. The most comfortable is to create and maintain a high degree of homogeneity among the constituents. This is much easier to achieve in the new congregation where the founding pastor continues for at least three decades.

The most challenging is to focus on one or two stages of the faith journey and rejoice in the fact that this usually means a ministry with a fast moving passing parade of constituents.

A third is to accept the fact that just as most adult Americans grow older, shorter, and fatter with the passage of time, the normal pattern for American Protestant congregations is to grow older and smaller.

A fourth alternative is to act on the conviction that the fourth economy, a world filled with more and more meaningful and memorable experiences, has arrived. In other words, agree with Pine and Gilmore that both work and ministry are now theater and that every church, as well as every business, should see itself as a stage. (No, I do not receive a commission for selling their book.)

To explain this fourth alternative, we need to follow those visits to prisons and secondary schools with two other trips.

How Do We Renew Downtown?

During the past five decades tens of billions of dollars and millions of hours of work have been devoted to the renewal of the central business district of scores of the nation's cities.

Therefore, our next visit is to look at the efforts to renew the central business district back in the third quarter of the twentieth century. We see the same basic formula was used in many cities.

The economic base of the old downtown often was organized around (a) the paperwork and financing required for the sale of commodities, (b) the manufacture of goods, and (c) the sale of goods via wholesale and retail outlets. In the years following World War II this was enriched by a modest increase in employment in legal, financial, and educational services plus restaurants, hotels, governmental offices, and entertainment.

By 1960 that led many experts in urban renewal to conclude that while the past had been built on turning commodities into goods and on wholesale and retail trade, the future was on expanding the service tier of the economy.

As manufacturing, wholesale, and retail operations abandoned the central business district for new and larger sites, the planners created a design for the renewal of that aging part of the city. A common practice was to identify three "anchors" for this plan. One was an institution of higher education, a second was an expansion of governmental office space, and a third was a cluster of health-care facilities centered on a hospital. In several cities this design included the state capitol, a new city hall or county building, a state university campus, a teaching hospital, and related facilities. Blank spaces on the map were filled with buildings for financial services, legal services, restaurants, and offices for agencies of the federal government.

The economic base of the old central business district had been built on the first two tiers of the economy—commodities and goods. The renewal plan rested largely on the third tier, the production and sale of services.

Unfortunately many of those providers of services could not compete, often because of transportation and parking limitations, with new competitors in outlying sections of that urban area.

As a result, when we make our next visit to examine contemporary plans for the renewal of the central business district, we discover a new economic foundation for the renewal plan.

The plan that emerged in the 1990s was designed to attract people to walk around, to listen, to sit around, to talk, to lie around, to eat, to network, to laugh, to applaud, to build an inventory of stories to share with the folks back home, to learn, to enjoy new experiences, to meet and make new friends, to drink, to sleep, to ingest too many calories, to relax, and to watch a few people take death-defying risks.

That paragraph could cause people to recall the conditions that accompanied the fall of Rome nearly sixteen hundred years earlier, so it was cleaned up for public presentation. The public presentation called for a new football stadium, a convention center, a variety of theme restaurants, a new baseball park, two or three museums, perhaps a casino, hotels and motels, gift shops, motion picture theaters, lots of off-street parking, one or two dinner theaters, perhaps a music hall, a new municipal library, bars, coffee houses, a large bookstore, perhaps a multi-use indoor stadium that could house basketball tournaments as well as concerts and a health club.

That new renewal plan rested on the fourth tier of the economy called experiences and entertaiment.

What About Old First Church?

For old First Church downtown the rapid pace of these changes provided a serious challenge. The alternative that required the fewest changes was "to follow our members" and relocate the meeting place to be closer to the members' place of residence rather than near their place of work. (In the 1950s a frequently heard comment was, "Since I work downtown, we go to church downtown. That enables us to be with our friends who also work downtown.")

The passive response was to grow smaller in numbers and older in the age of the constituency. An extremely challenging alternative was to build a new constituency with the people who now reside in the central business district. Another option, for those with a big endowment fund or access to generous denominational subsidies, was to concentrate on social welfare or social justice ministries. For others, the eventual decision was to close or to merge into another congregation.

A small number chose what many perceived to be a radical alternative. This is to concentrate on reaching, attracting, serving, welcoming, and assimilating members of the daytime population. (This contrasts with the primary focus of many suburban congregations to concentrate on reaching and serving a nighttime and weekend population.)

When this strategy is successfully implemented, it usually means that (a) two-thirds of the involvement of the "permanent" constituency occurs on Monday through Friday; (b) a substantial proportion of the Sunday morning worshipers are tourists and other visitors; (c) that congregation has earned a national reputation as "a church you must visit if you're ever in that city"; (d) the members are drawn from a very large geographical circle in terms of their place of residence to what is clearly a regional church; (e) that congregation projects very high expectations of anyone seeking to become a full member; (f) non-member constituents outnumber members by at least a two to one ratio; (g) members are challenged to do what they know they cannot do in ministry; (h) the ministry plan places a high value on the power of meaningful experiences in helping people progress from one stage to the next in their personal faith journey; (i) rather than promote partnerships with other congregations, the emphasis is on creating partnerships with employers, governmental agencies, social service organizations, and others concerned with the vitality of the central business disrict; (j) in smaller markets television is the number-one channel of communication for inviting strangers to come to share in this ministry; (k) a significant portion of the annual budget is contributed by people who are not members; and (l) a common criticism by leaders in other congregations is, "They're really in the entertainment business, not the church business." The response to that criticism is not to deny it, but to explain, "Those are highly compatible and mutually supportive components of our ministry plan."

In dozens of the successful efforts for the renewal of the central business district, one component is residential housing. One goal, of course, is to house some of the people who work downtown. Another is to increase the nighttime population. The easy segment of the population to attract to downtown residential accommodations are childless adults, including retirees.

Frequently, however, those who would like to live downtown include couples with school age children. For many of them, the first criterion in choosing a place to live is the quality of the schools. One consequence is that one or two of the downtown congregations place a high priority on a partnership with a nearby public school. A second is to enter into a partnership with parents, educators, and employers to create a new tax-funded charter school. A third is to enter into a partnership with parents, educators, and employers to launch a private tuition-financed Christian day school.

The moral of that story is very simple.

If the economic base of the central business district is being renewed by creating a variety of memorable experiences for visitors as well as the people who live there, a parallel road may be the path to the renewal of old First Church downtown. That includes high-energy, fast-paced, and participatory worship experiences that include the use of projected visual images to communicate the gospel, creating experience-driven learning communities and a consumer-driven, rather than a producer-driven, approach to designing a new ministry plan.

The creation of that tax-funded charter school or that tuition-based Christian day school is simply one component of a larger plan to respond to the agendas people bring to church. The partners may be employers and others seeking to respond to that new agenda, rather than other churches. The design of the physical facilities often requires three venues for worship: a traditional sanctuary, a big box that accommodates participatory worship experiences, and a theater. That building constructed in 1925 and designed for a passive presentation-type of worship service may not be appropriate in a downtown being renewed or that experience-based tier of the urban economy.

Children's Ministries

The arrival of the experience economy provides a useful conceptual framework for designing ministries with children.

What is one of the greatest personal victories for a child? The answer, of course, is gaining the skill to walk alone. Children rejoice in mastering a new skill. Mastering the skill of walking increases the mobility of that child and also raises the youngster's self-confidence. Equally important, it proves, "I can do it! I can master the skills required for independence in this adult-designed world."

Mastering new skills nurtures self-esteem, self-confidence, and a venturesome spirit. It is a road to prove, "I'm a winner!" This is a completely different road from acquiring and storing information.

This introduces the question for adults preparing children to enjoy an experience-dominated culture. What skills do we challenge youngsters to master as a part of our ministry with families that include young children?

Possibilities include tumbling, learning the American Sign Language, singing, dancing, skating, acting, baking, archery, listening, juggling, sewing, mastering a computer keyboard, painting, storytelling, photography, wood carving, writing the script and producing a play or making a videotape that retells memorable Bible stories, playing a musical instrument, skiing, pottery making, quilting, writing, sculpting, and reading aloud.

Mastering these and other skills enables a child to declare, "I'm a winner!" Enjoying the skill of winning is one path to becoming a winner in life.

Most of these and similar skills also can be part of helping a child enjoy being a member of a winning team in mastering social skills, in acquiring factual knowledge, and in discovering cause-and-effect relationships. The new American economy places a high value on the competencies required to be a contributing partner of a winning team.

The New Fifth Economy

In 1998 Pine and Gilmore labeled the arrival of the age of experiences as the new fourth economy. In their book they have expanded the economic pyramid to five tiers, commodities, goods, services, experiences, and transformations.

The Great Commission declares that Christian churches are in the transformation business. The history of the Christian religion makes it clear that meaningful, relevant, and memorable experiences represent the most heavily traveled road to the transformation of individuals. Therefore in this discussion we are combining experiences and transformations into one tier in the new American economy. The ultimate criterion for self-evaluation in the Christian religion is measured in outcomes, not inputs. Denominational agencies may place a high value on financial inputs in their annual reports, but congregations place a high value on an outcome called transformed lives. That may be measured in the number of nonbelievers who have accepted Jesus Christ as Lord and Savior or the number of new believers who are now eager learners or the number of learners who have been transformed, often by meaningful and memorable experiences, into disciples or the number of disciples who have accepted the challenge to become apostles.

The goal is not a bigger budget or a larger staff or more worship services or other means-to-an-end inputs. The goal is the transformation of the lives of people on a spiritual pilgrimage. In the new American economy, and more gradually in the new ecclesiastical culture, experiences are supplementing goods (Bibles, hymnals, pipe organs, meeting rooms, etc.) and services (study, pastoral care, etc.) as components in that larger strategy for transforming lives.

That is the argument for combining experiences and transformation into one tier.

The emergence of what appears to be a radically different definition of a new fifth economy can be introduced by a few statistics.

In the year 2000 the average annual salary for a full-time major league football player was $1.2 million, triple the 1990 average. For major league baseball players, that average had more than tripled to $2 million in eleven years. For major league hockey players that average in 2001 was nearly five times the 1990 figure. For major league basketball players, the average salary in 2001 was five times the 1990 figure.

One consequence is that more and more professional athletes are hiring someone to manage their finances and/or incorporating themselves as a for-profit corporation and/or creating a foundation to manage their charitable giving.

The number of American millionaires doubled during the 1990s. The number of Christians contributing at least $200,000 annually to charitable causes has quadrupled since 1980. That has produced a sharp increase in the number of family foundations.

Who Will Manage Your Money?

This rapid increase in the quantity of discretionary income and accumulated wealth has created that new fifth economy. It consists of institutions and people who manage other people's money.

One example is the Fidelity Investments Charitable Gift Fund. Nine years after it was created, it has accumulated $2.2 billion in assets from 22,000 donors. For calendar year 2000 the Fidelity Fund and the Salvation Army were the only two American charities to receive more than a billion dollars each in private support. That encouraged other financial institutions to create similar mutual funds in 2000 and 2001.

A second example is the 600 community foundations organized during the twentieth century.

A third example is the recent rapid increase in the number of people who turn to a paid financial adviser for advice.

A fourth example is the incorporation of thousands of family foundations.

A fifth is the increase in the number of national denominational agencies, regional judicatories, and congregations with a full-time development office staff to attract gifts and bequests to their foundation.

A sixth, and perhaps most impressive, is the number of private and public colleges and universities that have been able to increase the market value of their endowment to beyond a half billion dollars. As of June 30, 2000, that number stood at 86 colleges and universities.

Seventh, the emergence of this new fifth economy has radically changed the assumptions for financing the ministries of congregations, denominations, and parachurch organizations.

In simple terms this new fifth economy for congregations brings together deeply committed Christians, discretionary accumulated wealth, discretionary income, creativity, venturesome spirits, and folks who are more interested in creating the new than in perpetuating the old. The institutional vehicle is a separate 501(c)3 corporation called a foundation. These congregational foundations are not created to provide financial subsidies to subsidize the old. They are organized to bring together private, corporate, foundation, and governmental dollars with creative volunteers to design and implement new ministries in response to unmet needs.

To be more precise, the goal is not to gather money to fund an institution, but to challenge potential contributors to join a partnership in support of a cause.

An explanation of this new economy requires a side trip to look at the larger picture of the changing nature of philanthropy in America and chase a couple of other rabbits.

CHAPTER SEVEN

The New Face
of Philanthropy

What is the most significant change in charitable giving by individuals in the United States during the past three or four decades?

From this observer's perspective the answer to that question came on November 6, 2001, at a hearing before the House Committee on Energy and Commerce. By that date Americans had contributed in cash and pledges $564 million to the Liberty Fund created by the American Red Cross in response to that Black Tuesday eight weeks earlier.

Members of Congress objected to the decision to allocate $264 million to other needs and to use only $300 million to aid the victims of Black Tuesday. When he discovered that many of those dollars had been allocated to the long-term institutional needs of the Red Cross, such as improving its telephone and technology systems and providing reserves for future terrorist attacks, a Democratic Congressman from Michigan declared, "I think you took advantage of a very tragic situation." He contended that the donors had been led to believe their contributions would go to the aid of the victims of those four airplane crashes. The response of the Red Cross was that the donors knew their contributions would go to aid the families of the victims and also to "the emerging needs from this event." Several House members contended that their constituents believed all their contributions would go to the aid of the victims of that disaster of September 11, 2001.[1]

Those speaking from the old tradition of American philanthropy explained that when donors contribute their charitable dollars to a respected nonprofit institution, they expect and trust that institution to be a good steward and make wise decisions on who will be the ultimate recipients of those charitable dollars. In other words, the officials of that institution can and should determine the final destination of those dollars.

The new face on American philanthropy is donor-driven. Donors decide which causes they choose to support. The intermediary must either add value (see chap. 3) or forward those contributions to the designated recipients. The comments at that hearing suggest that the representatives of the American Red Cross were playing by the old rulebook, and the discontended donors assumed they were playing by the new rulebook. They thought they were contributing toward the welfare of the victims rather than to the treasury of a huge institution.

That generous response to the attack of September 11, 2001, illustrates the attractivenes of a worthy cause. At least 190 different organizations appealed for and received charitable contributions for the aid of the victims of that disaster. Many of these causes originate in the minds of the contributors, rather than in the deliberations of the policy-makers of an institution.

This change can be seen in the decision-making processes of foundations as well as among individual contributors. A new attractive cause has more appeal than perpetuating an old institution. The most attractive appeal today often originates in the mind of the contributor or in a collaborative process with a few other potential contributors or in response to a disaster.

Why?

Why did this happen? Is this change good or bad?

The answers to both of these speculative questions will be heavily influenced by one's perspective. This pilgrim has three answers to the why question. First, the affluence of the past three decades has created a new generation of philanthropists, and today's newly rich tend to feel an obligation to share their wealth with others.

Second, one of the great success stories of the American churches during the last third of the twentieth century was not simply to teach stewardship, but more particularly to inculcate the concept of responsible stewardship. The individual who has been richly blessed by God has an obligation not only to share those blessings, but also to be a good and wise steward. That means identifying what are truly genuine needs.[2]

A third factor is the product of two trends in the contemporary American culture. One is the rise of individualism.[3] Thus one has an individual responsibility to be a good steward. Instead of contributing to long-established institutions and letting others choose the ultimate recipient of that charitable dollar, the individual donor should decide.

Overlapping that is a culture that affirms, tempts, and rewards the individual entrepreneur. One evidence of this is the large number of women who have concluded that they no longer are interested in working for someone else and have launched their own business. A second is the number of women who are the chief executive officers of foundations or charitable organizations. A third is that huge number of younger adults who have decided to make a living off the World Wide Web. A fourth is the growing number of social entrepreneurs who create and finance a new benevolent organization in response to an unmet need. Instead of giving money to an existing charitable organization, they create a new one. It usually is easier to create the new than to reorder the priorities of the old!

Those of us who like to give credit to the teachings and ministries of Christian churches when and where we believe credit is due rejoice in this trend. We agree that individuals should accept and fulfill the responsiblity of being good stewards. That is one reason why we describe these as the best of times.

Those who are distressed by the declining interest in financially supporting institutions over causes tend to label this an unfortunate trend. They correctly describe this as a failure in stewardship education. Their definition of success would have motivated donors to contribute to institutions. This disagreement has produced the great debate discussed earlier in the third chapter. Who should determine the ultimate destination of those charitable dollars? The donor? Or the initial recipient?

What's Number Two?

The second biggest change in American philanthropy is far less subjective and far easier to measure.

This is the increase in the number of Americans with discretionary income and/or discretionary wealth. October 2001 did set a record for the sale of motor vehicles in the United States in one month! Despite the fluctuations in the American economy since 1970 and the economic recession that began in 2000, today there are more Americans with more money to contribute to charitable causes than ever before. The Center on Budget and Policy Priorities reported in early 2001 that an after-tax income of $83,225 was required to place a taxpayer among the top 10 percent of all taxpayers in 1998. At the beginning of the twenty-first century the American population included 300 billionaires—up from 13 in 1982—and more than 6 million millionaires. The net assets of American foundations increased by more than $100 billion dollars between 1995 and the close of the twentieth century.

More important than current income, however, is accumulated wealth. What should the individual or family do when their accumulated wealth exceeds what they will ever need to support themselves! Create a trust fund for their children and grandchildren? Give it to their church? Wait passively and let the estate tax take a big chunk of it? Purchase a big house? Give a large chunk of that accumulated wealth to the first persuasive messenger who represent what appears to be a worthy cause? Send a generous check to a college or university?

One attractive alternative is to incorporate the family foundation. To be economically feasible, that requires an initial gift of at least $2 to $3 million, depending on state laws. The number of family foundations increased from approximately 30,000 in 1990 to an estimated 48,000 at the end of 2001.

Another alternative is to turn to one of the 600-plus community foundations to manage the assets, but the donor retains the right to designate how the income from those assets will be used. A growing number of congregations and denominational agencies are now competing in this game by creating their own foundations and soliciting major gifts, bequests, and legacies.

In summary, there are more Americans with more money to give away than ever before, and many of them feel they are responsible for making wise and prudent decisions on identifying the ultimate beneficiary of those gifts.

Buildings or Causes?

Over a period of three decades Andrew Carnegie contributed the money to construct 2,509 public libraries in the United States. Many still stand.

While contributing to construction of a new building continues to have great appeal, for many Americans the worthy cause is even more attractive. One example came in the fall of 2000 when George W. Bush and Albert Gore raised a combined total of $10 million very quickly and very easily to finance their legal battle to determine who would receive the electoral votes of Florida.

What Have They Learned?

The combined market value of all college and university endowment funds in the United States at the end of 2000 was approximately $200 billion. The number of schools with an endowment of at least one billion dollars grew slowly from one in 1974 to ten in 1988 and then jumped to 34 in 1999 and 41 in 2000. Several of these are tax-supported public institutions.

Colleges and universities stand out as the number-one example of how to raise money in this new American economy. What have they learned that could be exported and adopted by churches and other religious institutions?

First of all, the most effective seekers of charitable contributions operate on the assumption that this is an era of abundance, not scarcity. Their financial planning is not driven by a Depression era ethic. Second, the most effective accept the fact that the competition for the charitable dollar is greater and more sophisticated than ever before. Third, they accept the responsibility to take the initative in asking for charitable contributions. While an occasional donor makes an unsolicited gift of several million dollars, that is a happy surprise, not the standard operating procedure. Fourth, each capital funds drive is designed to create a positive foundation for a later financial campaign.

Fifth, and perhaps most important, they do not depend on any one system or approach to motivate all potential contributors. What is the best way to encourage large financial gifts? To ask potential donors to contribute to the cost of a new building? Or to patiently build a long-term personal relationship with that potential donor? Or to ask for money to create a new program or a new course of study? Or to endow a professional chair? Or to seek gifts to the endowment fund? Or to allow the donor to choose from a list of needs? Or to assume the second or third contribution will be larger than the first, so don't worry about the size of that initial gift? Or to build on institutional loyalty with grateful alumni? Or to seek gifts for named scholarships? Or to look to foundations, corporations, and individuals who have a history of contributing to institutions of higher education?

The answer, of course, is all of the above and more.

A simple illustration of this is to look at who controls the naming of buildings. Once upon a time most of the buildings on a college or university campus were named for former employees. They were named for deceased presidents of the school or deans or famous professors. Only a few were named for donors. That decision-making authority has moved from the trustees to the development office.

What Does This Mean?

This new face of American philanthropy is distinguished by an unprecedented level of competition for the charitable dollar. This has created a new high stakes game in which only a few thousand charitable, educational, and religious organizations can play at that high level of sophistication.

For well over 90 percent of all Christian congregations, and the overwhelming majority of denominational agencies and parachurch groups, this means they will not be able to compete in that high stakes game.

The best response is to design a customized financial plan built on the strengths, assets, and distinctive role of that religious organization. That is the central theme of chapters 10, 11, and 12. In addition, it may be useful to look at three other powerful factors.

The Power of Performance

Americans prefer winners to losers. They prefer the proved to the untested. One example of this is that nineteen out of twenty members of the United States House of Representatives seeking reelection are returned to Congress every two years. In 1998 it was 98 percent. In 2000 it was 99 percent. The major league baseball team that won the World Series the previous year usually enjoys a higher attendance than the teams that finished third or lower in their division.

Likewise donors usually prefer to give their money to organizations with a positive track record. This can be illustrated by comparing requests for contributions from three different denominational agencies.

The first can be summarized in these words: "During the past decade we should have started ten new churches. Due to other pressing demands, we organized only two. The larger of those two now averages 125 at worship, and the other averages nearly 80 at worship. Our goal is to launch ten over the next five years, and we need to raise $1.5 million to be able to do that. We ask for your financial contribution to enable us to reach that goal."

The second recaptures recent history. "During the past decade our goal was to plant ten new missions. Thanks to your support and the contributions of others, we achieved that goal! The third oldest of those ten is now a flourishing congregation that averages well over 500 at worship. Unfortunately our first effort closed after six years. The second oldest now averages about 60 at worship. Of the other seven the two newest are exceptionally promising ventures with excellent ministerial leadership, another merged into a sister church two years ago, one dissolved after three years, one averages nearly one hundred at worship, a sixth, founded four years ago, is currently without a pastor, and the seventh just voted to merge with the congregation that sponsored it. We seek your support in raising $1.5 million to plant ten new missions during the next five years."

The third plea for financial contributions can be summarized in three sentences. "Ten years ago we adopted a goal of planting one new mission every year for a decade. Three of those ten now average more than 700 at worship, four average between 350 and 685, one dissolved after an unfortunate internal conflict, both of the two newest now report that their worship attendance exceeds 200, and both are financially self-supporting. We ask for your financial support to raise $1.5 million to plant ten more new missions during the next five years."

Which of those three requests for money is most likely to motivate potential contributors to give?

In the old ecclesiastical economy credibility often was institution-based. In the new ecclesiastical economy, credibility is increasingly performance-based. This is especially true for the generations born after World War II. Younger Americans are far more likely than older ones to challenge the credibility of corporations, governmental agencies, political parties, hospitals, military officers, physicians, denominational officials, professors, civil servants, the news media, and experts in general.

For most congregations this means improving the system of internal communication to help people understand more fully all aspects of the ministry. The guiding generalization is the larger the size of the congregation, the larger the proportion of the constituents who are unaware of most of what is happening.

The Power of Relationships

While information is helpful in building credibility on the basis of performance, for most people life is still organized around relationships. The guiding generalization is the greater the level of anonymity within a congregation, the more difficult it will be to achieve financial goals.

At the other end of that spectrum, the stronger and healthier the group life and the larger the proportion of adults who identify this congregation as "my primary social network," the easier it will be to achieve those financial goals.

The Power of Language

The final, and perhaps the most significant, consequence of this increasingly competitive climate for the charitable dollar is what colleges and universities do best. They take the initiative. They ask potential donors for money. They challenge people with big dreams. More significant, however, they carefully choose the words and formulate the sentences that will be used to communicate that dream. There is no such thing as a neutral way to describe the need or to state the question.

A common parallel is that whoever designs the agenda for a decision-making meeting usually can exert a tremendous influence on the eventual outcome by the choice of words in formulating the issues to be resolved.

In both congregational life and denominational agencies, the choice of the words to describe a particular financial need usually will have a powerful impact on the response.

The critics, of course, deplore this as one more example of how the advertising business is corrupting the church. A more realisic statement, however, is that one facet of the changing face of American philanthropy is the increased power of effective communication.

How Large Is the Pie?

How much money are we talking about when the discussion turns to charitable giving in the United States? What proportion of that goes to and through religious organizations? Have American churchgoers been increasing or cutting back on their charitable giving? Accurate answers to those three questions would provide an informed context for planning.

The only honest answer is that we don't know. A reliable and internally consistent data base on charitable giving in the United States does not exist. How large is that pie? The answer depends on who measures it.

One temptation is to examine the annual financial reports of denominations and congregations, use the Consumer Price Index, which overstates the level of inflation, to adjust for a decrease in the purchasing power of the dollar, and produce conclusions about what has happened to per member giving. That methodology is designed to produce bad news. Since bad news attracts a larger audience than good news, that methodology tends to dominate the communications marketplace.

One serious flaw in that methodology is that it overlooks the money given to that growing number of nondenominational megachurches. Another flaw is the absence of consistent definitions of the term *member*. A bigger flaw is that a larger and growing proportion of churchgoers contribute to charitable causes that are not reported in congregational or denominational reports. A common example is the church member who sends a check directly to a college, university, community ministry, missionary, home, theological school, ecumenical venture, nursery school, or other institution not affiliated with that person's denomination. This means that gift is not reported in denominational records.

The biggest flaw in that methodology, however, is the change in national policy in funding charitable causes.

One of the great philanthropists of all time was a Baptist Sunday school superintendent by the name of John D. Rockefeller. He died in 1937. He gave away well over a half billion dollars, $35 million of which went to found the University of Chicago. Eventually that was followed by another $50 million. Rockefeller's dream was a great Christian university with a divinity school at the center. That would create an environment in which the core values of Christianity could permeate every facet of higher education.[4]

Who is John D. Rockefeller's successor? Is it the Rockefeller Foundation, with assets of $3.7 billion in 2000? Or the Ford Foundation, with assets of over $14 billion? Or the Bill and Melinda Gates Foundation, with assets in excess of $21 billion? Or IBM, which contributed $126 million to charitable causes in 2000?

The Birth of the Big Gorilla

No! The big player in the game of philanthropy today is the United States government. During the 1890s approximately 45 percent of the total receipts of the United States government were appropriated for veterans' pensions.[5] Whether that should be described as deferred compensation for past service or charity is not the point. It clearly did provide a solid political base for the Republican Party and another precedent for the future.

For this discussion that increase in veterans' pensions following the Civil War was the second big step in a trend that had begun earlier in the nineteenth century. The first step was the big, bitter, and long quarrel over the control and funding of grammar schools. Who will teach children to read, write, and do arithmetic? For two centuries that was largely the responsibility of the parents and the Christian churches. The birth of the common school movement during the first four decades of the nineteenth century generated bitter political battles over control, curriculum, and funding. Eventually the decision was made to rely primarily on taxes, rather than on parental contributions, for the funding of both public and religious schools. Eventually, of course, the anti-Catholic spirit of the day eliminated the allocation of tax funds to religious schools.[6]

The third big step was the use of local tax dollars to fund pensions for needy widowed mothers.

During the twentieth century the federal government has become an ever larger force in the funding of charitable causes. It also has created huge inconsistencies in the reporting systems. A half dozen examples will illustrate this point.

Mary and Mike met while they were attending a Catholic parochial school. Both capital and operating expenditures were funded out of the parish budget. Their parents contributed to that parish budget. Their contributions could be deducted from their income in calculating their federal income taxes. Twenty years later Mary and Mike are married and the parents of two children enrolled in that same school. Mary and Mike Farrell pay $3,500 tuition annually for each child. Since this is a fee for services they cannot deduct that $7,000 from their income in calculating their federal income tax bill. When the Internal Revenue Service reports the total of charitable contributions by a taxpayer, that $7,000 is not in that total.

The Farrells' neighbor, Ted Olson, graduated from a Lutheran college. The church he attended offered generous scholarships to high school graduates enrolling in that Lutheran school. Ted's parents were members of that parish, and their contributions could be deducted from their income when they prepared their federal income tax form. Those scholarships also were reported and counted as a part of that parish's income and expenditures and thus were a part of that grand total of charitable giving by religious organizations for those years.

Ted is now married and has an eighteen-year-old daughter who has a $3,500 Pell grant to go to college. That Pell grant is partially funded by the income taxes the Olsons pay, but is not included in anyone's report on charitable giving.

Since they were married fifty-three years ago, John and Sarah Brown have accumulated far more wealth than they ever dreamed would be possible. Their only child, George, is the executive director of a Baptist retirement home in Texas. Every year John and Sarah contribute $25,000 to the budget of that benevolent enterprise. The check goes directly to the home. That $25,000 is not reported as a charitable contribution by either their church or their denomination, but they do deduct that $25,000 from their gross income in filing their income tax forms. Therefore it is included when the Internal Revenue Service reports the amount of charitable giving.

For well over one hundred years a Protestant congregation included in the annual budget a modest amount to pay pensions to retired pastors, or their widows, who had once served that congregation. Those payments came from contributions by the members. In 1953 that congregation, for the first time in its history, was served by a minister covered by Social Security. For the next forty-five years he paid his Social Security taxes. Unlike his predecessors he also received a tax-exempt housing allowance instead of living in a church-owned home. When he retired in 1998, he and his wife began to draw their Social Security payments. They also receive a monthly pension check she had earned for forty years of teaching in public schools. They sold the house, for which they had paid $16,200 in 1953, for $243,000. When they retired, they asked that congregation not to pay them a pension, but to allocate those dollars to combat world hunger. Their retirement years are funded by a combination of income from investments and checks from goverment agencies, plus the inflationary impact on the value of housing, not by charitable contributions.

A small congregation in Quincy, Massachusetts, dates its history back to the seventeenth century and once was the spiritual home of John Adams and his son, John Quincy Adams. The present meeting house was constructed in 1828. By 1998 the congregation realized that extensive restoration was needed. The problems were far more serious than any of the 120 members had anticipated. The bills kept coming in and eventually totalled $1.7 million! What could be done?

Between 1660 and the 1780s various members had given the congregation eleven silver cups for use in Communion services. The members knew these cups were not only sacred links with the past, but also valuable antiques. One estimate was that they could be sold for perhaps a million dollars to help pay for the restoration. Finally, after months of debate, in January 2001 they were sold. The auction netted the church $2.6 million dollars! That enabled the congregation to pay all its bills, create an endowment fund, and expand its community ministries.[7]

The federal government in effect contributed the equivalent of over a half million dollars by not requiring a tax on the capital gains. One reporting system could credit that congregation with per member giving of well over $20,000 for the year 2001. A more realistic financial statement would describe that $2.6 million as income from the sale of property, and it would not be classified as member contributions by either the congregation or the denomination.

Back in the mid-1920s a group of Methodists got together and raised the money to build and operate a nonprofit hospital. Thirty-five years later the hospital trustees decided the time had come to construct a large addition and renovate the old building. A Hill-Burton grant from Washington covered much of the cost. In one era that charitable cause was funded by religious contributions. In a later era the taxpayers picked up a big chunk of that capital expenditure.

A couple of years ago that hospital was sold to a national for-profit corporation. The net proceeds from that sale became the assets of a new foundation that uses the income from its investments to improve health. Grants are available to congregations that desire to add a parish nurse to their staff. In its annual report to their denomination one congregation's report of total expenditures for the previous year includes the compensation of all staff, including their parish nurse. Should the income from that Hill-Burton grant of decades earlier that now funds the foundation that helps to pay the compensation of that parish nurse be included in the total charitable giving for last year?

In the old American economy philanthropy was doing good. It was designed to fulfill what came to be called the Seven Corporal Acts of Christian Mercy—"feed the hungry, clothe the naked, shelter the homeless, care for the orphan, tend the sick, visit the prisoner, and bury the dead" (Matt 25:35-40).

Most of these acts of Christian mercy were funded by charitable contributions to religious organizations. Today taxes fund Medicaid and Medicare, which provide much of the care of the sick. The federal government, states, and local governments provide most of the dollars required to shelter the poor, the elderly, and the homeless. Municipalities own and operate hospitals and cemeteries.

In his second inaugural address on March 4, 1865, President Abraham Lincoln called for the nation "to care for him who shall have borne the battle and for his widow and his orphan."

Religious organizations responded to Lincoln's call by constructing and operating hundreds of orphanages and homes for widows. Today taxes provide most of the funding for children's homes, and Social Security checks and governmental subsidies pay for housing the majority of widows.

How Many Pies Are on the Counter?

Instead of trying to measure the size of that pie called "charitable giving," a better beginning point may be to count the number of pies on the philanthropic counter. In a vast oversimplification of contemporary reality, we limit the count here to three.

The largest pie by far is government. If one omits Social Security, higher education, research, Medicare, federal payments to distressed farmers, scholarships, and pensions, the total annual payments by various levels of government for charitable causes clearly exceeds $260 billion. That total does include food stamps, subsidies for housing, disaster relief both overseas and in the United States, public assistance, and several thousand other tax-funded programs.

The federal government, however, administers relatively few social-need driven institutions. Most of the federal dollars are used to pay for services that are outsourced to a variety of vendors. Medicare, research on diseases, grants to institutions of higher education, and billions of dollars in grants to state and local governments illustrate this reliance on outsourcing. A substantial proportion of those tax dollars pays for services provided by religious organizations.

The second largest pie lumps together all the charitable giving in the United States by individuals, foundations, corporations, and various other philanthropic organizations *exclusive of religious congregations.* This pie included at least $140 billion in 2001.

The smallest of these three pies consists of the estimated $65 billion contributed by individuals directly to and through religious congregations. An informed guess is that at least $55 billion of that $65 billion is contributed out of current income.

Caution! The two smallest of those three pies provide only a clue, not an answer to the question of how much money Christians contribute to charitable causes. This methodology greatly understates the contributions of church members to funding social ministries! For example, one church member may contribute $200 a year to fund a food pantry for the hungry, and $200 of that person's taxes go toward state and federal government programs to feed the hungry. Which is a charitable contribution?

Well over one-half of all those $200 billion-plus tax dollars in that first pie come directly out of the pockets of members of Christian congregations in the United States. Perhaps as much as three-quarters of the $140 billion dollars in that second pie also originated from church members.

Why Is That Third Pie So Small?

The contemporary marketplace to raise money for charitable, benevolent, and religious causes is far more competitive than ever before in American history. The big gorillas in that marketplace are governmental agencies that offer individuals two choices, "Pay up or else!" That explains why over one-half of all expenditures for what historically fell under the umbrella of acts of Christian mercy are funded by tax dollars. (If that definition is expanded to include education, health care, and all other forms of tax-funded assistance to the needy and the not-so-needy, the percentage funded by taxes goes above 90 percent.)

The small gorillas in that marketplace consist of those institutions that have created a highly sophisticated and effective system to encourage voluntary contributions. One example consists of several hundred institutions of higher education. Among those small gorillas are at least 5,000 religious congregations.

The pygmies in that marketplace feed on what the gorillas leave on the ground. Together the small gorillas and pygmies divide approximately $200 billion among themselves.

Three BIG Public Policy Questions

The dominance of the big gorillas (governments) in collecting money for what historically have been charitable causes raises three big public-policy questions for Americans in the twenty-first century.

The first focuses on who is the most effective agency in America for collecting the dollars needed to fund charitable needs. The current political consensus is government in general and the federal government in particular. Most of the benevolent dollars for aid to the victims of 9-11-01, for example, will come from the federal government. Has that issue been fully resolved? Or should greater efforts be made to encourage donors to contribute those charitable dollars directly to non-governmental organizations?

The second public-policy question is to gain agreement on who is most effective in disposing of those charitable dollars. Governmental agencies? Or non-governmental organizations?

Who is most effective in delivering services to help the needy? Who is the fairest in responding to that expanding agenda that calls for the redistribution of both wealth and income? Should the collector be assumed to excel in all areas of expertise? Or should governments collect and non-governmental agencies create and deliver the needed goods and services?

If the answer is government, should the primary burden for both collecting and spending be on the federal government? Or should the federal government collect and rely on state and local governments to spend most of those tax dollars for charitable causes? Or should non-governmental organizations be asked to carry a larger load in the creation and delivery of those services?

A third big public policy issue surfaced in early 2001 when President George W. Bush created the White House Office of Faith-Based and Community Initiatives. An early priority of John Dilulio, the first head of this new agency, was to secure a complete performance evaluation of federally funded social service programs in five major departments. Dilulio emphasized that peformance would be a crucial criterion in evaluating future federally funded programs. This is a radical departure from the traditional reliance on the pork barrel.

Another goal is to produce a level playing field so congregations and other religious organizations will be able to compete. Dilulio promised the game of allocating federal tax dollars in outsourcing social services will become more competitive. Will performance be more influential than patronage in outsourcing social service programs? Tune in to this debate in 2005 for clues.

The fourth policy question pits the producer of charitable goods and services against the consumer. Should those charitable dollars be used to subsidize the producers of goods and services or the consumers? The nineteenth century pattern was to concentrate largely on subsidizng the producers.

That began to change in the 1930s with Social Security and grants to distressed farmers. That pattern of sending those charitable dollars to be allocated by the consumer continued with the G. I. Bill of Rights, Medicare, Section 8 Housing subsidies, Pell grants, and other forms of scholarships plus new forms of public assistance to low income families, food stamps, and the Earned Income Tax Credit.

Will the primary recipient of these charitable dollars in the twenty-first century be the producers of goods and services? Or the consumers of those goods and services?

How Much Is $200 Billion?

A conservative estimate is that in 2001 the institutions represented by those two smallest pies received a combined total of $200 billion in benevolent contributions.

That is equal to the combined endowment funds of all the institutions of higher education in the United States. That is one-sixth the amount spent on legalized gambling in the United States in 2001. That is less than the $233 billion spent each year on toys in the United States. That $200 billion is approximately seven times the amount the federal government collects each year in estate taxes. It also is seven times what was spent in 2000 in federal aid to agriculture. Medicaid costs the state and federal governments well over $200 billion annually. That $200 billion is 190 times what was spent on candy for Valentine's Day in 2001. It is seven times the street value of cocaine imported each year from Colombia and five times the cost of operating the American prison system. Federal grants to state and local government also amount to $200 billion. It is six times the annual expenditures on business travel. It is 300 times what NBC paid for the right to broadcast the 2000 Olympics held in Sydney. It is one-third more than the $150 billion Americans now spend each year on home repairs and renovations. It is slightly more than double the combined net worth of the forty wealthiest Americans under age 40 in August 2000. That $200 billion is 125 times the combined total annual reciepts of the 10,800 congregations in the Evangelical Lutheran Church of America and forty-four times the combined total annual expenditures of the 35,800 United Methodist congregations in the United States. That $200 billion is twelve times what Americans spent on parking in 2001 including fees, garage rentals, parking meters, fines, and court fees. It is ten times the annual federal expenditures to combat the import, distribution, and sale of hard drugs. It is 200 times the retail sales for merchandise and souvenirs on the NASCAR racing circuit. It is the equivalent of the net worth of the six wealthiest Americans. It is one hundred times the amount Americans spend each year on runnning shoes and basketball shoes. It is 25 percent less than what was spent in the United States to correct for the now forgotten dreaded Y2K problem. That sum of $200 billion is but a big drop in that bucket called the domestic national product, but it also is such a big drop that it produces many income streams—and that introduces another issue.

CHAPTER EIGHT

How Many Income Streams?

The year is 1928. The place is a small town in Alabama. You are talking with the proud parents of a baby boy. You ask them, "Which of these events do you expect your son will see in his lifetime?"

1. The state of Alabama will fund part of its annual budget through the sale of whiskey.

2. The public schools of Alabama will be racially integrated.

3. Most of the states in this nation will operate state-owned lotteries as a source of revenue.

4. Mississippi and a dozen other states will depend on a tax on gambling as a substantial source of revenue.

5. At least forty states will levy a tax on personal income as a source of revenue.

6. Thanks to the strong support of white voters in the Bible belt a Republican will be elected president of the United States.

7. In that same election the Democratic candidate will receive enough support from American-born black voters to win a majority of the popular vote.

8. Your son will be able to travel to New York for a luncheon meeting and return home to Alabama the same day.

9. Hell will freeze over.

The obvious correct answer is all nine. Hell, a small town in Michigan, experiences many days of sub-freezing temperatures every winter.

Back in the old governmental economy in the United States it was understood that each level of government would have its own primary source of income.

The federal government would depend on income taxes, both corporate and personal, plus fees, tariffs, and a few excise taxes. State governments would rely largely on sales taxes, income taxes, and fees as the primary sources of revenues. County, city, and other units of local government would be financed largely from property taxes.

In the new American economy state and local governments depend on dozens of income streams. That list may include property taxes, income taxes, sales taxes, fees paid by land developers, private utility taxes, grants from the state government, grants from the federal government, fees and taxes from gambling establishments, motor fuel taxes, income from state-run lotteries, taxes on alcoholic beverages, amusement taxes, hotel, motel, and restaurant taxes, building permits, licenses, taxes on airline tickets, sewer taxes, profits from state-owned and operated beverage retail stores, building permits, water taxes, grants for naming a public building, fines, user fees, and income from investments.

The demand for public services has compelled governmental officials to expand the number and variety of income streams.

The Old Ecclesiastical Economy

For most of the history of Christian churches in America, the financial base consisted largely of five sources. One was taxes. A second was pew rents. A third was the offering plate. The fourth was the generous benefactor who might not be a member of that congregation. A fifth was and is a variety of fundraising activities such as dinners and bake sales.

The emergence of a variety of Christian parachurch organizations in the nineteenth century led to the promotion of special financial appeals. Foreign and home missionary organizations were the most numerous of these new Christian organizations, but a comprehensive list would run to at least a thousand names. Most of them identified congregations and churchgoers as their primary source of funds. Congregational histories describe how by 1880 it was not uncommon for a congregation to endorse dozens of special appeals. One pattern called for passing the offering plate twice during Sunday morning worship. The first time was to finance local operating expenses, the second was to collect contributions for the cause of the week, such as a college or orphanage or particular missionary or home or camp or to provide an honorarium for a visiting evangelist.

The Arrival of the Unified Budget

As the competition for funds increased in the early years of the twentieth century, several denominations decided to combine the approved causes into one unified budget. Congregations were urged to reduce or eliminate those designated appeals and contribute money to that unified denominational budget for missions.

One guiding assumption was that the old system often resulted in dollars going to the agency with the most persuasive messengers rather than to the most worthy causes. A second was that the national denominational leaders had the benefit of an overall perspective in evaluating needs against resources. That placed them in a better position than congregational leaders to make wise decisions in the allocation of scarce resources among competing demands. This was consistent with the American culture of that era, which placed a high level of trust in persons in positions of authority. In the contemporary American culture, the popular trend is to trust local leaders. That is one part of the explanation for the recent emergence of so many independent congregations designed to reach generations born after 1960.

While largely forgotten today, the agricultural recession that began in 1922 and the national economic depression that began on that Black Tuesday in 1929 had a tremendous impact on church finances. In the 1920s the vast majority of American Protestant congregations were located in rural and smalltown communities. For generations volunteers had provided much of the skilled labor required to construct, repair, and maintain the congregation's meeting house. A significant portion of the pastor's compensation was a rent-free dwelling, wood to fuel the furnace, and meat, fruits, and vegetables for the preacher's table.

Cash salaries were relatively modest. In 1936 the average annual salary for the pastor of a rural congregation usually was in the $100 to $800 range. The (mean) average annual salary for all rural pastors in the Lutheran Church-Missouri Synod was $693 followed by $688 for rural pastors in the Presbyterian Church in the United States of America, $662 in the United Lutheran Church, $553 in the Methodist Episcopal Church, $643 in the Congregational Christian churches, $587 in the Evangelical and Reformed Church, $583 in the Protestant Episcopal Church, $543 for the Seventh-day Adventists, $490 for the Norwegian Lutheran Church of America, $486 for the Presbyterian Church in the United States (Southern), $386 for the Church of the Nazarene, $295 for Southern Baptists, $540 for Northern Baptists, and $85 for pastors in the Mennonite Church.

Ministerial salaries in urban communities, of course, were substantially higher. In 1936 the average (mean) salary of a minister in urban churches in the Lutheran Church-Missouri Synod was $1,216 compared to $1,831 in the

United Lutheran Church of America, $1,786 for Episcopal priests, $1,745 for northern Methodists, $1,866 for southern Methodists, $595 for AME preachers, $2,235 for northern Presbyterians, $1,875 for southern Presbyterians, $1,850 for the Congregationalists, and $2,460 for the Reformed Church in America.[1]

For comparison purposes it should be noted that the Consumer Price Index in 2001 was nearly 13 times the index for 1936. Annual salaries of a public school teacher (all grades, both rural and urban) averaged $1,283 in 1936, but the typical salary for the teacher of a rural one-room elementary school in 1936 was in the $300 to $700 range. Small town public high school teachers were paid $700 to $1,200 annually. The average annual net income for nonsalaried lawyers in 1936 was $4,394, for nonsalaried dentists $2,726 and $4,204 for nonsalaried physicians.

By the early 1950s it was not uncommon for a pastor or the chair of the congregation's finance committee to explain, "With the exception of four special appeals a year, we fund all our ministries out of the offering plate."

A congregational version of the denominational unified budget had become the approved approach to church finances. Members were expected to tithe their income and return all or most of that tithe to the Lord via their congregation's financial system. That unified congregational budget was expected to include funds to finance not only the unified denominational budget but also causes that formerly had been supported by special appeals. That list often included a camp, a church-related college, campus ministries, a missionary couple, the local council of churches, a children's home, a retreat center, a theological school, and a local social welfare agency or a parachurch organization that employed a former member of that congregation. Some of these were now included in that unified denominational budget. Others were included in that congregation's unified budget.

Five of the guiding assumptions for the unified budget were: (1) members should and would trust the judgment of designated leaders to evaluate the merits of each cause, (2) the only significant source of potential contributions consists of the current income of members, (3) members should and would tithe their income and return all or most of that tithe to the Lord by way of their church, (4) the denominational system was the best channel for members or for the congregation to financially support worthy Christian causes beyond that congregation's local ministry, and (5) Christians prefer not to be bothered with repeated appeals for an endless variety of special causes.

The unified budget was a product of the evolving economic culture of America of the first half of the twentieth century. It was compatible with the depression-based assumption that the American economy is organized around a scarcity of resources. It was consistent with the trend toward the greater centralization of government and business of that era. The unified budget was a relevant response to the call for efficiency and economy. It is still a great model in the eyes of those who are convinced next year will be a carbon copy of 1954.

The Rise and Fall of Subsidies

Four trends coincided during the last two-thirds of the twentieth century to add a new income stream to the financial base of many organizations and institutions in general and to congregations in particular. One began in the 1930s. That was the use of financial subsidies to redistribute wealth and income. The New Deal, farm subsidies, college scholarships, Social Security, an expansion of public assistance to the poor, the G.I. Bill of Rights, unemployment compensation, and employer-paid health insurance were expressions of this trend. That quick decision by the United States Congress in September 2001 to subsidize commercial airlines with a poor business plan was simply one more example of the power of lobbyists to secure federal subsidies.

The second trend was the economic prosperity that followed the end of World War II.

The third was the peak of denominational influence and resources in the 1950s and early 1960s.

One consequence was several of the larger Protestant denominations had the resources required to fund new ventures in interdenominational cooperation, in promoting social justice, and in expanding both regional and national staff. In addition, the call to redistribute wealth and income made it relatively easy to add another stream of income for many congregations. This came in the form of an annual denominational grant. Most of these grants fit into one of eight categories.

1. An annual financial subsidy to enable a congregation to be served by a full-time and fully credentialed resident pastor.

2. An annual subsidy to cover part or all of the cost of the pastor's health insurance and/or pension. (This did not become a widespread subsidy until the 1980s.)

3. A one-time grant to help a congregation finance a capital improvements program.

4. A short-term annual subsidy for a few years to encourage a numerically shrinking congregation to design and implement a new outreach ministry.

5. A grant to enable an all-white congregation in a racially changing neighborhood to add an ethnic minority pastor to the staff.

6. An indirect subsidy to enable a congregation to pay less than its "fair share" toward the financial support of the denominational system. Thus if the "fair share," based, for example, on average worship attendance or total expenditures or membership, was $10,000, that congregation would be asked to contribute only $5,000 as its "fair share."

7. A substantial annual grant for several years to help fund the budget of a new mission. Instead of expecting a new mission to become self-governing, self-expressing, self-financing, and self-propagating within twelve months after the first public worship service, that target date was 36 or 48 or even 60 months down the road. (This long-term subsidy often turned out to be a powerful factor in the dissolution of that new mission before its tenth birthday.)

8. A one-time grant to encourage two small town or rural congregations to merge, purchase land for a new meeting place, and construct new physical facilities.

One unanticipated consequence was a change in priorities for congregational leaders. Instead of focusing on improving their competence in fulfilling the Great Commission, the top priority was to improve their skills in persuading denominational officials to enlarge and/or extend that financial subsidy.

The fourth trend emerged from research that suggested long term financial subsidies to noncompetitive farmers, noncompetitive steel companies, noncompetitive defense contractors, noncompetitive governmental agencies, noncompetitive savings and loan associations, noncompetitive public schools, noncompetitive retail stores, noncompetitive colleges, noncompetitive commercial airlines, noncompetitive miltary bases, noncompetitive railroads, noncompetitive churches, and noncompetitive newspapers were a costly investment in postponing the day when major changes would be made.

The old guiding assumption was that the winners in the new American economy could and should subsidize the losers. The new guiding assumption is that often does more harm than good to the victim. The expansion of public assistance was based on that first assumption. President William J. Clinton's legacy includes a growing acceptance of that new second guiding assumption.

The two big exceptions to this new guiding generalization are: (1) once a subsidy is in the budget it is difficult to remove it and (2) "emergencies" encourage people and institutions to join that line looking for financial subsidies.

That Big New Income Stream!

What is the greatest single change in church finances from the emergence of the new American economy? If measured simply in dollar terms, that is the easiest question raised in this book. It is a ten digit number—$1,000,000,000. In 1992 Protestant congregations received at least one billion dollars more in bequests than were received back in 1952 after allowing for inflation. In other words, after allowing for inflation, bequests to congregations have increased by a billion dollars in forty years. This does NOT include the value of bequests received by parachurch organizations, denominational agencies or Christian colleges or theological seminaries or other Christian organizations. For the calendar year 2001 Protestant congregations in the United States received well over $3 billion in bequests. That does not include cash contributions made by living donors.

For many congregations in which a substantial proportion of the adult members were born before 1930, bequests have turned out to be a welcome new income stream. Those who are comfortable balancing the operational budget of the congregation with gifts from the dead see these as the best of times. Those who are uncomfortable with the dead subsidizing the living call these the worst of times.

Today's generation of mature adults (1) were heavily influenced by the Great Depression that inculcated the virtue of "saving for a rainy day," (2) grew up in a society that lifted up deferred gratification as a virtue, (3) worked in a rapidly expanding economy during the post-World War II decades when personal income rose at an unprecedented pace, (4) devoted more effort to learning and practicing the skill of saving than was devoted to learning the skill of spending, and (5) benefited from national economic policies that rewarded borrowers at the expense of savers in the 1940–85 era and that rewarded savers during the 1985–99 era.

While those generalizations do not fit every adult born back before 1928, the American population today includes an unprecedented proportion of mature adults who are financially well off. In addition, the number of Americans, age sixty-five and over, more than doubled from 16.5 million in 1960 to over 37 million by the end of 2001.

It also should be noted that the generation born in the 1920s has turned out to be the most church-going age cohort in American history. That generation displays much stronger institutional loyalties, to both congregations and to denominations, than is reflected by any of the younger generations. They also are more likely to give a larger share of their charitable contributions to the church than are subsequent age cohorts.

One result is a growing number of congregations report that over a five-year period, bequests and income from investments now account for one-fourth to one-half of their total receipts.

One of the most highly visible consequences is the question that is increasingly seen in church bulletins. It often is in a box at the bottom of the third page and reads, "Have you remembered your church in your will?" Has your long-range planning committee suggested that box be included in your bulletin every week?

The User Fee Stream

From the perspective of the year 2025, what may appear to be the biggest change is the rapidly expanding reliance on user fees. The most obvious examples of user fees can be found in congregations that charge users all or part of the cost for what formerly was offered without direct charges. The Christian day school that once was financed completely out of the parish budget now charges tuition. A fee for materials and the instructor's time is charged those who sign up for that two-hour Bible study class on Tuesday evening. Many of the activities and trips designed for senior citizens are partially or entirely financed by fees. A fee is charged to participants in that aerobic dance class. A fee is charged for the weekday preschool program. A fee is charged for after-school ministries. A fee is charged for that children's drama class on Saturday. A fee is charged for use of the building by "outsiders." A fee is asked to cover materials and refreshments in many vacation Bible schools. A fee is charged to those teenagers who want to go on that ski trip.

One conflict over user fees is illustrated by many theological seminaries. One school seeks large financial gifts so it can be a tuition-free seminary. Another seeks contributions to a scholarship fund so it can offer scholarships to the most promising candidates, but continues to charge a high annual tuition. That debate really is over whether the donor's gift should go to subsidize the institution that provides the services or to the consumer of those services. For the past six decades the American culture has gradually been shifting from subsidies for the producers of services to subsidizng the consumer. Most Christian denominations still argue that the subsidies should go to the producer, not to the consumer of services. What is the attitude of people in your congregation on this issue?

How Many Streams?

Many of today's new supermarkets are designed to produce at least a dozen income streams. These include the sale of meats and groceries, receipts at the coffee bar, photo finishing, the sale of ready-to-eat foods, soft drinks, household supplies, flowers, office supplies, alcoholic beverages, greeting cards, magazines and newspapers, the pharmacy at one end of the store, rental from a branch bank, income from a small fast-food restaurant plus charges to manufacturers for the favorable placement of a new product or for the floor space for a demonstrator.

Perhaps the dramatic illustration of this multiplicity of income streams came in the weeks following Black Tuesday 2001. Within two months at least 190 organizations were seeking charitable contributions for the aid of the victims of that disaster and their families!

How Many Streams for Your Church?

In the new American economy the most frequently heard answers to this question are these three: "One! We are a high expectation church and that means every member by definition is a tither. Those tithes cover all our expenditures."

A second response is, "Three or four. Maybe that's why we run a deficit for the first ten or eleven months of our fiscal year and catch up in the last month." For a growing number of congregations, the answer is, "Seven to twelve, depending on what year it is." Today most American Protestant congregations depend upon several income streams such as (1) the offering plate; (2) bequests; (3) memorials; (4) one-time large gifts encouraged by the tax code, (5) user fees; (6) income from investments; (7) government grants for social services; (8) the small "nickel and dime" appeals twenty to sixty times a year; (9) rental income from use of the building or parking lot; (10) money-raising events such as plays, bazaars, dinners, auctions, rummage sales, and bake sales; (11) grants from corporations; (12) the one- or two- or three-year capital funds appeal; (13) the BIG "Miracle Sunday" appeal designed to raise a very large amount of money over a ten-day period (dozens of congregations have received over one million dollars in cash over two weekends); (14) grants from that congregation's own foundation; (15) denominational subsidies; (16) the sale of real estate or personal property; (17) the net income from a well-designed conference attended by several hundred outsiders; (18) grants from community or private foundations to finance a new community ministry; (19) the once-in-a-decade appeal to long time members who have retired in another state; (20) contributions from "snowbirds" in the South in the winter or summer tourists in the North; (21) contributions from constituents who are not members; and (22) "giving circles" (see chap. 10).

The Big Benefactor

What goes around comes around. The post-Civil War era saw the emergence of hundreds of wealthy entrepreneurs who made generous contributions to churches, educational institutions, libraries, museums, and other benevolent causes.

A new generation of wealthy benefactors appeared in the 1920s. Hundreds of colleges, congregations, and charitable institutions were rescued from oblivion by their gifts.

The new American economy has produced the largest and the youngest group of individual benefactors in history. Their gifts to educational and religious institutions are measured by seven or eight, and occasionally nine digits to the left of the decimal point. A common characteristic is a high level of skill in accumulating wealth, but many admit to a low level of competence in disposing of that wealth.

"God made you a millionaire," explained a forty-five-year-old pastor to an old friend from his college years. "He made me an evangelist. I believe I am called to plant a new mission in a community 500 miles south of here. I need a gift of $250,000 from you to be able to do that."

"Well, I don't know," replied the wealthy friend after a long pause. "I'm not sure you can start a new church for only $250,000. I'll tell you what I'll do. As soon as you incorporate your new church, we'll set up a special account for designated contributions. I'll contribute a million dollars to that account. You use what you need to plant your new mission. If you don't need it all, we can use it to start other new churches."

Five years later, that new mission was averaging over 700 at worship and had become a self-expressing, self-governing, self-financing, and self-propagating congregation. Thanks to compound interest, the balance in that special account had grown to well over a million dollars.

The benefactor came by and explained to that pastor. "First, you have been a good and faithful steward of what was given to you. Second, God has been good to me. I would like to bring the balance in that special account up to $5 million. What do you believe would be the best way to invest those dollars in building God's kingdom?"

Seven Questions

1. Using the list above as a beginning point, what are the potential income streams for your congregation?

2. How many of those potential income streams are now being utilized by your congregation?

3. Is that a satisfactory number? Or do you want to either increase or decrease the number?

4. What are the values that will guide your decision-making process as you make that decision?

5. What steps must be taken to add a new income stream to the financial base of your congregation?

6. Or do you prefer the alternative of creating a high-expectation congregation in which one of the requirements for membership is that every candidate for membership (a) must be a tither and (b) is expected to return to the Lord

via that congregation's treasury at least one-half of that tithe (see chap. 10)?

7. Another widely used alternative is to reduce proposed expenditures to match anticipated receipts.

Which alternative do you prefer?

CHAPTER NINE

How Competitive Is This New Ecclesiastical Marketplace?

"Why are you a member of this particular congregation?"

In the 1950s these were among the most frequent responses to that question. "I was born into this congregation." "I married a member." "This church is close to where I live." "I'm a third-generation member of this denomination, so when I moved here, I naturally chose this church." "Skin color. I'm a Negro and this is the only Negro church close to where I live." "I'm more comfortable worshiping in German than in English, and that's why I chose this church." "My husband (or father) is the pastor." "My grandfather helped found this congregation."

Kinship ties, inherited denominational loyalties, geographical proximity, race, nationality, language, and marriage were highly influential factors in choosing a church home as recently as the 1950s. Nationality, language, race, and marriage continue to be influential factors today for perhaps one-fourth to one-third of all American Protestant churchgoers today. Kinship ties and geographical proximity, however, are relatively minor influences for European-Americans born after 1950.

Perhaps the most highly visible cultural illustration of the increased competition for people's time, commitment, energy, and money in America appear on those beautiful Sunday mornings that feature a community walkathon. A group of people have decided to use the walkathon to raise money for a worthy charitable cause. Volunteers are enlisted. They are asked to secure sponsors who will contribute an agreed-upon sum of money for each mile that volunteer walks.

These volunteers are in direct competition with the churches for people's time and energy! These were rare events in the 1950s when it was culturally incorrect to enter into direct and open competition with the churches on Sunday morning. The Sunday morning walkathon and similar events are more common in the North than in the South, but frequently the organizers include several adults who are regular churchgoers. It is now culturally acceptable to compete. After all, that is one characteristic of a free market! It also is a big free market! A total of 745,000 charitable organizations qualified for tax-exempt status under section 501(c)3 of the Internal Revenue Code in late 2001. Approximately one-half were religious congregations.

The number-one recent competition for charitable dollars, of course, came in the weeks following 9-11-01, as 190 different organizations competed with one another to raise money for the victims of that disaster.

A reasonable to optimistic estimate was that a half billion charitable dollars could be raised for the families of the thousands killed on that Black Tuesday. By mid-November, however, it was announced that the cash and pledges would exceed $1.2 billion. That generous response illustrates three lesson in contemporary philanthropy.

First, Americans have tens of millions of dollars waiting to be given to worthy causes. Who gets it? Those who ask for it and make a persuasive plea on behalf of that worthy cause. Despite the blot on the public image of the Red Cross when the leaders refused to participate in creating a shared data base of the recipients of these charitable contributions, that organization raised more than a half billion dollars.

Second, television in particular and the public press in general represent the most effective channels of communication for persuading potential donors to be generous donors. Visual images not only are worth a thousand words, to paraphrase that old proverb, but they also may produce millions of dollars.

Third, congregations, denominations, and parachurch organizations that use a summer-to-summer program year for their fiscal year were not as adversely affected by that competition for charitable dollars as were those who use the calendar year for their fiscal year.

A New Level of Competition

From this observer's perspective, the most significant trend in American Christianity during the twentieth century was the emergence of an increasingly competitive ecclesiastical marketplace. Today when American-born Caucasians are asked, "Why are you a member of this particular congregation?" that evokes a new array of responses. Among the most common, six can be illustrated by these statements: "The ministry of this church speaks to my personal and spiritual needs." "We appreciate the emphasis on quality." "We were looking for a church that would help us transmit the Christian faith to our children, and we found it here." "I prefer to help pioneer the new rather than try to perpetuate the old, so when I was invited to help create this new congregation, I jumped at the chance." "This church offers us an array of attractive choices in worship, learning, fellowship, and being involved as a volunteer in doing ministry." "The church we left told us about the Christian faith, and they told us what we as believers should do. Here we experience what being a devoted follower of Jesus is all about, and we experience what that means." (While a surplus of conveniently located off-street parking rarely is mentioned as a factor in choosing a new church home, the absence of adequate parking often is cited as the reason for rejecting a particular congregation.)

These responses introduce what this observer believes is the first of a dozen reasons why the ecclesiastical marketplace is more competitive than ever before in the American church.

Consumerism and Higher Expectations

The number-one variable can be summarized in one word: consumerism. Americans coming to the marketplace bring higher expectations than ever before. It matters not whether they come to the marketplace looking for a new motor vehicle, health care, a college dormitory room, the public library services, public transportation, a new single family home, breakfast cereals, a preschool for their four-year-old, a retirement residence, a personal computer, a spouse, a new church home, the younger generations come with higher expectations than their parents or grandparents brought to the marketplace.

They come expecting the producers of goods and services to be sensitive and responsive to their needs and wants. A simple and highly visible example is the addition of Saturday evening worship to the weekend schedule.

The Impact of Ecumenism

Consumerism has affirmed the right of the individual to search among a larger number of vendors in the marketplace. The ecumenical movement has increased the number and variety of vendors in that marketplace.

For most of American church history, a major component of a Christian congregation's identity was in who we are not. This emphasized the differences among the various Christian bodies in America. Calvinists clarified their identity by emphasizing that they were not Armenians. Methodists explained that their pastors were sent, not called. Baptists were repelled by those who practiced infant baptism. Protestants found it easy to identify a dozen important differences between themselves and Roman Catholics. Others quarreled over whether a Christian could partake of alcoholic beverages or be a member of a lodge or play cards or dance or work on the Sabbath.

As was pointed out earlier, the ecumenical movement urged, "Instead of focusing on the differences that separate us, let's emphasize what we have in common." One consequence was that made it easier for younger generations to switch from one religious tradition to another. Third-generation Roman Catholics joined Protestant congregations. Methodists joined nondenominational churches. Lutherans joined Episcopal parishes. Presbyterians became Methodists.

That remarkable success of ecumenism since the mid-1960s has sharply expanded the range of choices a church shopper may consider in looking for a new church home. That has greatly expanded the level of competition. It also explains why so many pastors of non-denominational congregations report, "One-third of our new members were reared Roman Catholics, one-third had no previous church affiliation, and one-third are refugees from a Protestant denomination."

When Did People Stop Walking?

One of the best illustrations of the chicken-and-egg riddle (which came first?) is the disappearance of the American pedestrian. One reason why is that between 1970 and 2000 approximately 220,000 were killed by motor vehicles. The good news is that decrease in the total number of pedestrians has reduced the number killed annually by motor vehicles by nearly one-half since the early 1970s.

Why are so few Americans today walking to work, to school, to the doctor's office, to the grocery store, to the movies, to visit their friends, or to church? Is the basic cause the disappearance of neighborhood institutions? Or did neighborhood institutions disappear because people stopped walking?

One part of the explanation is the increasing geographical separation between the place of residence and the place of work or the place of entertainment or the place of shopping or the place for the delivery of medical services. Another is the consolidation of public schools and the decision to create large elementary schools and very large public high schools with large student parking lots.

A third factor is that between 1965 and 2000 the population of the United States increased by 45 percent, the number of licensed drivers nearly doubled, and the number of licensed motor vehicles more than doubled.

One consequence is that since most shoppers now drive to the supermarket, the sale of groceries is far more competitive than it was in 1965. A second is that since most churchgoers now drive to church, what's the difference between driving two miles and ten miles each way? The ten-mile journey may do less damage to the vehicle and its exhaust system than the two-mile trip.

More important, for many churchgoers there are only two attractive congregations within a mile or two of their place of residence, but there are a dozen highly attractive and three dozen attractive choices within a ten-mile radius.

What Happened to Woolworth's?

A fourth part of the explanation is sometimes referred to as the "WalMart Syndrome." The giant discount store with tens of thousands of items for sale and the giant parking lot in front has wiped out most of the variety stores on Main Street that depended on street parking.

Between 1975 and 2000 the number of "five and dime" stores in the United States decreased from over 30,000 to fewer than one thousand. They could not compete with WalMart, KMart, and Target.

Likewise the small neighborhood church with four off-street parking spaces, two adult classes in the Sunday school, and an average attendance of 85 at the one worship service on Sunday morning cannot be expected to compete with the megachurch with a combined attendance of 1,600 in those five weekend worship experiences.

This is a far different game from the 1950s when that same neighborhood church had only two competitors—old First Church downtown of the same denomination and perhaps a nearby small neighborhood congregation afffiliated with a similar denomination.

Instead of two competitors, that small congregation today has ten or twenty churches competing for the same assortment of potential future members.

The Big Cutback

During the 1950s and early 1960s most of the mainline Protestant denominations were expected to expand their agendas to include (a) the potential merger with another denomination; (b) the urgent need to reverse their withdrawal from the large central cities, especially in the North; (c) a variety of social justice issues including racism, poverty, and housing; (d) the revitalization of numerically shrinking and aging congregations; and (e) the call for increased financial support of church-related institutions such as colleges, camps, seminaries, and homes.

One consequence was to drop new church development to a lower place on that list of priorities. The resulting vacuum was, and is, being filled largely by new denominations and movements, entrepreneurial individuals who organize an independent or nondenominational church, large congregations that accept the responsibility to plant new missions as an integral part of their ministry, and the new congregations organized by immigrant clergy. In New York City, for example, at least 500 new Protestant congregations are created every year—most of them consisting of either recent immigrants or American-born adults under age forty.

These new congregations have provided a new group of aggressive competitors in the effort to bring the gospel of Jesus Christ to new generations of American-born residents and to recent immigrants.

From Generalist to Specialist

In the 1930s nearly every home in rural America contained at least three books. One was the King James translation of the Holy Bible. The second and third were the mail order catalogs from Sears, Roebuck and Company and Montgomery Ward. In some homes more time was spent studying the catalogs than was devoted to reading Scripture.

The catalogs distributed by Sears and Wards offered a huge variety of merchandise. In the late 1920s Sears even sold houses by mail.

What happened to those catalogs? Parcel post rates went up. The farmers' children moved to urban areas covered with attractive shopping centers. Consumers had more time to shop as the length of the work week was reduced. Buyers wanted to see and feel what they contemplated purchasing. The discount stores offered lower prices. The mailboxes were filled with catalogs from the specialty mail order houses. The variety of merchandise in the marketplace exceeded what any one catalog could offer.

On the ecclesiastical scene the congregations that had proclaimed, "We welcome everyone" could continue to articulate that slogan. They were prepared to welcome everyone, but they were not prepared to respond to the expectations people brought. Most did not offer a weekday preschool for four-year-olds. Most could not offer people a choice from among three different worship experiences on the weekend. Only a few had an orchestra. Most worshiped God only in English. Only a few could challenge people to go with fellow members and spend two weeks working with fellow Christians in a sister church on another continent. Only a few could guarantee a surplus of conveniently located off-street parking spaces on Sunday morning. Most did not offer a specialized ministry with new parents. Only a few scheduled yearly trips for members to the Holy Land.

In this competition between the generalist with limited resources and the one with huge resources, the latter usually prevails. One alternative, as illustrated by Kresge, is to replace the small five-and-dime variety stores with large discount stores. On the ecclesaistical landscape the counterpart is the open country church that has averaged between 35 and 60 at worship for a hundred years. Recently it transformed itself and has grown into a full service congregation averaging over a thousand at worship. That does happen, but not often.

A more popular choice has been to merge into another congregation or to close.

A middle ground is to choose a specialty in ministry and concentrate resources on excelling in that ministry. The most common example is the focus on creating a small, intimate, loving, caring, and comfortable fellowship for mature adults who prefer simplicity over complexity and predictability over surprises.

To compete in the ecclesiastical marketplace as a generalist-type congregation for the loyalty of large numbers of churchgoers born after 1960 usually requires an average worship attendance of 800 or more. That is necessary to be able to mobilize the resources required to offer the quality and choices younger generations expect.

From Teaching to Learning

Perhaps the most subtle arena in the competitive national marketplace is the change from teaching to learning. That old producer-driven economy concentrated on enlisting and training adults who could teach others. This concept peaked in usage in the United States military forces during World War II. It worked! Twenty-three-year-olds taught and nineteen-year-olds learned. Unfortunately most of those teachers and students no longer are around.

A similar, but less effective, system of a teacher/student model was used for decades in the public schools, in Sunday schools, and with undergraduates in colleges and universities.

The guiding generalization today for those seeking to reach people born after 1960 is, "It is extremely difficult to teach anyone anything that person does not want to learn." One response is to abandon the old concept of classes headed by a teacher and replace that model with the creation of egalitarian learning communities. That is an increasingly common model in graduate schools, in community colleges, and with four-year-olds.[1]

In the ecclesiastical marketplace, those congregations that focus on learning have a huge competitive edge over those that are still trying to attract younger generations to traditional forms of Christian education.

The Impact of Marriage

In the old economy when a Lutheran from Minnesota met and married a Lutheran from Wisconsin, they naturally went to a Lutheran church. When a Baptist from Texas met and married a Baptist from Florida, they naturally joined a Baptist church.

Today, when a Baptist from Texas meets and marries a Catholic from Louisiana, they often decide, "We will choose a church home that is new to each of us." Will it be Lutheran or Episcopal or Methodist or an independent church? When that Lutheran from Minnesota marries a Methodist from Iowa, they also may decide to choose a church home that is neither Lutheran nor Methodist.

What will they choose? A growing number chose a church that offers a specialized ministry with engaged couples and newlyweds on "how to build a happy and enduring marriage." That peer group meets for two hours every week for forty to forty-five weeks. The churches offering that have a huge competitive edge in reaching couples in an interdenominational or interfaith or intercultural marriage.

Incidentally, the least competitive arena in the ecclesiastical marketplace is among those churches seeking to reach, attract, welcome, and assimilate that large number of heterosexual couples who choose to live together but not marry.

The Competition for Time and Attention

Every voluntary association and charitable cause in America today is competing for the time, attention, loyalty, and support of younger generations. That fifty-page list includes lodges, bowling leagues, service clubs, veterans'organizations, political parties, walkathons, churches, and parent-teacher associations. The big winners in this competition are television, the Internet, and those religous bodies that project very high expectations of their constituents such as Islam, the Church of Jesus Christ of Latter-day Saints, and a variety of nondenominational Protestant congregations.

Oppose or Endorse Change?

Perhaps the second most subtle expression of competition in the ecclesiastical marketplace is between the tradition-driven congregations and those that find it relatively easy to adapt to the new environment of the new economy.

The guiding generalization is many religious bodies fall into one of two categories. One large group consists of those that are ideologically liberal and institutionally conservative. They tend to resist changes in their institutional systems, but are reasonably receptive to changes in their ideology. A slightly smaller but growing group consists of those that are ideologically conservative and institutionally progressive. They naturally tend to resist changes to their ideology, but are usually open to changes in their institutional system.

Everyone needs a stability zone. For the first, it is in their institutional conservatism. For the second, their stability zone is their ideology. (A third group is highly vulnerable because of the absence of an agreed upon stability zone.)

The fourth group, that are both institutionally and ideologically conservative, are able to welcome those who seek an island of stability and continuity with the past in a sea filled with change and discontinuity.

One expression of internal conflict is evoked when leaders of the ideologically conservative body propose changes in the ideology. Another is when leaders of the institutionally liberal body propose changes in the institutional systems.

The greatest source of internal conflict in religious organizations, and especially in denominational systems, arises when the leaders cannot agree on (a) whether their organization is ideologically conservative or liberal and (b) whether it is institutionally conservative or progressive. That absence of agreement on contemporary reality makes it extremely difficult to design a strategy for change that will maximize support and minimize opposition. That scenario is further complicated by the temptation nearly every sinful human being expresses, "My definition of contemporary reality is the only one that is accurate."

In dollar terms the lowest cost religious bodies are those that are conservative in terms of both their ideology and their institutional expression. Relatively few that are liberal in both ideological and institutional terms ever reach large numbers of people born after 1960. In a culture overflowing with pressures for change, everyone needs a stability zone!

The Power of Tenure

In the old American economy that was organized around work, kinship ties, survival goals, functions, continuity, frugality, and institutional relationships, it was common to depend on loyalties to institutions. Americans displayed a high level of loyalty to their country, to their state, to their employer, to their place of birth, to their church, to their denomination, and to their neighborhood institutions. These expressions of institutional loyalties may have peaked in influence during World War II.

Individualism and consumerism both affirm the concept that a person's number-one loyalty should be to one's self. Should a president's number-one loyalty be to the political party that placed him in office? Or to his own career? Is a pastor's number-one obligation to that congregation? Or to that pastor's career path?

In the new ecclesiastical culture, interpersonal relationships are extremely powerful. For many parishioners, their number-one loyalty is to their pastor, number two is to their social network, number three to that congregation, and number twelve to that denomination. For others, their number-one loyalty is to their own personal faith journey, number two is to their social network, number three is to their pastor, number six is to their congregation, and number eighty-four is to the denomination with which that congregation happens to be affiliated.

What are the implications in today's ecclesiastical marketplace?

How do we minimize the number of "our people" who leave us to go to some other church in this community?

The suspenders-and-belt theory offers the most competitive advantages. First, place a high value on a tenure of twenty-five to forty-five years for each pastor. Second, do not assume that "membership in this congregation" will be a powerful tie. Maximize the proportion of constituents who are deeply involved members of a social network of seven to twenty-five people that is an integral part of that congregation. Examples include vocal choirs that sing at least forty-five weekends a year, prayer cells, continuing Bible study groups, adult classes in the Sunday school that are closely knit social networks, a band, that team of mentors with teenagers, the worship team, a closely knit circle in the women's organization, mutual support groups, and mission teams. Conceptualize that congregation as a network of overlapping communities united around two or three common mission goals and reinforced by the continuity of ministerial leadership.

Long pastorates and the cohesive power of the group life of the congregation are valuable assets in a highly competitive ecclesiastical marketplace that encourages people to switch institutional affiliations. In this marketplace the most valuable brand name of a congregation is less likely to be the denominational affiliation and more likely to be the person and personality of that long tenured pastor or the community image of that church. Relatively short pastorates of five to twelve years seriously erode the competitive strength of a congregation in a culture that is organized around personalities rather than inherited institutional loyalties.

Customer Service

In the old American economy supermarkets sold groceries, airlines were in the transportation business, hospitals cared for the victims of accidents and illness, private liberal arts colleges were educational institutions, and the churches concentrated on religion.

In the new American economy all of these and most other institutions are faced with two alternatives. One is to accept the fact they really are in the customer service business. The alternative is a discontented and shrinking constituency.

One consequence of this new emphasis on customer service is the producers of commodities, goods, and services tend to conclude these are the worst of times. By contrast, many consumers view these as the best of times.

The congregations in today's highly competitive ecclesiastical marketplace that are reaching large numbers of people born after 1960 accept as a fact of life they must be sensitive and responsive to the expectations of these younger generations or watch passively as their constituency grows older in age and fewer in numbers. They are ready to master a new rulebook in order to play what has become a new game.

These are a dozen reasons why the competition among the churches to reach, attract, serve, assimilate and retain younger generations has become increasingly competitive. A different perspective looks at other arenas in the contemporary ecclesiastical marketplace. Seven of these are worth cutting down a few trees to discuss here.

Other Arenas of Competition

One increasingly competitive arena is the ministries with high school, college, and university students. A second is on what some call the world missions arena. For most of American church history, that scene was dominated by independent nondenominational or interdenominational mission sending agencies plus the denominationally organized and financed foreign mission boards. In recent years, however, hundreds of congregations are enlisting, training, sending, and supporting their own missionaries, both short term and long term to serve Christ on other continents.

A third highly competitive arena is the competition among theological schools for "the best and the brightest" among younger generations contemplating the ministry as their vocation.[2]

A fourth represents another huge change since the 1950s. This is the abundance of resources available to pastors and congregational leaders on "how to do church better." These include books, monographs on single issue concerns, motion pictures, videotapes, the Internet, planning consultants, professional fundraisers, architects plus specialists in music, learning, youth ministries, worship, projected visual imagery, evangelism, church planting, and other subjects.

Once again the key criteria in choosing from among the competitors are quality, relevance, reputation, price, and the ability to customize.

Overlapping that is the increasing competition among those providing continuing education opportunities for congregational leaders, both lay and ordained. The old ecclesiastical economy called for the potential learners to come to the teacher's turf. This was a natural reflection of the academic culture which assumed students should come to the teacher's turf.

One result was the classroom learning environment usually was a college or seminary campus or a retreat center or a denominational center.

The affluence of the 1980s moved many of these learning environments to a hotel where people could eat, sleep, socialize, and learn under one roof.

In the 1960s researchers began to lift up the influence of the physical setting on the total pedagogical environment.

One current example is that the very large public high school frequently is organized to increase the degree of anonymity, isolation, and complexity. One consequence is anonymity, isolation, and complexity tend to feed alienation and increase the proportion of students who are self-identified losers. A predictable consequence is an increase in anti-social behavior.[3]

By the mid-1990s it began to become apparent that the best pedagogical environment for continuing education experiences for congregational leaders (this emphasis on the change from opportunities to experiences is extremely significant!) is the physical facilities of a congregation which has been an innovative and effective pioneer in creating new expressions of ministry as well as perfecting traditional forms of ministry. When these experiences are staffed, not by outside experts, but by the staff and volunteers of that teaching church, it has a built-in level of credibility that cannot be matched by a cadre of experts in a hotel ballroom.

One slice of the competition in this arena is between this emerging network of self-identified teaching churches, where learning occurs in the physical, social, cultural, pedagogical, and religious environment of a worshiping community, and those organizations that schedule continuing education in hotels.

A sixth, which is far from new, is that huge number of entrepreneurial individuals and congregations who are competing with denominational agencies in planting new missions in the United States and on other continents.

Finally, while it is not the most important arena of competition in the contemporary ecclesiastical marketplace, one of the most interesting is the intradenominational competition for the loyalty of congregations. In the early years of the twentieth century, one expression of this was the competition among several agencies within the denominations for financial contributions from congregations. Several denominations decided to reduce that by a unified national denominational budget. (Recently, however, denominational agencies have begun to compete with congregations for the financial contributions of that congregation's members—but that is a subject for chapter 11.)

During the 1990s the competition also has increased between the regional judicatories and the national denominational budget for financial support from congregations. Typically the agency that is institutionally closest to the congregation wins that battle.

During the 1990s, however, the criteria were revised. Ask congregational leaders this question.

"Which level of the organizational structure of your denomination are you most happy to support?" Most of the responses to this question fall into one of these five categories:

1. The one in which we know and have a good personal relationship with the paid staff.
2. The one that has earned our trust.
3. The one that has been sensitive, responsive, and helpful in resourcing our needs.
4. The one with which we have had no disagreements on theological, doctrinal, policy, social, or political issues.
5. The one that displays a high level of commitment, competence, and performance in fulfilling its responsibilities. (The denominational pension board usually heads this list.)

In this arena, as in much of life, relationships, trust, and performance are foundation stones in building loyalty.

At this writing the most interesting arena of internal competition is in the Evangelical Lutheran Church in America (ELCA). A debate over institutional pluralism surfaced there in 2000. Will it be possible for a Lutheran parish to retain its membership in the ELCA and also be a full member of WordAlone? Will a Lutheran parish be able to be a member of WordAlone, "a renewal movement...with an educational focus," and also a full member of the Lutheran Congregations in Mission for Christ, as well as a full member of the ELCA?

This contemporary intradenominational competition for the loyalty of congregations has produced two responses. The old ecclesiastical economy response was, "Take your choice. In or out!" The new ecclesiastical economy has generated a stronger affirmation of accommodation. "Sure. Why not? Congregations have the right to chose their own affiliations."

The big expression of this response is the increasing number of African American congregations that are dually affiliated with a black denomination and a predominantly white denomination. For at least forty years hundreds of white congregations have been full members of two different predominantly white denominations.

Another contemporary expression of this spirit of accommodation is the Southern Baptist congregation that has terminated its affiliation with the Southern Baptist Convention, but continues to be affiliated with the local Southern Baptist Association and a state Convention of the Southern Baptists.

At this point a few readers may protest, "That's all very interesting, but where we live, the greatest competition is for the charitable dollar! When do we get to that?" The answer is that requires three more chapters.

The Impact
on Congregations

"We really have only one very simple question," explained the chair of the finance committee at the Oak Grove Church. "How can we improve our system so we're always be able to pay all our bills on time?"

The best answer to what is a complex subject is to begin by first looking at several other questions. After these issues have been resolved, it will be relatively easy to design a financial system for the twenty-first century.

What Are Your Assumptions?

As your leaders design that customized financial system for your congregation for the twenty-first century, it may be useful to begin by reaching agreement on a dozen assumptions.

1. What is our assignment? To improve the present system? Or to start with a blank sheet of paper and design a new system?

2. What will be our time frame for the budget preparation process? Will we use the traditional three-column format with the first column, "Actual expenditures for last year" followed by a second column, "Actual and estimated (expenditures) for this year" and "Budgeted for next year"?

Or will we use a four- or five- or six- or seven-year time frame in order to plan at least three years ahead?

3. Will our fiscal year coincide with the calendar year? Or with the program year, which for most congregations is summer to summer?

4. Do we expect everyone will contribute approximately the same number of dollars? Or do we expect that 60 to 80 percent of the total receipts will come from 20 to 30 percent of our contributors?

5. When we ask our people to tithe, do we expect that to be a tithe of current income? Or a tithe of net assets? Or both? Today many adults have considerable accumulated wealth, but only a modest annual income.

6. Do we expect the offering plate will produce most of our receipts? Or do we plan on several income streams (see chap. 8)?

7. Do we believe it will be easier to motivate our people to contribute to "underwriting a unified budget"? Or to motivate them to contribute to specific causes?

8. Do we expect our mail box, the Internet, and direct withdrawals will bring in as many dollars as we receive in the offering plate?

9. Do we expect the users to pay for the cost of many specialized ministries, activities, and programs? Or do we believe most or all of these should be financed out of a unified budget?

10. Do we identify as "missions" investing current resources to expand the capability of this congregation to reach generations not yet born? Or do we reserve that term for sending money to hire someone else to do missions on our behalf?

11. Do we believe the system we use to raise money for operating expenses should be the same system we use for funding capital expenditures and missions?

12. Do we expect all or nearly all of our total expenditures will be funded by contributions from our members? Or do we expect non-members to contribute to our ministries?

The answers to many of these questions tend to create self-fulfilling prophecies.

Taxes to Pew Rents to Chickens to Tithes to an Endowment Fund?

"My first wife and I joined this church back in 1786, two years after the Act of Toleration of 1784 was adopted by the legislature," recently recalled the 252-year-old Henry A. Harder, a longtime member of a United Church of Christ congregation in Connecticut. "At that time churches were supported largely by property taxes. The Act of Toleration called for each town to choose the minister and the church the taxpayers wanted to support. It was called the Act of Toleration for two reasons. First, no one church could be subordinated to any other religion. Second, your taxes went to support the minister and the church chosen by the majority in that town. If, however, a taxpayer was a member of another church and could prove financial support of that other church, he was exempt from the church tax."

"Yeah, I remember that," added a 252-year-old deacon, "but the Baptists objected to it even though in a few towns a Baptist church received that church tax. They fought it for years and finally killed it in 1818. The next year we adopted a system of pew rents to pay the bills."

"Our congregation depended on the church tax until it was abolished in 1833," added Henry's 261-year-old brother, Benjamin, who was visiting from Massachusetts. "While we Congregationalists were the chief beneficiaries of the religious tax because of our numbers, the Baptists, Methodists, Episcopalians, Unitarians, and even the Universalists shared in that tax after 1780. That was the year Massachusetts adopted a constitution. Article III of its

Declaration of Rights required the legislature to authorize the towns to levy a property tax that would support the ministers. The legislature also was authorized by that constitution to make church attendance compulsory" (see chap. 1).

The common thread was that a town or other local government could, by a majority vote, establish its own religion, but it could not exclude any other religion. In most of the colonies, however, it was clear that only Protestant Christian churches could enjoy public support from the local tax levy. One exception was Maryland, which had a large Catholic population, where the state constitution authorized the levying of taxes for any Christian religion. That was referred to as a "multiple establishment."[1]

"We abandoned pew rents in 1880," continued the still vigorous Henry Harder. "I recall the year because that vote was taken a week after the death of Grace, my third wife. Grace died in late May, and we voted to abandon pew rents the following week."

"No, Henry," corrected his 249-year-old younger brother, James. "Grace was your fourth wife. It was Abigail who died in 1880."

"Yeah, I guess you're right," agreed Henry. "The point I was trying to make is that during my years in this church, I've seen lots of ways to raise money come and go. It was Margaret, my fifth wife, who helped organize the Ladies Aid here in this church. The ladies raised a lot of money for missions, but they also chipped in one time when we needed money to replace the roof. The Ladies Aid also agreed to pay half the cost when we decided to install indoor plumbing back in the 1930s. It was my sixth wife, Agnes, who persuaded the trustees to go ahead with that project. I was a trustee at the time, and the first time around we voted it down, but when the ladies promised to pay half the cost, they shamed us into it. They raised most of their share through Tuesday chicken dinners every noon. I remember it was twenty-five cents for adults and fifteen cents for the high school kids to have dinner here every Tuesday for a couple of years. I don't recall how many chickens gave their lives to pay for those toilets and sinks, but it must have been way over a thousand.

"During the time we've been members here, we've sure used a lot of ways to raise the money to pay our bills," continued Henry. "We've depended on taxes, pew rents, tithes, legacies, auctions, plays, dinners, bazaars, special appeals, the sale of Christmas trees, and all kinds of other money-raising activities. Back in the 1950s, when we had a lot of farmers in the congregation, several of them set aside one acre of land. They called it God's acre. Whatever that acre produced they sold, and the money was given to the church.

"Back in 1960 we got a new minister who introduced the goal that every member should tithe and give at least half of that tithe to the church," recalled Henry. "I know it was 1960, because his first wedding here was when Laura and I were married that June. Unfortunately, his goal of this becoming a tithing church never was widely accepted. Maybe it was because he left after only five years to accept a call to a bigger congregation in Ohio. It did boost our income some for a few years, but our next minister never promoted tithing, so that goal was soon forgotten."

"Our four big sources of income in recent years, outside the offering plate," added Henry's younger brother, James, "have been bequests, income from the endowment fund, capital fund campaigns, and special appeals for missions. When Henry's sixth wife, Agnes, died in 1943, Henry took the initiative to start a memorial fund in her name for scholarships for our young people going to college. A year later a young man from our congregation was killed in France. His parents contributed that $10,000 G.I. insurance payment on condition that the memorial fund be expanded to become a general endowment fund. In 1945 we received another $10,000 G.I. insurance payment from the parents of a boy who was shot down over the Pacific. We also received a couple of other big bequests for the endowment fund. In 1950, when Henry's seventh wife, Doris, was treasurer of the endowment fund, she reported it had slightly over $50,000 in assets. That would be the equivalent of $350,000 in today's dollars."

"Today, our endowment fund, thanks to many more bequests and the stock market, has assets of nearly $2 million," interrupted Henry. "At last month's annual meeting, Laura, she's my eighth wife and chairs our finance committee, reported they were budgeting $40,000 for various kinds of scholarships plus $20,000 for missions and $60,000 for the church budget out of income from our endowment fund. If that fund keeps on growing, by the time of my funeral in another fifty years, we can have a well-financed church with a well-paid minister, even if we don't have any members."

"That bothers me," commented a young fifty-three-year-old who had joined in 1977. "Our membership and our church attendance have been going down for at least twenty years. Is it reasonable to believe that we can have a healthy and vital congregation that lives off the dead? That $60,000 will cover nearly half of our church's expenses this year."

"Back in the 1930s it was a lot of dead chickens that kept us going," retorted Henry. "In those days nobody objected to killing chickens to buy toilets! We've been living off the dead since long before you were born."

"This is the first time I've ever heard that our church once was funded out of local property taxes," inquired a member who had been born in the same year John F. Kennedy was assassinated. "How was that justified? Why was it terminated?"

"Those are two easy questions," explained Henry. "It initially was justified on the basis that this was a Christian country. Most of the immigrants from Europe, including both my mother and father, came from countries where there was an established church funded out of the public treasury. In the seventeeth century and the early part of the eighteenth century, most of the colonies had an established religion financed with public funds. In the northern colonies it usually was the Congregationalists. In Virginia and a couple of other places it was what today we call the Episcopal Church. The notable exceptions were Rhode Island, Maryland, Delaware, and Pennsylvania. What was new came in the latter part of the eighteenth century. The first step was to make the process more democratic. Instead of the ruler of the land declaring what the established church would be, in each town the male property owners chose, by a majority vote, what would be the established church in that community. Second, in most of the colonies, and later the states, no religion should be subordinate to any other. In several states they even allowed the other Protestant churches to receive tax funds. In earlier years only one religion could receive tax funds. That policy was liberalized, here in Connecticut in 1784, as I pointed out earlier, after 1784 it was a democratic and equitable process."

"If it was equitable and democratic, why was it terminated?" challenged a thirty-three-year-old member. Was it the separation of church and state policy?"

"No," replied Henry, "you're referring to the first amendment to the Constitution of the United States. The Bill of Rights was approved by Congress in 1787 and ratified by the states in December 1791. The First Amendment begins with the words, 'Congress shall make no law respecting an establishment of religion.' That places a restriction on the actions of the Congress, not on the states. Earlier, in the Northwest Ordinace of 1787 Congress had included a guarantee of religious liberty for residents of that territory. The states in existence in 1787, however, were free to continue an establishment of religion. It was not until more than a hundred years after the deaths of Thomas Jefferson in 1826, and James Madison ten years later, that the restrictions on the establishment of religion in the First Amendment were interpreted to apply to the states. As you may recall from your study of American history, two hundred years ago church services were held in the Treasury building, in the Supreme Court chambers, and in the War Office. The First Ammendment was far less influential here in Connecticut a hundred and fifty years ago than was the growth of tolerance, democracy, and egalitarianism following the Revolution. The big factor, of course, is that by 1818, when the church tax here in Connecticut was terminated, most of the people who had grown up with the old exclusionary establishment were dead. My kid brother, James, over here, and I are among the few around today who were alive back in 1784 when the Act of Toleration was adopted. Remember, it took thirty-two years after the Act of Toleration was adopted before the church tax was abandoned. That used to be the normal interval between when a new idea was introduced and when it was widely accepted. Here in this church, for example, we began to see people coming to church in automobiles in the 1920s, but it was 1958 before we paved our parking lot. I remember the year because a week later Doris's funeral service was held here, and the funeral director complimented us on our new parking lot."

"That's right," added older brother Ben, "you usually need a lot of funerals between the date when a new idea is first introduced and when it can be implemented."

"That's not what I meant," stormed Henry Harder in an angry voice. "Doris was a wonderful wife, and she was always open to new ideas."

"Rather than talk about all your wives, I would like to return the discussion to why tax dollars cannot be used to finance the ministries of religious organizations," demanded a young member.

"Let me respond to that while Henry takes a breather," offered James Harder. "In very simple terms there are three answers. The first is billions of tax dollars are allocated every year here in the United States to fund the work of Christian organizations" (see chap. 7).

"Second," continued James, "that is not the big battle. The current quarrel is over whether tax dollars can go to a worshiping community to finance job training or to shelter the homelesss or to cure the drug addict or to feed the hungry or to care for the sick. One side declares that is acceptable. The other side says those funds must go to a separate legal corporation, not through the congregation's treasury. Another side of this is the distinction between federal tax dollars going directly to a religious organization versus state and local tax dollars. The big battle is over federal funds. Another facet is whether the tax dollars follow the consumer of the services or go directly to the producer of the services who recruit the consumers. The G.I. Bill, for example, called for the funds to follow the consumer. The same is true of Pell grants, Medicare, Social Security, and other tax-funded programs. For example, there is no restriction on a recipient of a Social Security check, which is funded by federal tax dollars, from contributing those dollars to the recipient's church or to rent an apartment in a church-owned retirement village. In the old days the tax dollar went to fund the veterans' home or the county farm where the elderly poor lived."

"You've overlooked the biggest factor in this whole debate," interrupted Henry's older brother, Ben. "Instead of placing that third as I expect you were about to do, this should be placed first. It is anti-Catholicism! I'm a Protestant and I've lived in Massachusetts now for well over two hundred years. Today three-quarters of the church members in Massachusetts are Catholic, but it wasn't always that way. James Madison's arguments for separation of church and state included his conviction that would be a healthier relationship for the churches. Over the years I've come to agree with him. Madison's argument also was against establishing one national religion as the government-supported religion. That is what the First Amendment was intended to forbid. For two hundred years no one seriously objected to tax dollars funding church-owned and operated grammar schools on the basis of separation of church and state. Those who did object were mostly property owners without school age children. They simply didn't want to pay to educate someone else's child.

"The separation of church and state issue first came up when the issue of equity was interpreted to mean tax dollars could be used not only to fund Congregational or Methodist or Baptist churches but also Roman Catholic parishes. That was where people drew the line in the sand!" continued Ben. "During the first half of the nineteenth century, the issue was redefined. Tax funds had been used to fund church-owned grammar schools, but when it was suggested that tax funds should go to Catholic schools to educate the children of the Irish immigrants, that was proclaimed as a violation of the separation of church and state. For most of our history the big dividing line has not been between church and state. It really has been a Protestant/Catholic division. Up until recently, Methodists, Baptists, and other Protestant denominations used anti-Catholicism as a central organizing principle. I remember when the Methodists sent Bishop G. Bromley Oxnam from Omaha to Boston. Catholics in Nebraska warned their Catholic friends in New England they should be prepared for attacks by a remarkably articulate Methodist. Oxnam used the separation of church and state as a basis for many of his anti-Catholic speeches.[2] For younger people, however, that era of anti-Catholicism began to fade away in the 1960s after the election of John F. Kennedy, the assassination of the Kennedy brothers, and Vatican II. Even though Massachusetts is now a predominantly Catholic state, I still see lots of traces of the anti-Catholic sentiments of the pre-1960 era. Once again, however, funerals are changing old traditions. In the 1920s, when Al Smith was a candidate for president, or in the 1950s it was not unusual for a liberal Methodist bishop to be anti-Catholic. That was a part of the Methodist culture. Today the Methodist culture calls for the liberal bishop to be a leader in ecumenism. The culture influences the ideology."

"How do you feel about faith-based initiatives being supported by tax dollars?" asked a young woman in this gathering.

"I'm with James Madison on that one," replied Ben Harder. "I'm opposed to the idea of establishing any one church as the national religion, but that's never going to happen here. Madison had seen that in Europe and in the colonies, but it is not on today's agenda! I also agree with Madison that tax funding of the worship and teaching ministries of any one religion would be unhealthy for that religious body. What we have today that James Madison never anticipated is the decision by all levels of government to outsource to both nonprofit and for-profit corporations a huge variety of social services and programs to help people.

"That Act of Toleration of 1784 here in Connecticut was a guideline I could live with today. It emphasized equity, local control, and a level playing field. I also, however, am comfortable with the Everson decision of 1947 in which the United States Supreme Court ruled the First Amendment ban on the establishment of religion also applies to the states, thanks to the Fourteenth Amendment. In that landmark case the Court approved the use of public funds to bus children to parochial schools since the public purpose was safety, not religious instruction. I am comfortable with the Court's decision in the McCollum case of 1948 that limited religious instruction in public school buildings. I have no problem with veterans using their educational benefits to go to a Christian college or a Medicare recipient being treated in a Baptist hospital or a job training program for security guards being adminstered by an inner city Pentecostal church or funding a Salvation Army program for teenage substance abuse or using tax dollars to enable Lutheran Social Services of America to resettle political refugees from Asia in Minnesota or buying computers for use by children in a Christian day school. I am, however, opposed to using tax dollars to fund worship or teaching ministries.

"My central point," concluded Ben, "is that for at least the fifth time in my long life, we have to take a new look at how we finance the life, ministry, and outreach of congregations like this one and mine back in Massachusetts."

Nine Lessons

This narrative overflows with relevant lessons. The most important may be that in the new American economy, despite the longer life expectancy of Americans, fewer funerals are required between the date when a new idea is first introduced and when sufficient support can be mobilized to implement it.

Second, the older the age of the man, the more likely he will prefer to talk about the past rather than the future. Why? As Henry Harder acknowledged, his future may be only fifty years while his past is five times as long. We all naturally tend to focus on what we have in the largest quantity. The twenty-six-year-old talks about the future. The seventy-six-year-old prefers to talk about the past. The father of four and the grandfather of seven will spend more time talking about his grandchildren than his children. The aging leaders of the dying congregation will devote huge quantities of time and energy to next year's celebration of the one hundredth anniversary of the founding of that church, but display limited interest in designing and resourcing a new future for it.

Third, premature deaths undermine the perpetuation of the oral tradition in tribes, churches, and political discussions.

Fourth, births, deaths, and weddings often are more useful benchmarks than the calendar for recalling the date of a particular event.

Fifth, some men are luckier than others. The majority have only one wife in a lifetime. Others have two or three or more. Who are the fortunate ones?

Sixth, the idea of using tax dollars to finance the ministries of religious organizations did not originate in New England or Virginia in the seventeeth century. It did not originate more recently with Franklin D. Roosevelt or Lyndon B. Johnson or George W. Bush or Jesse Jackson. It did not originate when the twenty-three-year-old governor of the Massachusetts "Great and General Court," Henry Vane, set aside 400 pounds sterling in 1636 for the founding of Harvard College where "Everyone shall consider the main end of his life and studies to know God and Jesus Christ which is eternal life and . . . exercise himself in reading the Scriptures twice a day."[3]

That concept was brought to North America by the reformers from western Europe. It has survived in several provinces in Canada but has been under attack in the United States for many decades. Most recently the objections have focused on using tax dollars to fund the educational, social, and community programs of black urban congregations or of non-Christian religions.

Seventh, the distinctive contribution of the political and religious leaders of the late eighteenth century in America was that funding should be equitable, locally decided, and nondiscriminatory.

Eighth, as that new minister who arrived back in 1960 discovered, it takes more than good intentions and five years to change the culture of a congregation that has been in existence for centuries. To transform it into a tithing church means replacing the old low commitment culture with a high expectation culture. Today that is an especially challenging assignment in New England!

Ninth, as Benjamin Harder recognized, as the decades roll by, churches are called to redefine their identity, role, ministry, and constituency. Few congregations are able to retain the same constituents for more than six or seven decades. Ben, Henry, and James are exceptions! One component of that process of planning for a new era often means replacing the old system for paying the bills with a new system. There is a shortage in the new American economy of chickens eager to sacrifice their lives to pay for the new plumbing in the church. There is an even greater shortage of women eager to work in church kitchens to cook and serve those chicken dinners!

The culture does shape the ideology, and the new ecclesiastical culture in America is reshaping the systems used to finance congregational life, ministry, and outreach. Several other factors, however, should receive serious consideration when the time comes to design a customized financial system for your congregation. High on that list is whether your congregation specializes in high-cost or low-cost ministries.

High Cost or Low Cost?

How much money does an American Protestant congregation require to finance its ministries? The only good answer is that depends on local circumstances. A broad generalization is the annual expenditures usually average out to somewhere between $500 times the average worship attendance and $4,000 times the average worship attendance. One exception is the house church where that average may be $50 to $100. A second exception is the very large congregation that is able to fund the total cost of a new meeting place in one year. For that one year, that congregation's receipts may be $10,000 times the average worship attendance for that year.

One common variable is the difference between high-cost ministries and a low-cost approach. The total cost of offering a particular ministry (including the cost of staff time, a fair share of the real estate costs, and the overhead plus the program expenditures) can be determined by dividing that total by the average number of people reached and served by that particular ministry. That makes it possible to arrive at an average cost per person served.

At one end of that spectrum are the exceptionally low cost ministries such as adult Sunday school classes, the emphasis on celebrating the past rather than investing in the future, the traditional women's missionary organization, and the lay-led house church. At the other end of that spectrum are the very high cost ministries. These include many of the campus-based ministries with undergraduates, most ministries with formerly married single adults, many ministries with large numbers of teenagers, short pastorates of two to five years, pastoral care, ministries with young never-married adults, the total ministry of the low-commitment congregation in which the average worship attendance is less than one-half of the confirmed membership, and the specialized ministries that are funded out of the parish budget rather than by fees such as a Christian day school or a recreation ministry or a ministry with shutins.

Between these two are the moderate cost ministries such as a ministry with families that include teenagers staffed largely with volunteers, the theologically homogeneous congregation with a program staff-to-average-worship attendance ratio of 1 to 300 rather than 1 to 200 or 1 to 150, the ministry with married couples with young children or a ministry focused on creating and nurturing small groups.

The ministry of worship does not fit into this discusion. First of all, in most Christian congregations, it is "the cash cow" or "the profit center." The dollar receipts generated by those worship services subsidize most of the other ministries. Second, and more important, the ministry of worship should be evaluated by a different set of criteria. First, is it pleasing to God? Second, what is happening in the lives of those worshipers? Third, from a long term perspective, the quality and relevance of corporate worship often is one of the crucial factors in determining the numerical growth or decline of a congregation.

How Costly Is Diversity?

"Our strength is in our diversity!"

That is an increasingly common slogan among Protestant congregations in the United States.

At least occasionally it is proclaimed as an explanation for the relatively small size of the congregation. When megachurches dominate the religious scene, how does one defend the existence of the congregation averaging eighty-five at worship? One response is to highlight the demographic diversity.

What Is Demographic Diversity?

The most common expression of demographic diversity is generational. These congregations are able to point out the age distribution of their membership resembles the age distribution of the American population. This means that approximately 16 percent of the members, age fourteen and over, have passed their sixty-fifth birthday, another 30 percent are ages forty-five to sixty-four, 34 percent are twenty-five to forty-four, and 20 percent are ages fourteen to twenty-four. The median age of those fourteen and over is approximately forty-six years.

A second definition of demographic diversity reflects racial and nationality categories. Thus the congregation that reflects a cross section of the American population would report 82 percent of its constituents (all ages) are white, including white Hispanics, 13 percent are blacks, and 4 percent are Asians. If Spanish as the first language is substituted for Hispanic, the white non-Hispanic category drops to 70 percent.

With the one major exception of that rapidly growing number of Pentecostal or charismatic churches, it is rare to find a congregation averaging more than 135 at worship that reflects that degree of cultural diversity.

A third definition of demographic diversity appeared after World War II. The first stage consisted of congregations that welcomed adults who were divorced and remarried. Today, it is easy to find congregations that have a divorced and remarried pastor as well as many divorced and remarried members.

The next stage focused on the growing number of single never-married adults age eighteen and over. That total nearly tripled from 18.2 million in 1965 to 49 million in 2000. That means the congregation that is truly demographically diverse reports about one-fourth of its active constituents, age 18 and over, are never-married adults. (A specialized ministry with the one-sixth of the American population, age 18 and over, who are formerly married usually differs in several respects with one focusing on never-married adults.)

The third stage came when congregations openly and eagerly welcomed self-identified gays and lesbians. The unifying and redemptive central organizing principle often was the ministry around the death of a loved one.

The newest definition of this version of demographic diversity helps to explain why marriage is becoming the "hot" social justice issue. A survey completed by the National Opinion Reserach Center of the University of Chicago in 1998 reported that of all households consisting of a heterosexual man living with a hetereosexual woman, 32 percent (up from 16 percent in 1972) were unmarried couples without children at home, 30 percent (up from 29 percent in 1976) were married couples without children at home, 26 percent (down from 45 percent in 1972) were married couples with children under age fifteen at home, and 12 percent (up from 10 percent in 1972) were unmarried couples with children under fifteen at home. The number of unmarried couples with children under fifteen at home quadrupled from 431,000 in 1980 to over 1.6 million in 2000.

At this writing it is extremely rare to find a Christian congregation in the United States that reflects that version of demographic diversity!

A fifth expression of demographic diversity is based on the place of birth of the current constituency. That rare congregation that models this form of diversity reports that approximately 90 percent of the current constituents were born in the United States, 3 percent in Mexico, 2 percent in Asia, and 5 percent in Central America, the Caribbean and elsewhere.

In several very large central cities, such as New York, Chicago, and Los Angeles, the big contemporary wave in new church development is the creation of new congregations serving recent immigrants.

Theological Pluralism

A completely different definition of diversity is expressed by those congregations that rejoice in the diverse religious backgrounds of the constituency. A common example is reflected by the statement, "At least one-fourth of our current adult constituents were reared in the Roman Catholic Church, nearly a fourth had no previous church relationship, about a fourth came by letter of transfer from a church of our denomination, and the others came here from a variety of other Protestant churches."

That statement really represents the past, not the present. It describes the religious background of the present constituency. If it is a large and rapidly growing congregation, today's members probably share a common theological position. If it averages fewer than 135 at worship and if most of the members share in the corporate worship of God on fewer than 26 weekends a year, it may be a truly theologically pluralisic congregation.

A second expression of theological pluralism is the congregation that includes people scattered all along a belief system, but the unity is in kinship ties or in the fact that nearly every adult either is a second- or third- or fourth-generation member or married to a second- or third-generation member.

Another is the theologically pluralistic congregation bound together by the combination of a long-tenured loving shepherd, social class, and affection for that historic meeting place.

From a pastoral perspective, the most difficult assignment is to serve a theologically pluralistic congregation that also includes great diversity in the level of Christian commitment. To illustrate this point, imagine a congregation consisting of two hundred husband-wife couples, each with two children at home and an annual family income of approximately $75,000. Every adult was born in the United States but comes from a western European ancestry and has completed four to eight years of post-high school education. There is very little diversity in terms of race, language, educational attainment, income, or ancestry. None of the adults are the children of members of this congregation.

Two years ago at a congregational meeting, it was decided by a 143 to 24 vote of those members present and voting that one-half of all dollar receipts would be allocated to missional causes. That left a budget of $335,000 for operational expenditures.

Out of those four hundred adult members, 20 percent attend worship on at least 45 weekends a year. Their financial contributions to this church range between $7,000 and

$10,000 per household annually. A second 20 percent attend worship on 35 to 44 weekends a year, and their financial contributions range between $3,500 and $6,000 per household per year. These two groups account for well over 90 percent of the volunteer time by members as teachers, committee members, worship leaders, musicians, and other workers.

A third 20 percent attend worship between 20 and 35 weekends annually, and their financial contributions range between $2,000 and $3,400 per household per year. The remaining 40 percent attend worship on somewhere between 2 and 19 weekends annually. Their financial contributions range between $500 and $1,900 per household for the year.

Last year worship attendance by adult members averaged 214 per weekend. The most committed 40 percent accounted for 65 percent of the member attendance, and they also contributed 80 percent of the $670,000 received from members.

With the exception of that strong financial commitment to missions, this picture resembles worship attendance and financial support patterns reported by thousands of Protestant churches in the United States. It is not at all unusual for 40 percent of the member households to account for two-thirds or more of the adult worshipers on the typical weekend and for 70 to 80 percent of the total dollar receipts from members.

In other words, perhaps the most widespread expression of diversity in American Protestant congregations today is in the level of Christian commitment.

So What?

At this point the reader may ask, "What has all of this to do with the impact of the new economy on church finances?"

One useful clue can be found by a brief look at two congregations in the same city of 40,000 residents. Church A was founded in 1889. Last year it averaged 450 at worship. In generational terms it is a demographically diverse parish with a disproportionately large number of mature adults. All of the constituents trace their ancestry back to western Europe. There is a modest degree of theological pluralism among the members. In the last presidential election nearly one-half voted Democratic, nearly one-half voted Republican, and about 3 percent chose a third party candidate. The paid program staff included four full-time persons plus five part-time. That averages out to the equivalent of one full-time program staff member for every 75 people at worship in the typical Sunday morning.

This congregation projects relatively low expectations of anyone seeking to become a member. The basic requirement is completion of a class offered for one hour per week over five consecutive Sunday mornings. One result is a confirmed membership of 1,600 including 300 non-resident members.

Meeting in a building on a thirty-acre parcel of land two miles away is congregation B, founded in 1957, which now averages 2,900 at worship. It operates a Christian day school for children age three through grade eight. All the operating costs of the school, including staff compensation, custodial services, supplies, utilities, and insurance are paid from tuition. The congregational budget covers all capital costs for the school. This is a theologically evangelical congregation. The other big point of commonality among the members is a powerful conviction of the value of a Christ-centered education for children.

This is a congregation that projects high expectations of anyone seeking to become a full member. One result is a lot of tithers. Another is a total of 790 members age eighteen and over.

The program staff of the church, exclusive of the school staff, includes nine full-time and two part-time persons—a ratio of one full-time equivalent for every 290 people at worship.

While at the extremes in terms of the program staff-worship attendance ratio, these two congregations illustrate a common pattern. Demographic divesity and/or theological pluralism usually costs money! Homogeneity costs less than heterogeneity in building a constituency.

How Do You Define Missions?

"While this is not a day of rejoicing, every one of us should be able to walk out of here today holding our head high," declared the seventy-three-year-old lay leader at the Madison Avenue Church. As you all know, we haven't quite made it to our one hundredth anniversary, but I've been told that fewer than one-half of all Protestant congregations in existence in 1900 are still alive today, so we have done better than most. Far more important, however, is that we have kept the faith. Forty years ago this past spring, our pastor of that time, the Reverend Charles Harrison, challenged us to triple tithe for missions. With only two exceptions, every year since then we have allocated at least 30 percent of our total expenditures for missions. In at least a dozen years that proportion has exceeded 35 percent, and twice it went over 40 percent. Our basic goal has been to send 20 percent of our total expenditures to our denomination and another 10 percent to other Christian organizations. Reverend Harrison is long gone, may God rest his soul, but his passion for missions has lived on in and through this congregation."

The occasion was the last public worship service for this congregation that had been founded in 1904. Their first permanent church home was a wooden frame building that had been destroyed by fire in 1937. Despite the financial problems created by the Great Depression, the congregation had decided to construct a new and modern three-story brick building on that same site. That mortgage finally was paid off in 1954. At that time the members purchased two single-family homes to the west of the church, razed the houses, and paved a parking lot that could accommodate 34 vehicles. The debt on that expansion effort was retired in 1958. The following spring the Reverend Harrison challenged the congregation to set that lofty goal for missions.

A year later, a widow who was a second-generation member left a $100,000 bequest to the church. A prudent trustee insisted that should be the nucleus for an endowment fund. Thanks to an aggressive effort to encourage more bequests, plus some fortunate investments, the market value of the endowment fund passed the million dollar mark in 1982.

The worship attendance peaked in 1927 at 164, dropped to 135 a year after the fire, recovered to 158 in 1957, and gradually declined to between 110 and 130 in the ten years following the retirement of the Reverend Harrison in 1973. The next pastor turned out to be a disastrous mismatch, and he left in 1976. The successor was well received, and it appeared the worst was in the past when, without warning, that minister suddenly announced one Sunday in June 1983 that this would be his last Sunday. He was leaving and moving to Colorado. It turned out he did not depart alone. He was accompanied by the wife of the chairman of the governing board.

That event coincided with the retirement to the Sunbelt of several longtime pillars plus a general exodus of residents with an Anglo ancestry from that part of the city. The arrival of a large number of Latino newcomers in the neighborhood was accompanied by a sharp drop in the membership. For 1991 the average worship attendance was down to 55.

For several years, thanks to that endowment fund, this congregation had been able to enjoy the leadership of a full-time resident pastor and also allocate at least 30 percent of all expenditures to missions. The last full-time minister departed in 1989. For the next decade the congregation depended on a passing parade of retired ministers and supply pastors. The remaining $21,000 in that endowment fund was used in 1998 with $13,000 allocated to missions and $8,000 to balance the operating budget.

For the first six months of 1999 worship attendance averaged twenty-two while the members considered merging with a much larger church of their denomination. When their initial overtures were rejected ("Why should we take on your problems?"), they decided to dissolve. That last public worship service was scheduled for the third Sunday in September 1999, on the ninety-fifth anniversary of the formal organization of the Madison Avenue Church.

In her final report, the treasurer noted that slightly over $350,000 from the endowment fund had been allocated over the previous sixteen years to balance the operating budget while more than three times that amount had been allocated to missions. Pastor Harrison's passion for missions had dominated the financial planning at the Madison Avenue Church for four decades!

"A few of our critics have complained that we have sacrificed the life of this congregation for missions," concluded this lay leader. "I don't agree! I believe the church should be organized around missions, and that often requires sacrifice. For forty years we have been organized to support missions, and I'm proud of the response of our people to that challenge. We have fought the good fight for missions."

Three Lessons

This account illustrates three important differences between congregations operating in the context of the old economy and churches that are comfortable with the new economy.

The old economy called for congregations to raise and send money to other Christian organizations that would do ministry on behalf of those sending the money. The new paradigm congregations in the new economy are responding to the admonition, "Find ministry in your own backyard and do it." Some are investing those discretionary resources in ministries with nearby residents. Others are investing those discretionary resources in providing the physical facilities and the ministries required to reach new generations of American-born residents and/or recent immigrants or to become multisite congregations.

In the old economy congregations invested in subsidizing the ministries of others even at the risk of eventually closing. In the new economy future-oriented churches choose to invest in the future and to strengthen and expand their own ministry.

A second change illustrated by the Madison Avenue Church is that in the old economy congregations were challenged to send money. One characteristic of the new economy is the ease of travel. Instead of simply sending money, the new paradigm congregations challenge volunteers to go and spend a week or two or three or four to be engaged in doing ministry with fellow Christians in a sister church in another culture. The big fringe benefit is that the volunteers who return are not the same people who went. Believers have been transformed into disciples.

A third lesson from this account is that it is extremely difficult to create and perpetuate a healthy, vital, and deeply committed worshiping community that lives off the dead. The crucial fork-in-the-road decision in the history of the Madison Avenue Church was not in accepting the challenge to triple tithe for missions. The critical decision came in the 1980s when the leaders began to "borrow" money from the endowment fund to balance the operating budget and, later, to pay that triple tithe for missions.

Whether they are subsidized by the denomination, by other congregations, or by the dead, long-term financial subsidies and congregational health and vitalilty tend to be incompatible goals. The missionary imperative of self-governing, self-expressing, self-propagating, and self-financing congregations is relevant to Christian churches in North America as well as in the Third World. Long-term dependency on others is not healthy for children, for aging parents, for institutions, or for worshiping communities.

Another Scenario

In 1903, one year before the formal organization of the Madison Avenue Church, and three blocks to the east, another new congregation was founded by a different denomination. Grace Church grew rapidly through the early 1920s, and the average worship attendance peaked at 235 in 1922. That was followed by thirty years of gradual decline. When the owners of the neighboring homes refused to sell their property so Grace Church could provide off-street parking, the leaders decided to relocate. A three-acre parcel two miles to the west was purchased and a two-story building with 24,000 square feet of floor space was constructed. It was occupied in 1958.

The pastor, who had arrived in 1951, was the leader in persuading the congregation to launch a new era in its history by constructing modern facilities on a larger site at a far better location. When he retired in 1986, worship attendance averaged 465 for that year. The proportion of total expenditures allocated to denominational causes and missions had climbed from 10 percent in 1951 to 15 percent in 1986.

Three pastors and ten years later, worship attendance was averaging slightly under 300. One group of leaders advocated relocating to a larger site at a better location.

"We're competing with four big regional Protestant churches, each one of which was founded since 1970, and each one has an abundance of off-street parking as well as better facilities. We're in an obsolete forty-year-old building with only 150 parking spaces and no room to expand. We have an aging and numerically shrinking membership. We either make a break and start at a new location, or we keep on shrinking in size." That was the rational plea of this group of a dozen future-oriented young leaders. The overwhelming majority of the members, as well as most of the other leaders, however, categorically opposed relocation.

The current senior minister, who had arrived in 1994, suggested a compromise. "It will cost an estimated $300,000 to make the overdue repairs to maintain this building. One of our members owns a twenty-seven-acre parcel of land fronting on a state highway that she has offered to sell us for $650,000. It has been appraised at slightly over one million. We should be able to raise a million dollars in a capital funds campaign from November through March. That would enable us to make the necessary repairs to our present property and purchase that second site. Instead of relocating, we could become a two-site congregation with one staff, one name, one culture, one theological position, one governing board, one budget, and a demographically more diverse membership."

The lay volunteer chairing the capital funds campaign explained to the members, "The motion before us is to make major repairs to our present property and to purchase additional land that will enable us to become a two-site church. That motion has been seconded. The motion requires one million yes votes to carry. The votes are a dollar a piece and you may vote as often as you wish."

By March 1997 a total of slightly over 1.3 million yes votes had been cast. That twenty-seven-acre parcel was purchased. The needed repairs were made to the old meeting place. The first unit of the new facilities on that second site was ready for occupancy in September 1999. A year later worship attendance at the old location was averaging 265, and the combined attendance of the three services at the new site was averaging 430.

Ten Lessons

1. The old economy that dominated American culture for nearly four centuries was based on assumptions of scarcity. This led to the two-choice option of "Take it or leave it." Decisions were framed in either/or terms. Even in war time the new economy continues to be based on assumptions of abundance. This allows decisons to be framed in both/and terms. Should we send our eighteen-year-old to college, or should we trade our five-year-old car in for a new one? Should the retiree continue to live in Pennsylvania or move to Florida? Should I accept that offer of a new job twenty miles from where we live, or should I turn it down so we can continue to live here? Should our congregation repair our forty-year-old building, or should we buy land and construct new facilities to enable us to reach and serve new generations? Should we focus our resources on taking good care of our present membership, or should we make a priority the goal of reaching the unchurched?

The new economy encourages "both/and" responses to these and other "either/or" questions.

2. By far the most significant lesson in these two accounts can be summarized with two words: *inputs* and *outcomes*.

For forty years the financial planning at the Madison Avenue Church was dominated by the high priority given to allocating at least 30 percent of all expenditures as inputs into the ministries of other organizations. That was consistent with the older economy that placed a high value on inputs into a system.

The new economy places a high value on outcomes or results.

The old ecclesiastical economy placed a high value on money sent away. In a few religious traditions that was the number-one criterion in evaluating the performance of each congregation. Did that church send more money to head-quarters this year than it sent in the previous year? A high priority in the evaluation process also was given to how much denominational headquarters received.

The new ecclesiastical economy focuses on outcomes. How has this congregation utilized its resources to help fulfill the Great Commission?

3. The old ecclesiastical economy declared a congregation's identity was in its denominational affiliaton, its meeting place, its pastor, its ethnic heritage, and its membership. It was almost universally assumed that the ideal goal of a congregation would be to own and maintain one meeting place.

The new ecclesiastical economy affirms the concept that one congregation may have one, two, three, four, or two hundred meeting places.[4] That is simply a means-to-an-end issue, not a goal. The identity is in its ministry, not in its real estate.

4. The old ecclesiastical economy called for congregations either to (a) send money to someone else who would plant new missions to reach new generations and/or recent immigrants or (b) sponsor what soon would become a completely self-governing congregation.

The new ecclesiastical economy encourages strong and mission-driven congregations to become multisite churches as part of a larger strategy to reach and serve people who could not or would not come to that congregation's meeting place.

5. The old ecclesiastical economy offered a rule of thumb that a three-acre parcel for a new mission or for a relocation site was somewhere between adequate and extravagant. By 1960 that was expanded to five acres.

The new ecclesiastical economy suggests, "If you buy too much land, you can always sell the excess, but if you purchase too little, you may not be able to expand."

6. The old ecclesiastical economy assumed that a "big church" was one averaging approximately 350 to 500 at worship.

The new ecclesiastical economy suggests that if the goal is to be competitive with other large regional congregations in urbanized American counties, the minimum size is an average worship attendance of at least 800—and some contend that number really is 1,500 to 1,800. (One definition of "competitive" for congregations is that the majority of first-time visitors will return at least once. Another is the number of new constituents annually will be equivalent to at least 15 percent of the average worship attendance. A denominational definition is that when our members change churches, at least one-half of them will choose a congregation affiliated with our denomination.)

7. The old ecclesiastical economy declared that location, location, and location were the three crucial variables in shaping the future of a Protestant congregation in metropolitan America.

The new ecclesiastical economy declares that the three crucial variables are visionary leadership, relevance, and quality.

8. As was pointed out earlier, the old ecclesiastical economy declared that sending dollars to fund the ministry of others was an essential characteristic of a healthy church.

The new ecclesiastical economy affirms that sending people to be engaged in doing ministry in another culture and in investing in the future of that congregation are equally valid signs of health.

The old ecclesiastical system measured congregational health in dollars. The new measures congregational health in transformed lives and in fulfilling the Great Commission.

9. The old ecclesiastical economy assumed congregations would be the primary source of money for denominational systems.

The new ecclesiastical economy assumes that denominational systems, retreat centers, theological schools, and parachurch organizations will depend primarily on fees for services and resources, individual donors, foundations, income from investments, corporations, governmental agencies, and matching grants for their financial base.

10. The old ecclesiastical economy was organized largely around functions, inputs, and tasks (worship, Christian education, administration, budgets, stewardship, evangelism, missions, meetings, and committees). This was consistent with survival goals, with short pastorates, and with a one- or two-year time frame for planning.

The new ecclesiastical economy places a far higher value on relationships and outcomes. This is consistent with long pastorates, an emphasis on the personal and spiritual journey of the individual, and a five- to ten-year time frame for plannng.

How does your congregation define missions? That answer should influence the design of your financial system for the twenty-first century.

Why Give?

"Terry, a couple of us delivered the winter clothing we had collected to that shelter for the homeless our congregation helps support," explained Pat Jenkins. "While we were there, we talked with the person who is the head honcho for the shelter. We discovered they need a thousand dollars for some unexpected plumbing repairs. They operate on a very tight budget, so we told her to go ahead and make the repairs and we would pick up the tab. We figure we need twenty donors to give us $50 each. Are you interested in being one of the twenty?"

"Yeah, I guess I can do that," agreed Terry. "To whom do I make out the check?"

"Make it out to our church. That will simplify the record keeping. The shelter is in our community outreach budget for $3,000, but that was paid a couple of months ago. This is over and above that. Mark your check 'Homeless' so the treasurer knows where it should go."

Why did Terry quickly agree to contribute $50 to that shelter?

Peer pressure? The return of a favor to a friend Terry had asked for a contribution to another cause several months earlier? Terry had an extra $50 that could be contributed with no pain? Because the request was a specific cause which Terry affirmed and came from a trusted friend who could be believed? Because Terry felt a twinge of guilt about living in a $350,000 home while other people were homelesss? Because Terry daily gave thanks to God for the many blessings Terry enjoyed and therefore gave out of gratitude? Because Terry is a member of that community oureach committee and already was a strong advocate of providing shelter for the homelesss? Because this was Tuesday morning and Terry still remembered and was motivated by last Sunday's sermon based on Matthew 25:36? Because Terry was a volunteer member of the governing board for the shelter? Because Terry's employer is one of the five corporate sponsors of that shelter and encourages employees to support the shelter? Because Terry is a volunteer on the 5:00 P.M. to 10:00 P.M. shift at that shelter once a month and therefore has an experiential motivation to suppport it financially? Because Pat and Terry are two of twenty members of a giving circle that raises a thousand dollars a month for a specific cause identified by one or more members of that giving circle?

The correct answer, of course, is that Terry probably was motivated by at least three or four or more of those facors.

The number-one motivation behind "second-mile" giving over and above a person's regular financial commitments to a religious, educational, charitable, or political cause is because they have been asked to contribute by a trusted friend with whom they have a positive one-to-one relationship. That motivation often is reinforced by the donor's conviction this is a worthy cause.

The number-two motivation is an expression of the dependency path. We do what we do because we have done it before. Yesterday's work schedule influences today's work schedule. The time we eat each meal usually is determined by the hour we ate a similar meal yesterday. The church schedule for next Sunday usually is the same as for last Sunday.

An ancient bit of wisdom among budget officers declares, "It is extremely difficult to add new items to the budget for the coming year. It is even more difficult, however, to delete any position, organization, cause, need, or line item that has been included in the budget for the past several years."

When he was a candidate for the presidency of the United States in 1976, Jimmy Carter promised to introduce and implement the concept of "zero-based budgeting." Every expenditure item from earlier years would be deleted. The new budget would begin with a blank sheet of paper. Every proposed expenditure would have to be justified to be approved and included. After he became president, Mr. Carter discovered that only rarely does rationality overcome precedent.

The parallel is with donors. Many contribute, often generously, because they have contributed to that cause or organization in previous years. A similar pattern of the power of precedent influences the annual allocation of funds in many foundations, governmental agencies, congregations, corporations, denominations, and families.

A Crucial Fork in the Road

The central assumption of this chapter is every system produces the outcomes it is designed to produce. Those responsible for designing a financial system for congregations in the twenty-first century face several fork-in-the-road questions in designing that system. Each path at that fork leads to a different set of probable consequences. One of these is the power of precedent. How influenial will local and/or denominational precedents be in designing that new system? A common example is the definition of the fiscal year. Should the fiscal year run from January 1 through December 31? Or should it coincide with the program year that often runs from summer to summer and also has the big advange of covering two tax years for individual donors? Who will make that decision? What criteria will they use in making that decision?

Far more important, however, is another fork-in-the-road. One path calls for congregational leaders to accept the responsibility to motivate their constituents to contribute money to finance the institutional life, ministry, and outreach of that congregation. That is a far more difficult assignment today than it was in 1966 or even 1985! One reason is a large proportion of the church members who could be motivated by loyalty, guilt, pressure, a sense of obligation, and exhortation are in nursing homes or cemeteries and thus are difficult to reach.

So what's the alternative? One is yell louder. Another is to yell longer. A third is to beg more often. A better choice is to choose a new path at that fork in the road.

Individuals or Circles?

The old ecclesiastical economy called for asking individuals or households to make a financial commitment or pledge to their church. That usually required designing a once-a-year financial campaign directed at individuals and families. That was based on the assumption the few could and should motivate the many. A task force of nine might be asked to motivate five hundred members. That is a huge responsibility to place on the few!

This new model is based on the conviction the old hierarchical structure of society is being replaced by a culture that encourages horizontal relationships. One example is called a "giving circle." Some describe it as a mixture of an investment club, a book group, and a social network.

Typically seven to twenty individuals share a common concern. This may be to help relieve world hunger. It may be to purchase additional property to enlarge the parking lot. It may be to raise the money to add a badly needed position to the staff. It may be to help finance the costs incurred when a dozen members go to work with fellow Christians for a couple of weeks in a sister church on another continent. It may be to finance the overdue expansion of the meeting place. It may be to acquire the land for a second site to enable their congregation to become a multisite church. It may be to provide scholarships for young people responding to a call from God to full-time Christian service. It may be to create a new ministry with parents of children age birth to three.

The members of the giving circle identify the need, research the alternative responses to meeting that need, agree on a budget for that response, and raise the required money from among themselves. In one giving circle, each member contributes $100 a month and once a year they give the appropriate amount to that agreed-upon ministry. Another consists of eight teenagers. Each contributes $25 a month to their pool. A third giving circle consists of eleven families. Each family contributes $200 a month to the pool. Each family also hosts the group for dinner once a year. Approximately two-thirds of the evening is spent socializing and one-third is spent on deciding where that $26,400

will go. The five giving circles in that congregation contribute a combined total of approximately $85,000 a year to
special needs.

Many other giving circles do not expect everyone to contribute the same amount. The circle identifies the need,
designs a response, prepares a budget, and sets out to raise
that amount from both members and nonmembers of that
giving circle. Several large youth ministries include one or
two giving circles as they design that youth ministry to be
a collection of groups, teams, circles, choirs, and task forces.

This concept of giving circles has a longer history among
immigrants from Asia, Latin America, and the Caribbean
than among Americans whose ancestors came from Europe.

Why do giving circles work?

Among the most influential motivating factors are (1)
"This was our idea, so we are eager to support it," (2) the
attractiveness of designated second-mile giving, (3) peer
pressure, (4) fulfilling a group goal, (5) for some the giving
circle becomes their favorite social network, (6) the opportunity to "make a difference," (7) the dependency path theory, (8) "this is what helps tie our group together," and (9)
kinship ties.

While exceptions do exist, most giving circles are organized on the assumption that members will contribute out of
their current earned income. That introduces two other
fork-in-the-road questions in designing a congregation's
financial plan for the twenty-first century.

Signed or Anonymous?

A big theological fork-in-the-road divides congregations
into two groups. The traditional system calls for members
to complete a pledge card for the coming fiscal year and
sign their name on the card. This provides the budget committee with a basis for estimating income for the coming
year. It also enables the financial secretary to mail monthly

or quarterly statements to each person who pledged. That statement reports on whether the member is up-to-date on their payments.

One consequence is that signed pledge card reinforces the concept the line of accountability is from the individual to that church.

A different system calls for unsigned pledge cards. That provides the budget committee with a data base to estimate future receipts. The reason it is unsigned is to reinforce the conviction that the line of accountability is from the individual Christian to God, rather than to the church.

Which of thse two systems is consistent with the theological position of your congregation?

Capital or Operating?

One of the most widespread impacts of the new American economy is based on the distinction between capital expenditures and operating costs. For many decades municipal governments and public school districts have recognized this distinction. Most of the current operating budget was financed out of the annual receipts from income, general property, and sales taxes. (In a few places revenues from casinos or lotteries are now supplementing those traditional sources.)

By contrast, the major capital expenditures, such as new buildings, bridges, and an expansion of the water supply system, were financed by bond issues with a twenty or thirty year maturity. The explanation was these expenditures were for long term improvements and future users should help pay for them from taxes and fees for their use. It simply is not fair to ask today's taxpayers to pay the full cost of a new school that will be used by tomorrow's taxpayers.

In the old economy and the old ecclesiastical culture, it was not uncommon to combine the second or third capital

funds campaign to pay off the mortgage on a recently constructed building or an addition to the meeting place with
the campaign to secure pledges to underwrite the operating
budget for the coming year. A widespread practice was to
ask for two pledges, one to finance the operating budget
and one to the building fund.

For most congregations this was consistent with that old
American economy. Most adults lived from paycheck to
paycheck. Only a tiny fraction had accumulated substantial
wealth. Therefore both financial campaigns were designed
to encourage churchgoers to pledge a percentage of their
future weekly or monthly income to the operating budget
and a similar percentage to the building fund. For most, the
big difference was the pledge to the operating budget was
a one-year commitment and the pledge for the building
fund was a two- or three-year commitment.

Other congregations asked for three pledges, one to the
operating budget, one for missions, and one to the building
fund. In either system, however, the assumption was nearly
every pledge would be paid out of current income.

In this new American economy the constituency of most
Christian congregations can be divided into five groups.
One group lives off current income from their current
employment. Beyond their home and motor vehicles, they
have very little accumulated wealth. A second group also
lives off income from current employment, but that income
exceeds their taxes and regular expenditures. In most
months of the year, they are able to increase the value of
their accumulated wealth beyond their home and motor
vehicles. This takes the form of savings or investments in
stocks, bonds, or real estate. For many it is a more intangi-
ble investment through formal education designed to
increase their future earning power.

A third group consists of those who live with the fact
their total annual expenditures exceed their total annual
income from all sources.

A fourth and growing group pay their weekly bills from two sources and usually have money left over. One is current income from employment and/or investments. The second is converting some of their accumulated wealth into current income. Reducing the equity they have in their home by refinancing the mortgage or borrowing against an insurance policy or cashing a monthly check from Social Security or an IRA or Keogh Account or their pension fund are examples. Others make regular or occasional withdrawals from a savings account.

A fifth and growing group of Americans enjoy several income streams that, together, exceed their total expenditures including charitable contributions. Their total accumulated wealth increases year after year, give or take the blip for a brief slowdown or recession in the economy.

In operational terms these distinctions are significant. If, for example, every household in that congregation is living off current income, it makes sense to use a system that encourages people to pledge a percentage of their weekly or monthly income to the operating budget and/or to the building fund. One system does fit all.

If, however, that congregation includes a substantial number of families from three or four of those five categories, a more complicated system probably will be more productive.

The first step is to recognize that the appeal to ask people to contribute out of their current income usually involves sharply different dynamics than encouraging them to shift some of the assets in their accumulated wealth to a long-term investment in the ministry of that congregation. Asking someone to contribute $50 a week out of their $40,000 salary (income before taxes) is not the same as suggesting to a family that they contribute those 400 shares of stock in a for-profit corporation, for which they paid $20,000 seven years ago but now have a current market value of $100,000, to the fund to construct a $2 million addition to this ten-year-old church building.

A one-size-fits-all group appeal can be made to encourage those $25, $50, $75, and $100 weekly one-year pledges out of current income.

A customized series of one-to-one visits or three-to-three conferences may be required to receive those large contributions to a capital improvements program. One difference, of course, is the distinction between asking people to contribute to the annual operating budget out of current annual income versus asking people to donate capital assets to a capital investment.

A second is the difference between a $2,000 to $5,000 contribution and a $100,000 gift. A third is the difference in the agenda—one is to ask people to contribute out of an income stream that will be replenished next week or next month. The other is to ask people to surrender a capital asset that may not be replaced.

One pastor explains his system for asking for gifts from capital assets. "I ask several of our families whom I believe have the potential to be major contributors to set aside on their calendar two consecutive Tuesday evenings. Three of these couples or individuals are invited to come to our house for dessert with my wife and me on the first of their two Tuesday evenings.

"I explain in detail our next proposed building program. We talk about why it is needed, what it will cost, and how it will enable us to expand our ministry. We try to answer every question, and we chase every rabbit. These are sharp people! Within an hour they realize that I am about to ask them for a big commitment. Usually one of them introduces that before I have to raise the question.

"The typical question is, 'Well, how much do you want from us?' I reply, 'What do you believe the three of you can do?' At that point they begin to talk among themselves. One suggests a combined figure for those three families.

Another usually declares, 'Oh, I believe we can do better than that!' Within a half hour, they usually have each made a specific commitment. Incidentally, I believe peer pressure can be productive.

"After a few comments of satisfaction about accomplishing two evenings' work in one, someone will suggest, 'Well, I guess this means you aren't expecting us back here next Tuesday evening.' My response is, 'No. The reason I asked you to set aside two consecutive Tuesday evenings is that we do want you back next week. We need you to help explain this to three other couples who plan to be here next Tuesday evening. Our goal is to enlist those who are committed to the dream to help sell that dream to others in a setting where they have the support of those who already have committed themselves to that dream. Each couple or individual comes on their first Tuesday to be introduced to the need, and they return a week later to help introduce it to three other couples.'"

At that point in the conversation, I interrupted, "I'm a pragmatist. Tell me how this has worked for you."

"We're still on the learning curve," replied this pastor. "We first tried it back in 1989 with nine families, and our second experience with it was in 1994 with thirty-six households. In retrospect I regret that we weren't on schedule to do it in 1999. That probably would have been our greatest success. Last year, however, we ran our capital funds campaign from October through March. We are on a June through May program year, so we ask for pledges for the new operating budget in late April and early May, which I believe is the ideal time of the year to do that. We ride on the updraft of the Eastertide, plus the days are getting longer, the flowers are blooming, the grass is green, and everyone is looking forward to summer.

"So, to get back to your question, our last building program cost $1.7 million. Incidentally it was all paid for the day we got our occupancy permit from the city. In terms of the sources of that $1.7 million, we set a new record as 76 percent of it came from the sixty families involved in those Tuesday evening conversations. Our previous record back in 1994 was 73 percent. Those five dozen Tuesday evening households last year represented 22 percent of the households who contributed to the building program.

"After we completed that series of Tuesday evening conversations in which the guests in one evening became the salespeople for the program with three new households the following week, we ran a traditional one-size-fits-all-please-contribute-out-of-your-current-income campaign for that other 78 percent of our constituents."

Who Is Looking After Grandma?

The affluence of the new economy has had a tremendous impact on the definition of what traditionally have been described as "community outreach ministries." Among the highly visible examples are the congregationally owned and administered weekday childcare programs, the prekindergarten school for two-, three-, and four-year-old children, the once or twice a week senior citizens' luncheons, the community outreach of the parish nurse, a growing variety of recreation ministries that include nonmembers, and other ministries to shelter the homeless, feed the hungry, visit those in jail, and clothe the naked.

One of the recent additions to that list is the widowed grandmother. One of her three adult children now lives 900 miles away, a second 1,500, and the third 1,800 miles away. How can they look after their aging mother? One alternative is to take turns making weekly or monthly visits in person. That is time consuming and expensive.

A long time ago one of the three children offered, "Mother, why don't you come live with us. We have an extra bedroom that will give you privacy, and we'll be glad to have you."

Grandma replied, "Before you were born, I decided I would never become a burden on any of my children. Besides that, I've lived in this same house for nearly forty years. I'm comfortable here, and I don't want to move."

Another alternative is offered by the church in the community where Grandma resides. They offer those adult children four options. The lowest cost is a daily telephone call by a volunteer to Grandma and a personal visit if a problem is identified. Two or three times a week each of those three adult children receives an email lettter that summarizes Grandma's health, state of mind, needs, and current activities.

The next level includes that daily telephone call to Grandma plus a regular once or twice a week personal visit plus those email letters.

The third level includes four or five or six personal visits weekly to Grandma plus a once-a-month visit by the parish nurse on that church's ministry staff, plus transportation when needed to the store or the doctor plus those regular email reports.

The fourth level consists of responding to Grandma's needs when she enters an assisted living facility or a nursing home plus those regular emails.

The monthly checks from those distant children cover that share of the paid staff's total compensation that can be attributed to providing this ministry including that paid staff member who enlists, trains, and supports the cadre of volunteers required to staff it.

These checks are part of the income stream called "fees for services."

In the old economy, nearby kinfolk, neighbors, and friends looked after Grandma. In the new economy, the nonresident adult children outsource that responsibility to a congregation's community outreach ministry team.

The grapevine, and perhaps a feature story in the local newspaper, provide the new constituents required to maintain that ministry.

Less common is the very large congregation that decides either to relocate its meeting place or to become a two-site congregation. An 80- to 200-acre parcel of land is purchased for that new site. One portion is land set aside for a financially self-supporting retirement community designed for several score residential units including one- or two-bedroom units for grandparents. In addition to providing a caring community for mature adults, this can be a source of volunteers for the ministries of that congregation including staffing the community outreach ministry described above. A significant fringe benefit is that the twenty-four-hour, seven-day-a-week presence of the residents in that retirement village usually reduces vandalism.

A Learning Center?

In the old ecclesiastical economy, denominational agencies often owned and operated camps, retreat centers, and theological schools. In this new ecclesiastical economy an increasing number of very large congregations own and operate camps, retreat centers, and the church-based ministry that is replacing the old concept of campus-based theological education. This church-based program of theological education is especially attractive to second-career adults who have mastered the skill of being a self-taught learner and are fulfilling a call to a specialized ministry in the parish. The combination of a live instructor in the classroom for some courses plus the availability of distance learning classes enables a person to hold a full-time job locally, live at home, and earn a seminary degree.

One interesting sidelight, if the door is opened, is that a significant number of grandparents prefer to enroll in these classes rather than to play cards, watch television, quilt, take a nap, or go to the movies. A common consequence is that they become more self-confident, energetic, competent, and valuable volunteers. This usually is financed on a fee-for-service basis.

A parallel is the growing number of Christian congregations that are not related to a tradition that includes parochial schools that are opening tuition financed academies.

This introduces another variable that should be an influential factor in designing a financial system for a congregation.

The Economy of Scale Myth

The assembly plant that can turn out 1,200 motor vehicles a day operates at a lower per unit cost than the plant that assembles only 300 vehicles a day.

The supermarket that sells $400,000 of merchandise a day can make a profit with a smaller markup than the corner grocery that on a good day takes in only $5,000 in sales.

Everyone understands the economy of scale concept. A dairy farmer milking 15 cows needs a wife with a full-time job in town while the dairy farmer with 600 cows can make a comfortable living through hard work, long hours, and good luck.

"Two can live more cheaply than one" was a reason to marry back in the days when young people married.

Therefore, it logically follows that the congegation averaging 1,500 at worship should enjoy a lower unit cost and financially more efficient ministry than the church averaging 150 at worship. Economic logic dictates cost should go down as the numbers go up.

The one big objection to that assumption is that it does not reflect contemporary reality. The reality is that expenditures rise with size. The congregation averaging 150 at worship usually reports annual expenditures that average out to $700 to $1,500 times the average worship attendance. The congregation averaging 1,500 at worship usually requires somewhere between $1,500 and $4,000 times the average worship attendance to match the annual expenditures.

Why are unit costs higher in the very large congregation? Seven reasons stand out in the explanation.

Quality Is Expensive!

First, why has that very large congregation attracted so many people? One part of the answer is the emphasis on quality. In the new American economy people are attracted by high quality and repelled by low quality. The higher the quality, the higher the cost. That generalization applies to hospitals, clothing, universities, motor vehicles, food, housing, passenger comfort on a commercial airline, hotels and motels, restaurants, legal counsel, furniture, and churches. One major exception is the compensation for major league baseball players.

Choices Cost Money

A second reason why costs in American Protestant congregations increase with size is the larger the congregation, the greater the number and variety of ministries and programs offered. An increase in choices increases costs. This can be seen in the cost of providing choices in worship, learning, music, off-street parking, opportunities to be involved as a volunteer in ministry, fellowship, restrooms, recreation ministries, and especially in ministries with children and youth. The easiest way to reduce expenditures is to reply, "No, we don't do that here."

While the out-of-pocket operating costs of that ministry with Grandma described earlier and the learning center are covered by fees for services, both add to the total expenditures as well as to the cash flow of the congregation.

More significant, however, most of the additional choices offered by the larger churches are not covered by fees. They must be financed out of the receipts from contributions.

Diversity Costs Money!

Overlapping that is a third factor discussed earlier in this chapter. Demographic diversity costs money. The very large congregations tend to display a greater degree of diversity in the constituency than do smaller churches.

Customizing Costs Money

A fourth factor is the call to customize. This is a consequence of what has been described as the fourth great religious reawakening in America. The past three or four decades have brought a resurgence of interest in religion in the United States. That has increased since September 2001. The number of people gathered on the average weekend in Protestant congregations in America for the corporate worship of God in 2001 was at an all-time high. The most highly visible components include what Robert W. Fogel describes as the "enthusiastic" religions, the increase in the attendance in Islamic mosques, the rapid growth in the number of black megachurches, the launching of thousands of new religious congregations every year, the attention given by the public press to the church attendance habits of presidents, that growing number of congregations with one weekly worship experience owned and operated by high school students, and the impact of parachurch ministries on college and university students.

A substantial proportion of these churchgoers see themselves on a self-identified religious quest or journey or pilgrimage. As was mentioned earlier, many larger congregations are offering two or three or four or five or six or seven different worship experiences every week. Each service is designed for people at a specific stage of their personal faith journey. Customizing is more expensive than offering "one size fits all" services, events, and classes.

$3,000 or $12,000?

A fifth part of the explanation is reflected in what it costs a Protestant congregation in America to own its own meeting place. The experiences of four congregations will illustrate this point. When a fire destroyed the meeting place of a smalltown congregation averaging 155 at worship, they decided to relocate to a larger site on the state highway on the west side of town. Three acres of land cost $30,000. The improvements to the land and the cost of a new two-story building with a 180-seat sanctuary, a fellowship hall that seats 90 people at tables plus classrooms, the pastor's office, furnishings, restrooms, and a paved parking lot cost $1,070,000. That total expenditure of $1.1 million averaged out to slightly over $7,000 times the average worship attendance.

A year later a new independent church finished construction of their first meeting place on a five-acre site on the other side of town on land donated by a member. Thanks to thousands of hours of volunteer labor by skilled tradespeople in the congregation, their out-of-pocket costs were only $600,000 for a larger building. Several months after moving into their new church home, they reported an average worship attendance of slightly over 200. Their new church home cost $3,000 times the average worship attendance.

A few years earlier in another state what had been a rural church for well over a century began to experience rapid numerical growth as the surrounding farms were being transformed into shopping centers, residential subdivisions, new schools, parks, office buildings, and apartments. In ten years their average worship attendance quintupled from 65 to nearly 350. That led to the decision to relocate to a much larger, fifteen-acre site and construct new facilities. That led to an expenditure of $1.5 million for the new site at a superb location, a $3.5 million first-stage construction program, mortgage payments of well over $1,000 per day, and a second building program costing $3 million. A year after it was completed, that relocated congegation was averaging 800 at worship. Their relocation decision had cost approximately $10,000 times their average worsihp attendance.

A few miles to the north a megachurch averaging 2,500 at worship has launched a relocation plan. Their first step was to purchase a 48-acre site for $5 million. They estimate that over the next decade they will spend another $40 to $45 million on construction and be averaging at least 4,000 in weekly worship attendance. That projection means the cost of housing this minisry will average out to approximately $12,000 times the average worship attendance.

How Much for Benevolences?

While many exceptions exist, the general pattern is the larger the congregation, the larger the proportion of total annual expenditures allocated to missions, community outreach ministries, social service projects, denominational budgets, and other benevolences. In the smaller churches that proportion typically is between 5 percent and 20 percent of all expenditures. In the large congregations that proportion is more likely to be in the 15 percent to 40 percent range.

Who Sets Up the Tables?

Finally, the last of these seven reasons to explain why the economy of scale theory does not apply to Protestant congregations in America can be illustrated by looking at the budget. This line often is carried in the annual budget as the

"trustees' account" or "building maintenance and operation."

Who sets up the tables and arranges the chairs in that
new fellowship hall for the forty people expected to begin
the evening program with a meal? In that small congregation the answer probably will be either "the pastor" or "a
couple of volunteers." In that very large church, the answer
is more likely to be "the custodial staff." In that small
church a group of volunteers spend a Saturday painting a
classroom. In the very large congregation professional
painters do that as part of a larger renovation project. Add
the costs of utilities, insurance, custodial staff, longer hours,
and security, and it is easy to see why the total annual
expenditures for the congregation averaging 1,500 at worship will be not ten, but twenty to sixty times those of the
church averaging 150 at worship.

Another Fork in the Road

A common pattern in reporting the level of member contributions in congregations or denominations is to divide
the total financial contributions by the membership. Thus
one 1,000-member congregation with annual receipts from
member contributions of $600,000 reports an average of
$600 per member. Another 1,000-member church reports
annual contributions of $2,400,000 or $2,400 per year per
member. Why such a big gap?

One part of the explanation is the first church averages
400 at worship so contributions average out to $1,500 per
average attender. The second congregation averages 800 at
worship, so contributions average out to $3,000 times the
average attendance.

One divisor produces a four to one ratio between these
two congregations. The second divisor produces a two to
one ratio. Which comes closer to reflecting reality?

Another part of the explanation is that first congregation projects relatively low expectations of anyone seeking to become a member. It clearly is a voluntary association. Each member determines his or her own level of participation.

That second church responds to requests to become members with the following challenge. "First, you must complete a thirty-six-hour class for prospective new members. We do not want anyone to join our fellowship unless we are sure they understand and agree with what we believe and teach, with what we are convinced the Lord is calling us to be and to do, and with what we expect of members. After completing that class, you will be in a position to decide whether or not to ask to become a member. We expect every member to share in our weekly worship of God, to participate in one of our small groups, to tithe your income and to return at least one-half of that tithe to the Lord via the ministries of this congregation, to engage in a process to identify your spiritual gifts, and to be prepared to complete a training experience designed to prepare you to use your gifts in ministry. If you do not choose to become a member, you will still be welcome to worship with us, and to participate in learning opportunities and in other ministries. Only members, however, are able to serve as policymakers or teachers here."

Many of these high expectation congregations encounter two normal and predictable financial problems. One is the two-year lag between the numerical growth and financial receipts. The typical pattern is next year's receipts will be adequate to meet last year's level of expenditures. The second common problem is that the need for expanded physical facilities arrives before the debt on the last building program has been retired. This is an especially serious problem in those high expectation churches that are composed largely of people under age forty who have yet to reach their peak earning power.

On the other hand, they also enjoy three big advantages. First, since nearly every member is actively involved in doing ministry, it is relatively easy to explain, "Where does all that money go?" Second, that huge cadre of volunteers usually means fewer full-time program staff and more part-time staffers per 1,000 constituents so staff compensation is a lower proportion of total expenditures. Third, when by definition all members are tithers, that makes a big difference even if only one-third of the worshipers are members.

From a financial perspective the "comfortable" size is when the average worship attendance is less than the confirmed membership. The financial "discomfort" comes when (a) the average worship attendance is double or triple or more than the confirmed membership and (b) the average worship attendance is increasing by 15 percent or more year after year after year.

Stewardship Education or Raising Money?

From a congregational perspective the most significant single impact of the new American economy on church finances is in the definition of the primary constituency for stewardship education.

In the old ecclesiastical culture of the middle third of the twentieth century, it was widely assumed that stewardship education should focus on all members of that worshiping community including children and youth.

While few church leaders appear interested in celebrating it, one of the big success stories in American Christianity has been stewardship education. A reasonable estimate is that at least one-fourth of all Protestant churchgoers, plus millions of adults who are not churchgoers, believe they should be responsible stewards of both their annual income and their accumulated wealth. For many the issue is not the obligation to contribute time, energy, creativity, and money to worthy causes. Their problem is how to do that responsibly. What are the truly worthy causes?

One consequence is to complicate life for congregational leaders. One assignment is to design and implement an effective stewardship education program for somewhere between 25 and 90 percent of their members. These are the folks who are still at a relatively low point on that learning curve called faithful stewardship. The other assignment is to design and implement an effective educational ministry with those constituents who are high on that learning curve. They are completely convinced of their obligation to be good, faithful, and responsible stewards of the blessings the Lord has bestowed on them.

They are tithers, perhaps double or triple tithers. Many of these tithers, however, have yet to be persuaded they should return that entire tithe to the Lord via the treasury of this congregation. Is this church really a responsible and worthy cause that deserves their whole tithe?

What does this mean in operational terms?

A common response is to design a fundraising strategy to be implemented in the spring of the year. The primary focus will be on persuading those faithful stewards that this congregation's ministries represent worthy causes. The typical response is that 25 to 30 percent of the contributing households will account for 60 to 75 percent of the dollars received in cash and financial commitments. In simple and pragmatic terms this design reflects an effort to raise money. A widely used tactic is to secure a large commitment from one or two or three or four or five potential contributors. That legitimatizes the need and the size of the goal. That is followed by an effort to encourage a larger group to match those initial gifts. Thus when the goal is publicly announced, it can be accompanied by the assurance, "This is possible! We already have commitments for 30 or 40 or 50 or 60 percent of the total. Climb on the bandwagon."

Several months later a stewardship education is launched. This is designed for the folks who are not fully persuaded that a committed Christian is, by definition, a responsible steward of the blessings God has bestowed upon that individual.

A better design is to make stewardship education a continuing theme in that larger learning ministry that is a central component of the life of that worshiping community.

The key point, however, is to recognize that maintaining a healthy cash flow and stewardship education are two related, but separate concerns. Progress in maintaining that healthy cash flow is evaluated weekly, monthly, quarterly, and annually by objective criteria. Stewardship education is a responsibility that is never completed and cannot be measured by simple objective criteria.

What Is the Best System?

Only a litle imagination is required to identify at least a score of ways to finance the life and ministry of any one congregation. Several have been described in this chapter.

The best approach, however, is to begin with a larger perspective that conceptualizes every congregation as a collection of systems. Each system produces the results it is designed to produce. The one BIG exception to that generalization is when the outcomes of one system are adversely affected by another system designed to undermine one or more other systems. For example, in many congregations the ministry of music competes with the educational ministry for people's time and attention.

The best system for financing ministry is to conceptualize it as one component of a larger strategy to challenge constituents to a higher level of commitment. One variable in this system is preaching. Another is the strategy for missions. Does this congregation ask people to contribute money to missions? Or is a larger focus on contributing time, energy, creativity, and skill? A third component is the system for the assimilation of newcomers.

For this discussion one of the crucial components of the larger system consists of the expectations projected of people who seek to become full members of that worshiping community. A common pattern is a relatively low threshold into full membership. One example is the ten-hour class for prospective new members spread over several weeks. That is consistent with low commitment expectations.

At the other end of this spectrum is the system designed on the foundation of high expectations. One component of that system consists of the expectations projected of people who seek to become full members. One example is the system described earlier which opens the door to requests for membership to any person, age eighteen and over, who has been worshiping with that congregation on a regular basis for several months.

The first step in this strategy is the invitation to join a class for prospective new members. This class usually meets for sixty to ninety minutes every week for thirty-six to forty-five weeks. A major focus in that class is to discuss, "This is what this congregation believes and teaches." One reason for that emphasis is to discourage anyone who is not ready to subscribe to and support our belief system.

In addition to this emphasis on clarity of the belief system, a second focus is on behavior. The details vary, but a common expectation can be summarized in five sentences. We expect anyone seeking to become a full member will have been a regular participant in our weekly worship of God for at least one year before asking to be considered for membership. We also expect that person to have been an active participant in one area of ministry for at least one year such as a learning experience, our ministry of music, a mutual support group, a prayer cell, et al. Third, we expect that person will be a tither and return at least one-half of that tithe to the Lord via the treasury of this congregation. Fourth, we expect every prospective member to have completed the process for discovering their spiritual gifts. Finally, we expect every prospective new member to at least have begun a training experience to equip that individual to use his or her spiritual gifts through the ministries of this congregation.

This high threshold into membership eliminates many of the usual problems encountered in creating a worshiping community that shares a common theological position, in the assimilation of newcomers, in generating the cash flow required to pay the bills, in filling all the slots for volunteer staff, and in minimizing problems of internal communication.

The obvious downside of this approach is that it is far easier to install this high threshold in a new mission than to win acceptance for it in a low commitment church with a low threshold into membership. A second is some newcomers who want to transfer their membership from another congregation conclude that this violates their rights under Section 1, Article IV of the original Constitution of the United States. (The full faith and credit clause.) Third, when the worship attendance averages three or four times the membership, as is frequently the pattern in high commitment churches, the demand for volunteer leaders, teachers, and workers may exceed the supply.

One consequence of those three characteristics is that this high-threshold, high-commitment system will not fit every Protestant congregation in North America. That is one reason this has turned out to be such a long chapter. Both the new American economy and the new ecclesiastical culture have told Americans they have a right to choices. That is one more reason to design a customized financial system!

Four Customized Responses

The first guiding generalization is that low-expectation congregations, those in which the average worship attendance is less than 70 percent of the confirmed membership, usually need more income streams than are required in the high expectation churches. The large low-expectation church typically has to invest more resources in internal communication, in reinforcing the level of trust, and in greater compensation for professional program staff members than is the pattern in high expectation congregations. Frequently they also find it rewarding to encourage constituents to give to a variety of specific causes rather than to unified budget. The low expectation church may rely on a dozen or more of the income streams identified in chapter 8.

By contrast, the high expectation church may cover most expenditures from as few as six or seven income streams.

1. Contributions from constituents for missions.
2. Contributions from constituents for operating expenses.
3. Contributions from constituents for capital expenditures.
4. User fees.
5. Investment income from that congregation's foundation. (One big advantage of incorporating a separate congregational foundation is that it can be an effective tactic in a larger strategy to encourage deferred contributions such as bequests. The big argument against the foundation is the temptation to "borrow" money from the foundation to cover operating deficits of the congregation. This temptation can be overcome by trustees of the foundation who make only matching grants and limit these to missional causes and the initial funding of new ministries.)
6. Giving circles for special needs and causes.
7. Designated second-mile contributions.

A second guiding generalization describes most of the exceptions to the first. Congregations that allocate a large proportion of their total resources (including the time of volunteer and paid staff) to community service ministries tend to cultivate more income streams than do those congregations that allocate most of their resources to the spiritual, personal, and social concerns of their members.

Examples of these communiy service ministries include the Christian day school in which one-half or more of the students come from non-member households, the after-school ministry with children from the local public schools, housing the homeless, feeding the hungry, providing job training for the unemployed, operating the shelter for battered women, the "looking after Grandma" ministry described earlier, the daily or twice weekly ministry with residents of a nursing or assisted-living home, the recreation ministry in which the majority of the participants are not constituents, the tutoring program staffed with volunteers at the local public school, the retreat center for marriage counseling, the 168-hour-a-week ministry with "crack babies," the operation of the halfway house for felons released on probation, the ministries with substance abusers, the weekday preschool for young children, the ministry with first-time parents, and community development programs.

These congregations usually depend on fifteen to twenty different income streams including four or five governmental sources, corporations, family foundations, philanthropists, user fees, and social service agencies.

Which of these four categories describes your congregation? High expectation and member-oriented? High expectation with many community outreach ministries? Low expectation and member-oriented? Low expectation with many community outreach social services?

That may be one of the first questions to be asked as you design a customized financial system for your church.

Another question, if you are a denominationally affiliated congregation, is, what is the impact of that denominational system? That, however, requires another long chapter, but before moving to that discussion, it is necessary to conclude with what appears to this observer to be the highest line of demarcation separating underfinanced congregations from adequately financed churches.

What is that line? Is it theological stance? Or the income level of the constituency? Or the size of the congregation? Or the level of Christian commitment of the members? Or the age of the constituents? Or the curve on the chart reflecting numerical growth or decline? Or the theological training of the pastor? Or how long that congregation has been in existence?

While those and other variables often are influential, the key factor can be summarized in two sentences. First, the world of charitable giving is an increasingly competitive marketplace. Second, does the quality of that congregation's system for asking for financial contributions enable it to compete with other highly sophisticated systems?

Those two sentences also introduce the subject of how denominational agencies compete for money in this new American economy.

CHAPTER ELEVEN

The Impact on Denominational Systems

"What Texans have done, added to what Virginia Baptists have already done, demonstrates that we are in the midst of denominational upheaval," declared Thomas McCann, the president of the Baptist General Association of Virginia in the fall of 2000. "A revolution began in the seventies. It was based on the appointive power of the (SBC) president. A counterrevolution began in the nineties. It was based on the budget power of the state associations and local churches.

"It is clear to me that historic Virginia Baptists and the Southern Baptist Convention are on divergent paths.... While we used to walk side by side, it is clear that the distance between us is growing.... The Southern Baptist Convention holds title to vast amounts of property, but it cannot hold title to our hearts."

What will be the impact of the new economy on denominational systems?

The Regional Judicatories

The simplest way to answer that question is to begin by dividing the Protestant denominations into two groups. One group is organized on the assumption that a high priority for every congregation is to resource the denominational program. That includes sending volunteers to serve on denominational committees as well as to send money to underwrite the denominational budget. Every once in a while a pastor or a gifted staff member is "promoted" to a denominational office.

The dominant flow of resources is from congregations to denominational headquarters. Instead of investing resources in expanding the ministry of their own church, congregational leaders are encouraged to allocate those discretionary resources to help implement denominational priorities.

In recent decades the responsibilities of several national denominational agencies have been enlarged to include a greater regulatory role over congregational life and practices. The costs of this regulation, of course, should be borne by those being regulated.

An alternative design for denominational systems is based on the assumption that denominations exist to serve congregations. That assumption is challenged by those who insist that denominations in the United States originally came into existence to (1) combat heresy; (2) perpetuate the orthodox Christian faith; (3) oversee the preparation and ordination of the clergy; (4) enlist, equip, send, and support missionaries to proclaim the gospel on other continents; (5) plant new missions in North America; (6) create the institutions designed to respond to other needs such as colleges, homes, hospitals, pension systems, camps, retreat centers, theological schools, and publishing houses; and (7) serve as the primary partner in interchurch cooperation.

These responsibilities cost money, and congregations are the logical primary source of those dollars.

This second group, however, insists that the heart of the institutional expression of the Christian faith does not consist of denominational agencies or church-related institutions or ecumenical organizations. They contend that the core component of the institutional expression of the Christian faith is the worshiping community.

This second group contends that the health of any denominational system should be measured, not by the financial resources of religious institutions, but rather by the health, vitality, and relevance of congregations.

In recent years it has become increasingly apparent that denominational leaders in these two groups are choosing sharply different paths into the twenty-first century. Those choosing one path begin this discussion by concentrating on a different question than the one chosen by those walking down the other path.

What Is the Question?

Denominational policymakers in that first group ask, "How will this new American economy and the war on terrorism impact the income side of our denominational budget?"

Their counterparts in the second group ask, "What will be the impact on how we resource congregations as they seek to fulfill the Great Commission?"

The wording of the question always shapes the outcome of any discussion, planning process, or effort to agree on priorities.

What Is the Strategy?

The first group, those who place a high value on congregations resourcing the denominational program, might design a strategy for that regional judicatory that includes these seven points.

1. Since one-fifth of the congregations often account for most of the dollars sent to denominational headquarters, a high priority should be given to encouraging congregations with the potential for rapid numerical growth to fulfill that potential. A reasonable ten-year goal would be to double or

triple the number of congregations averaging over 800 at worship. During the past three decades very large churches have become the "cash cows" that provide a very large share of the total annual receipts from congregations.

In the allocation of the time, energy, and creativity of the program staff of that regional judicatory, nurture the elephants and largely ignore the ants.

2. Design ministry plans for new missions that are consistent with the goal that by the end of five years at least one-half of those new missions will be averaging at least 500 at worship. At least one-fifth should be averaging one thousand by their tenth birthday. Create, train, and equip the mission development teams of three to five people required to implement that design.

3. For the annual self-evaluation of that regional judicatory use a simple formula. How much money was budgeted to be received from congregations? How much was actually received? Does that ratio exceed 100 percent? If not, why not?

In quarterly or annual public statements evaluating the performance of congregations, use the amount of money sent to denominational headquarters as the number-one criterion. In a couple of mainline denominations the regional judicatory sends these statements that list these financial contributions of all congregations in that region to all congregational leaders every quarter. Make "Are we paying our share?" the number-one question for congregational self-evaluation.

Shame can be a powerful motivational force!

Affirm, celebrate, and award plaques to those congregations that send the largest percentage of their total receipts to denominational headquarters.

4. In selecting volunteers to serve on denominational boards and committees, give preference to both lay and clergy who are members of congregations that are generous supporters of the denominational budget.

5. At least one-third, and perhaps one-half, of the time and energy of the chief executive officer of that regional judicatory should be devoted to building close relationships with individuals and families who possess the financial capability to be generous contributors to the ministry of the denominational program.

One circle might consist of 20 to 100 individuals who have the interest, loyalty, and financial capability to contribute at least $50,000 annually to specific causes and needs. A larger circle would consist of those able to contribute at least $25,000 annually directly to that budget. A reasonable goal would be that after five years of cultivation, one-fourth to one-half of the total income for that regional judicatory would come from these loyal supporters.

This could be Plan B for those who are convinced that the degree of alienation between congregations and their denominations is (a) increasing and (b) undermining the reliability of a system that calls for congregations to finance denominational goals.

6. As part of a long-term strategy, create a foundation with its own board for that regional judicatory as a separate legal entity. Aggressively encourage individuals, families, family foundations, and others to make gifts to that foundation. In addition, design a well-publicized program to encourage people to include that foundation in their will.

7. As rapidly as politically possible, delete from the budget of that regional judicatory annual grants to denominationally related institutions created by earlier generations. That list includes colleges, theological schools, hospitals, retirement centers, etc. In the new American economy each one should be able to build its own financial base from constituents and loyal friends. Implement the slogan, "Every tub floats on its own bottom."

Dedicate those scarce resources to giving birth to the new, not to keeping the dying alive for another year.

An Alternative Strategy

Those who believe denominational agencies exist to resource congregations begin with a different question and a different set of priorities. How will this new American economy influence the strategic planning for this regional judicatory? The answer to that question could include these eight components.

1. Our number-one priority will be responding to requests from congregations for help in designing and implementing customized ministry plans for fulfilling the Great Commission. Our role is not to do ministry, but rather to resource congregations seeking to improve, strengthen, and expand their ministries.

2. A high priority will be given to responding to creative initiatives and a low priority to those congregations seeking help in perpetuating the past.

3. We are prepared to help aging and numerically shrinking congregations founded before 1980 identify a new constituency and design a ministry plan to reach, attract, serve, and assimilate newcomers. We also are prepared to help those small congregations eager to build a new future to find a large church that will partner with them in implemening that ministry plan.

We are prepared to resource congregations meeting in functionally obsolete buildings on inadequate sites and/or at poor locations to relocate their meeting place as part of a larger strategy to write a new chapter in their history.

We are prepared to resource congregations that have concluded the time has come to redefine their role and to design a customized ministry that will enable them to fulfill that new role. (One example is the neighborhood congregation founded in 1955 that is convinced that the time has come to become a large regional church.)

We are prepared to resource congregations that are ready to accept a role as teaching churches and help them design a ministry plan appropriate for their role as a teaching church.

When a pastoral or program staff vacancy occurs, we are prepared to help that congregation and to review its ministry plan and the staff configuration required to implement that plan before beginning the search for a new pastor or staff person.

4. Rather than close or merge numerically shrinking and weak congregations, we will encourage and resource larger churches to adopt them. The typical relationship calls for that small congregation to accept and carry full responsibility for the care of its real estate. That small church also will be expected to design a ministry plan that will evoke the interest of leaders in larger congregations who are willing to become partners in implementing that plan. We believe partnerships can be more valuable than financial subsidies channeled through denominational agencies.

One alternative scenario is for that missionary church to enlist, train, and assign a husband-wife couple or a team of three lay volunteers who will provide Sunday morning leadership for that "wounded bird." The twin goals are (a) to enable that congregation to become a fully self-expressing, self-governing, self-financing, and self-propagating worshiping community, and (b) for that team of volunteers to be replaced by indigenous leaders. A common practice is for that volunteer team to consist of a lay preacher, a worship leader or musician and a visionary leader. That team works with the indigenous leadership in developing a ministry plan designed to reach and serve a new constituency, not simply to try to perpetuate yesterday. One by one those volunteers from that missionary church will be replaced by indigenous volunteer leaders and/or paid staff.

5. The number-one criterion for the annual self-evaluation of this regional judicatory will not be to review what we have done. That number-one criterion will be to ask how the congregations in this regional judicatory are doing.

How many report an increase in their worship attendance? How does that compare with the previous year? How many have sent at least three lay volunteers to spend at least ten days doing ministry with a sister church on another continent? How does that compare with the previous year? How many of our congregations have launched or helped to pioneer a new off-campus ministry to reach a new constituency? How many of our congregations have received as new members a number that is equivalent to at least 15 percent of the membership of that congregation? How does that compare with the previous year?

Those are examples of measurable criteria that could be used for self-evaluation.

6. Instead of accepting the unilaterial responsiblity for planting new missions, that regional judicatory could focus its resources on making that happen. This could include these five alternative approaches.

a. Encourage larger congregations with a limited physical plant to become two-site churches. When the question is raised, "Should we relocate or remain here?" the answer is yes.[1]

b. Monocultural congregations could be encouraged to become multicultural parishes by establishing off-campus ministries with those who view that congregation's real estate and ministry as sending a message, "You don't belong here." That is a tested tactic that enables a congregation to become both multicultural and multigenerational.[2]

c. Prepare "Requests for Proposals" (RFPs) that solicit detailed proposals by pastors, congregations, potential staff teams, adult Bible study groups, and others for the planting of a new mission. Instead of assuming that all the necesssary wisdom and skill is located in the headquarters of the regional judicatory, tap into that vast reservoir of energy, creativity, and commitment that is waiting to be asked.[3]

d. Encourage individual congregations or coalitions of congregations to sponsor new missions.

e. Perhaps the most productive alternative is to encourage numerically growing congregations that average more than 800 at worship and have mastered the art of "how to do large church" to plant new missions designed to be large churches from day one. This often means bringing the future leaders of a church planting team to serve on the staff of that very large congregation for three to ten years to fully comprehend the distinctive culture of the very large church and to acquire the necessary leadership skills for that role.[4]

7. For perhaps one-half of all the regional judicatories in American Protestantism, a high priority should be given to challenging what once were rural congregations in farming communities to become exurban churches.

Four of the more common examples are (a) the farming community congregation in what is now becoming suburbia, (b) the rural church in a community increasingly populated by people who commute an hour, more or less, each way to a city job, (c) the church in what has become largely a retirement community, and (d) the church in what has become a destination for tourists and vacationers.

8. A crucial component of this strategy is for the executive of that regional judicatory to present an annual "State of the Church" report that is realistic, challenging, and filled with specifics. This can serve as the larger context for the preparation of customized ministry plans by each congregation.[5]

A recurring theme of that state of the church report is, "We are not in the business simply of maintaining the old. Our primary business is to help give birth to the new."

This strategy is based on the fact that the most effective way for any institution to fund its budget is to provide relevant and high-quality services to its constituents.

A National Perspective

A persuasive argument can be made that the combination of the new American economy[6] and the new American ecclesiastical culture has had a greater impact on national denominational systems than on either congregations or regional judicatories. One reason this is a difficult subject to discuss is because of the overlap between single issue changes and the combined impact of several changes. One example is in the financing of the budgets of national denominational agencies. Another reason is the widespread denial that old systems are becoming obsolete.

One example of the obsolescence of old systems is in the difficulties encountered recently by the National Council of the Churches in Christ in the U.S.A. A second is the difficulties encountered recently by the National Association of Evangelicals.

One example of denial is that while the institutional context for raising money for denominational agencies has been undercut, tens of millions of dollars continue to flow from and through congregations into national treasuries. So why change it?

Diverging Paths

While it is but one of many changes that have transformed the life of national denominational agencies, perhaps the best place to start is to go back to the quotation at the beginning of this chapter. In the Southern Baptist Convention, the Evangelical Lutheran Church, the United Methodist Church, the Presbyterian Church (U.S.A.), the Episcopal Church, and at least a dozen smaller denominations, the degree of divergence in those paths is increasing. The denominational leaders are walking down one path. The people in the pews are walking down another path.

Once upon a time those two paths were parallel and close. In a few denominations, the path chosen by the laity followed the one already blazed by denominational leaders. Today each passing year finds the gap is widening.

That pattern reflects what is happening in public high schools as parents send their teenagers to enjoy what the parents believe should and will be challenging learning experiences, but the majority of teenagers describe it as the road to boredom. A growing number of seventeen-year-olds complain that high school conflicts with their part-time job paying $800 to $1,200 a month.

The larger the size of that public high school, the greater the divergence between the expectations of the parents and the priorities of the faculty. The parents place a high priority on learning. The school places a high priority on order. Many of the parents believe the local public high school should be modeled on an academic learning center. The majority of the students are convinced it is modeled on a correctional institution.[7]

Similarly denominational leaders place a high priority on institutional loyalty. In some denominations the vows taken by new members of congregations include a vow of loyalty to that denomination.

By contrast, most of those adults taking a vow of membership believe the top priority is for that congregation to provide meaningful, relevant, and high quality responses to their personal and spiritual needs. Many display little interest in even knowing the name of the denomination, much less in learning what it means to be loyal to that particular religious tradition. The paths followed by newer members often are quite distant from the paths chosen by national denominational leaders.

This divergence in the paths followed by former partners who once shared a high degree of interdependence also can be seen in the relationships of physicians with health maintenance organizations, the federal government with the states, General Motors with its new car dealers, university administrators with the faculty, the United States Department of Agriculture with farmers, major league baseball club owners with their players, parents with their adult children, and scores of other sectors of our society.

The first page of chapter 7 describes the divergence of views between the American Red Cross and the donors to the Liberty Fund in late 2001.

The two guiding generalizations are (a) the greater the gap between those paths, the more fertile the climate for the growth of adversarial relationships and (b) the greater that gap, the less supportive the institutional climate for persuading the people going down one path to send money to finance the goals of the leaders going down a different path.

Liberty or Equality?

One of the great contemporary political debates on this planet often is articulated in either-or terms. Which should be the primary goal of a just society? To optimize individual liberty? Or to promote equality among all citizens? The political philosopher John Rawls insists on the priority of liberty. Ronald Dworkin argues this is not an either-or issue since liberty is a requirement for equality.[8]

A similar choose-up-sides debate is going on all across the American Christian church landscape. One factor in explaining the rapid numerical growth of independent congregations is they are organized around local control. They are unencumbered by denominational rules, regulations, and requirements.

This debate introduces an important issue in determining the priorities of any denominational system. What are the criteria in defining the central purpose of a denominational system?

The goal of promoting egalitarianism, if equality is defined as condition, usually includes the redistribution of wealth and other resources. If, however, egalitarianism is defined as equality of opportunity, that may require a greater emphasis on opening doors rather than redistributing wealth.

Which is the higher priority in your denominational system? To promote equality by collecting money from congregations and redistributing those dollars? That almost automatically carries with it a decrease in local autonomy since the dollars sent usually are accompanied by clearly defined expectations on how they will be spent. Or to enhance the liberty or local control of congregations by gathering resources (wisdom, skills, energy, creativity, money, etc.) from outside that system and making those resources available to congregations?

Or does the denominational agency define its mission as converting nonbelievers and transforming believers into disciples? Or is that perceived to be the mission of congregations, and the denominational agencies exist to resource congregations as they seek to fulfill the Great Commission?

Which side of this debate describes the position of your denominational agencies? To gather and provide resources that will enhance the capabilities and freedom of congregations? Or to gather and redistribute money to increase egalitarianism? Or to gather resources to implement a denominational strategy that is in continual flux?

The answer to that question will influence both the inputs side and the outcomes side of the denominational strategy.

The Erosion of Institutional Loyalties

A second and less visible change has been the eroding of inherited institutional loyalties. That is one reason why General Motors is closing out the Oldsmobile division. That is one reason so few major league baseball and football players spend all or most of their career with one team.

That is a part of the explanation for the increase in the number of American voters who classify themselves as "Independents." That is one reason why the two predecessor denominations of the United Methodiost Church reported their congregations received 320,000 new members by intradenominational letters of transfer in 1956 compared to only 130,000 in 2000.

A guiding generalization that must be injected into the discussion at this point can be summarized in six words. Trust is the foundation for loyalty. When the constituents do not trust the leadership, loyalty is vulnerable to rapid erosion. That generalization applies to infantry companies, football teams, religious organizations, university faculty, political parties, charitable organizations collecting and disbursing contributions, medical clinics, and a variety of other voluntary organizations.

Reinforcing Trust and Loyalty

How can a denomination reinforce the loyalty of its clergy and laity to that denomination? Historically among the most influential forces have been these:

1. The denomination projects a clear, precise, and relatively narrow doctrinal stance. This is the opposite of theological pluralism.

2. Most of the members share the same nationality ancestry.

3. All pastors have graduated from (a) a college affiliated with that denomination and (b) the same theological school. At a minimum they all attended a seminary affiliated with that denomination.

4. All congregations depend solely on teaching resources produced by that denomination.

5. All congregations use the same edition of the denominational hymnal.

6. Most of the members receive the magazine or newspaper published by their denomination or by the local regional judicatory. (*The Banner* and *The Baptist Standard* are two exemplary models.)

7. The number-one source of unity is a widely accepted definition of a common enemy. Number two is doctrine. A close third, and with some this is number one, is a commitment to one mission board for world missions and one mission board for home or national missions.

The only major exception to that generalization is that the central organizing principle for the women's organization still may be missions. A strong argument can be made that this means an organization that is a partner with, but not subordinate to either of those two denominational mission boards. Merging the three into one is one way to (a) create a "cleaner" table of organization for the denomination as a whole, (b) centralize authority, (c) weaken support for missions, (d) undermine denominational loyalty, and (e) encourage the growth of parachurch and/or congregational ministries designed to offer relevant and meaningful responses to the concerns women bring to church.

8. The organizational structure includes both geographically defined and culturally defined regional judicatories. For example, the twelve congregations in one county might be affiliated with nine different judicatories. The four Anglo congregations would be affiliated with the geographically defined regional judicatory including that county. The Haitian congregation would relate to the nongeographical Haitian judicatory. The Hmong church would relate to the nongeographical Hmong judicatory. Likewise the Vietnamese, the Korean, the African American and Mexican American, the Ecuadorian and the Filipino congregations would be affiliated with their own monocultural nongeographical judicatories. This improves the capability of that denomination to reach and serve recent immigrants by organizing new monocultural congregations.

9. Many of the members enroll their teenagers in a college or university that is closely related to that denomination. One reason is to transmit the denominational belief system and culture to the next generation. Another reason is to encourage intradenominational marriages.

10. Every congregation sends a significant number of the laity to a large two- or three-day annual mission conference. This event greatly overshadows the impact of the one- or two-day less well-attended annual "business meeting" where controversial or divisive issues are discussed and resolved.

11. These brief mission trips of seven to twenty-one days by lay volunteers to serve in ministry with members of a congregation on another continent are always with a sister church of that same denomination.

12. While clergy do transfer out to serve in other denominations or in independent churches, only rarely is a minister invited to transfer in and serve within this denomination.

13. Mergers with other denominations are limited to one every five hundred to eight hundred years.

14. Congregations are so happy with the resources supplied by their own denomination that the possibility of purchasing resources or counsel from a parachurch organization or outsider never occurs to anyone.

15. All campus ministries financed by that denomination are carried out unilaterally by worshiping communities related to that denomination.

16. All continuing education experiences for both the laity and the clergy are designed and administered by teaching churches affiliated with that denomination.

17. While the design bears only a minimal resemblance to a few decades earlier, summer camp experiences continue to be offered for children, youth, adults, and families and are well attended.

18. The denomination has at least one national religious radio program and at least one national religious television program.

19. The denomination operates an interactive web site that is designed to be responsive to a huge variety of needs and questions.

20. When a member announces a change of place of residence to a more distant location, that member's congregation sends a letter to the church or churches near that member's new place of residence advising them of this move.

21. At both the local and regional levels, intercongregational cooperative ventures in ministry should be intradenominational, not interdenominational or interfaith.

22. Outsiders often refer to this denomination as "uncooperative" or "isolationist" or "sectarian" or "out of the mainstream."

While far from exhaustive, this list helps to explain why several denominations have decided not to pay the price required to reinforce the loyalty of the laity and clergy to that religious tradition.

It is a free country, so that is a completely acceptable decision. The price tag on it, however, is the weaker the loyalty of the members to that particular religious tradition, the more difficult it will be to persuade them to send money to national headquarters.

The Impact of Competition

Another factor is a central theme of this book. In war time, in the contemporary American economy and in this ecclesiastical culture the competition for the charitable dollar today is both greater and more sophisticated than it was in the middle third of the twentieth century.

Likewise the competition among parachurch organizations, denominational agencies, for-profit corporations, web sites, individual entrepreneurs, teaching churches, theological schools, retreat centers, and publishing houses to resource congregations is far, far greater than it was in the first couple of decades after World War II.

One of the most effective ways for a denomination to strengthen its relationships with congregations is to provide relevant and high quality resources. The current demand is to add value to congregational ministries. That is far more difficult today than it was in 1955! The number-one example is in music and worship resources closely followed by helping congregations become intentional learning communities, resourcing ministries with families that include teenagers and resourcing caring communities composed of newlyweds and couples engaged to be married.

Which Arena?

When it seeks money to fund its budget, every denominational agency enters a highly competitive arena. Which arena should be chosen? The arena overflowing with charitable dollars to be given away, but that is the most competitive! Or an arena with fewer dollars but less competition?

One choice is to compete in that arena subsidized by state and federal governments. The federal government, and most states, provides financial incentives to encourage individuals, foundations, and corporations to contribute money to charitable causes. This is a highly competitive game! It is dominated by several hundred institutions of higher education plus scores of single purpose causes. This rich arena requires a very high level of skill to be a winner. The upside, however, is that this is the arena with the most dollars! Every national denominational agency should consider the possibility of developing the skills required to compete in this rich arena.

A much smaller arena with limited resources is to compete for a place in the budgets of congregations affiliated with that denomination. This game has one upside and six downsides for denominational agencies. The upside is it requires a low level of skill. One downside is congregations do not receive any financial reward from the federal government for sending money to denominational headquarters. A second is this resembles a zero sum game. Every dollar sent to the denominational headquarters is one less dollar to be spent by that congregation to expand and enrich its own ministry or for other benevolent causes.

A third, and far more serious, downside is this resembles the farmer who in the winter ate the seed corn he had saved to plant in the spring. A common practice is for congregations, instead of investing those dollars to strengthen the future of their parish, send 10 percent to 20 percent of their total annual receipts to fund the current operating expenditures of the denomination.

A fourth, and nearly as serious, downside, is this practice reinforces the conviction that a top priority of every congregation is to collect and send money for others to spend. That is a different perspective than the conviction that denominational agencies exist to help congregations fulfill the Great Commission!

A fifth downside is this design places the regional judicatory and the national denominational budget in competition with one another and with a growing variety of benevolent causes and needs for a place in each congregation's budget.

Finally, a sixth downside is choosing this arena for funding the denominational budget is compatible with the values and practices of the old American economy, but it is not supported by the values and reward systems of the new economy nor the values of younger generations.

A different arena of competition for denominational agencies is to fund their budgets from user fees. As described several times earlier, this is a highly competitive arena! The players include publishing houses, parachurch and paradenominational agencies (councils of churches, ecumenical caucuses, etc.), teaching churches, colleges, theological schools, entrepreneurial individuals, profit-driven corporations, and many others.

To be a winning player in this arena requires an exceptionally high level of competence, but it can be highly productive!

A fourth arena calls for regional judicatories to create their own constituency of individuals and families who are (a) committed supporters of the ministries and work of that agency and (b) able to make substantial annual financial contributions directly to that regional judicatory. This model is widely used by church-related colleges, theological schools, universities, homes, parachurch organizations, and single purpose benevolent causes. The winners in these arenas excel in building relationships, earning trust, and effective communication.

Which arena is the first choice for your denomination? Is that a wise choice for the future?

New Generations Bring New Agendas

While nothing can be done about it, a strong argument can be made that the most influential factor in changing the context for financing denominational agencies was the death of approximately 77 million Americans in the 1965–2000 period inclusive.

They have been replaced by approximately 126 million children born during those thirty-six years who were still alive and residing in the United States at the end of 2000 plus approximately 37 million immigrants living in the United States at the end of 2000. In other words, for every twenty residents of the United States lost by death during that thirty-six year period, ten were replaced by immigrants and thirty-five by births. The "extra" births and immigrants beyond the needed replacements produced that net gain of 86 million in the nation's population between 1965 and the end of 2000.

The key point for this discussion is that nearly all of those 77 million who died were born into and socialized into the old American economy and the old American ecclesiastical culture. Their replacements, who outnumber the 118 million survivors of the United States population of 195 million in 1965, by nearly a three to two ratio, have been and are being socialized into the new American economy and a substantially different religious culture.

Equally important, the babies born in 1965 and subsequently probably will outlive those Americans born in the pre-1965 era. These younger Americans bring a substantially different worldview, value system, and set of expectations than were carried by earlier generations. One illustration of this is the number of heterosexual unmarried couples living together with children under fifteen years of age nearly quadrupled between 1980 and 2000. By contrast, during the same two decades the number of married couples with children under age fifteen at home increased by slightly over 12 percent.

The systems that worked with adults born in the 1910–40 era are not working as well with the generations born in 1965 and later. One alternative is to build a constituency from among adults born before 1940. Another alternative is to change. A third option is to accept a gradual shrinkage in "market share."

Regulate or Resource?

A central factor in the context for denominational policy-making can be described as the counterculture. One of the central components of the new American economy has been deregulation. The deregulation of commercial airline travel, the stock market, long-distance trucking, the sale of electricity, telecommunications, and the emergence of charter schools are among the most highly visible examples.

The counter trend in several denominations has been to expand their regulatory role.[9] Five arguments are heard in support of this enhanced regulatory role for national denominational bodies. The historic one is to combat heresy and to perpetuate the orthodox Christian faith. This is most highly visible in the Reformed traditions. While it is impossible to prove a single cause and effect relationship, the Reformed traditions emphasize regulation and also have experienced scores of schisms.

A second argument is uniformity. This is one of the classic arguments in favor of expanding the role and authority of the United States government. This opens the door to uniformity among the states in such functions as public assistance, health care, education for grades K-12, law enforcement, election procedures, interest rates, social justice, laws governing marriage and divorce, the conservation of natural resources, traffic regulations, land use controls, the ownership of guns, pensions, the legal incorporation of for-profit corporations, and judicial procedures.

The parallel argument for a strong regulatory role for the national denominational headquarters is to encourage uniformity in standards for ordination, in the organizational structure and governance of both congregations and regional judicatories, in reporting systems (use of the calendar year rather than the program year), the criteria to be followed in adding and deleting the names of people to a congregation's membership roster, and in the pension systems available to the clergy.

The third argument is the fast food restaurant theme. Customers know exactly what to expect when they order at a MacDonald's or Burger King restaurant. Both have spent tens of millions of dollars to guarantee that hamburgers and servings of French fried potatoes will taste the same in

Pennsylvania as the identical order served in California. Churchgoers have an equal right to expect that when they move from Pennsylvania to California and choose a new church home carrying their favorite brand name, they will experience the same belief system, governance, and practices that they enjoyed before moving.

The fourth argument has been around for at least three thousand years and is a favorite of dictators. The people cannot be trusted to make wise decisions on their own behalf or on behalf of the common good.[10] Headquarters knows best. The leaders at headquarters are able to see the larger picture while local leaders are limited by a more parochial perspective.

This fourth argument wins more adherents in bad times than in good times. It wins more supporters in time of war than in peace times. It also wins more adherents from among those in centralized positions of authority than from local leadership.

A fifth argument represents an outside perspective and is supported by leaders in independent or nondenominational congregations and parachurch organizations. They contend that in the new American religious culture every expansion of the centralized regulatory role of denominations eventually increases the constituency of the independent churches and parachurch organizations.

In the old American ecclesiastical culture it appeared that an expansion of the regulatory role of the denomination was compatible with asking congregations to send more money to denominational headquarters.

From this observer's perspective, it appears those are becoming incompatible expectations. An expansion of that regulatory role probably will require denominational agencies both regional and national, to depend on sources other than congregations for most of their financial support.

That, however, is only one of several questions to be raised when the time comes to design a new denominational financial system for the twenty-first century.

Has That Time Arrived?

Every national denominational system and every regional judicatory has a system for financing its work. That system may be a collection of procedures accumulated over the years. Or it may be a carefully designed and relatively new system devised to replace what the leaders had concluded was an obsolete system. Or it may be a product of the merger of two or three denominations.

A reasonable assumption is the combined impact of the new American economy and the arrival of the new ecclesiastical culture raises this question. Has the time come to revise or replace the old system? If the answer is yes, it may be helpful to reflect on these sixteen questions in preparing a new financial system for the twenty-first century.

1. Do you believe dollars generated in congregations should represent a majority of the receipts used to fund the budgets of national denominational agencies? Or only a tiny proportion?

If the answer is, "A large proportion," that may mean the top priority is to strengthen the level of trust between the people in the pews and the national denominational leadership. Another high priority will be to encourage the emergence of more large churches.

If the answer is, "None or only a tiny proportion," the divergence in paths described in the opening paragraph of this chapter may not be significant. In the new American economy, national denominational agencies need not be dependent on the financial support of congregations. Like hundreds of church-related institutions founded in the nineteenth century and the early decades of the twentieth century, they now can turn to other sources of income to pay their bills and choose their own path to the future.

2. Do you believe your regional judicatories can and should be the primary place for resourcing congregations? Or should most of that responsibility rest with national denominational agencies? Or with a network of teaching churches in your denomination? Or should your congregations be encouraged to contract with parachurch organizations and other "outside" sources for help?

That question does not have a "right" answer.

The appropriate response in a denomination with several very large regional judicatories, such as the Southern Baptist Convention, will not be appropriate for those denominations in which the large regional judicatories include fewer than 100,000 confirmed members.

3. Which is the greater responsibility of your national denominational system? To resource congregations? Or to regulate the belief systems, behavior, polity, governance, actions, ministries, and practices of congregations and local church leaders?

The right answer is not, "Both." The greater the emphasis on regulation, the lower the receptivity of congregational leaders to turn to the regulators for resourcing. The BIG imbalance in the American population today is a surplus of people who want to regulate the practices of others and a shortage of people who want to be regulated!

4. Is the redistribution of income, or wealth, perceived to be a major responsibility of the national denominational agencies? Or is that a responsibility of the regional judicatories? Or does your denomination operate on the principle that every congregation should be self-expressing, self-propagating, self-financing, and self-governing?

5. Is the design of your system for funding the budgets of national denominational agencies based on the old economy assumption of a shortage of financial resources? Or on

the new American assumption of an abundance of financial resources?

6. Do you believe the annual receipts for your national denominational system originate with congregations and regional judicatories? Or do you believe those contributions originate with individuals?

The answer will suggest whether the primary relationship in building trust is with institutions or with individuals.

7. Do you believe younger generations are comfortable sending their charitable dollars to an institution that will forward some of those dollars to another institution which will forward some of those dollars to another institution which will distribute those dollars among other institutions which will decide on the ultimate recipient of those dollars? Or do you believe that younger generations prefer to send their charitable dollars directly to the institution or cause that will use them in ministry? (That turned out to be a polarizing question for the American Red Cross in late 2001!)

This question is based on two assumptions. First, it is assumed that a system devised by and for white males born before 1920 may not be acceptable to adults born after 1960. Second, it is assumed that people born after 1960 will outlive those born before 1920.

8. What do you believe are the most pressing scarcities of resources in your denomination?

From this observer's perspective, the answer in at least a couple of denominations is the most serious shortages are, in this order of severity, (a) a shortage of ministers who are effective visionary leaders; (b) a shortage of entrepreneurial pastors; (c) a shortage of self-identified "career associate pastors" with a very high level of competence in one or two specialized areas of ministry; (d) a shortage of trust by congregational leaders in their denominational operations; (e) a shortage of ministers with the gifts, skills, personality, vision, energy, experience, and productivity required to be an effective team leader or senior pastor of a very large church; (f) a shortage of "ideal matches" between the needs of the congregation and the gifts, skills, priorities, and experience of a long tenured pastor; (g) a shortage of pastors able to lead in the renewal of congregations with an aging and shrinking membership; (h) a shortage of creativity in the denominational system that is required to create the new for a new era; (i) a shortage of denominational staff members equipped to help congregations design a ministry plan that is customized for their situation; (j) a shortage of effective systems to help pastors "reinvent" themselves for a new pastorate; (k) a shortage of adults born after 1960 who are eager to help perpetuate institutions founded by people born before 1920; and (l) a shortage of dollars for ministry.

The point of that long list is that a scarcity of money ranks no higher than twelfth on the list of contemporary pressing shortages.

9. Do you believe that an unprecendentedly large number of adults in your religious tradition have discretionary financial resources they would prefer to give to a worthy Christian cause than to spend on themselves or transfer to their children?

10. In resourcing congregations, do you believe in the old economy guideline that one size can fit all? Or do you believe in the new Ameican economy guideline that calls for customizing to fit the need? Does that distinction also apply to the funding of congregations and regional judicatories?

11. Do you believe the largest single share of the responsibility for planting new missions to reach new generations and recent immigrants should rest on (a) the national denominational agencies; (b) the regional judicatories; (c) those congregations averaging at least 500 at worship, (d) clusters of congregations of all sizes; (e) independent or nondenominational congregations, movements, and;

societies; (f) wealthy Christians and those who are financially able and eager to fund new missions; (g) the first constituents of that new mission; or (h) members of lay-led house churches?

Is your answer consistent with the polity, governance, and financial system of your denomination?

12. If you are a leader in a predominantly Caucasian denomination seeking to become a multicultural body, what is the number-one component of your strategy? To become a federation of largely monocultural regional judicatories? To become a federation of multicultural regional judicatories composed largely of monocultural congregations? To become a multicultural denomination composed largely of multicultural congregations?[11]

13. Do you believe that the most effective way to maintain a relationship between the institutions created by your denomination in earlier years (colleges, homes, camps, theological schools, hospitals, etc.) and your denomination is a continued annual financial subsidy by your denomination to these institutions?

14. Do you believe today's congregations have a responsibility to help fund the budgets of these institutions? Or should these institutions be encouraged to rely on direct financial support from other sources including corporations, foundations, investment income, governmental bodies, individuals, and/or user fees?

15. While exceptions do exist, in broad general terms several expressions of specialized ministries require an exceptionally high level of staff competence and/or substantial financial subsidies. Others require competence but no subsidy. For example, a weekday prekindergarten program requires competence but usually little or no financial subsidy from the church. Church-based ministries with college and university undergraduates usually require a much lower financial subsidy than campus-based student min-

istries. Both, however, require a very high level of competence.

High cost (in terms of competence and/or money) specialized ministries include (a) ministries with young and
childless adults, (b) campus-based student ministries, (c)
ministries with teenagers, (d) ministries with developmen-
tally disabled adults, (e) sending one person out to plant a
new mission, (f) one-to-one counseling, and (g) planting a
new mission that is designed to be, from day one, a congregation that displays a high degree of demographic diversity
and also is theologically inclusive.

Comparatively low cost specialized ministries include (a)
ministries with married couples with children, (b) ministries with healthy mature adults who are life-long
Christians, (c) ministries with families that include
teenagers, (d) sending teams of two or three full-time specialists with a couple of trained volunteers or part-time staff
specialists to plant a new monocultural mission, (e) organizing intensive and long term adult Bible study groups, (f)
weekday vacation Bible school, and (g) operating a food
pantry to feed the hungry.

Is the financial system for your denomination designed
to encourage and support the high cost and more difficult
specialized ministries? Or to encourage and support the
less difficult and lower cost specialized ministries?

16. Finally, and most important, what is the bias in your
current financial system? One example of a bias is to subsidize incompetence, poor stewardship, failure, numerical
decline in congregations, inability to compete, reluctance to
change, irrelevance, a passion to perpetuate yesterday,
obsolete programs or institutions, early retirement for
clergy, and expensive in-house operations that could be
outsourced at lower cost.

A radically different bias is to affirm and reward success,
creativity, high levels of productivity, innovation, visionary

leadership, new ventures in missions, and effective evangelistic strategies.

Can you identify a bias in your present financial system? If so, are you comfortable with that bias?

What Have We Learned?

The last third of the twentieth century taught denominational leaders a half dozen lessons in church finances that justify the sacrifice of a few trees to summarize them.

1. Don't try to be an ecclesiastical savings and loan association!

Several regional and national denominational agencies decided that one source of financing could be to borrow money from church members and congregations. They guaranteed a 3 percent to 8 percent return on those short term loans. Those funds were loaned to congregations to finance building programs on ten- to thirty-year mortgages at 5 to 10 percent. The interest curve assumed that long-term interest rates always would be substantially higher than for short-term deposits. The spread between the interest paid and the interest received not only would finance this whole venture but the surplus could help fund the national denominational budget.

In the new American economy, however, interest rates turned out to be remarkably volatile. One result was the depositors asked for their money back on those short term low interest loans. Thus the denominational agency found itself forced to pay 10 percent or more to replace money it had loaned out earlier at 6 to 8 percent.

Taxpayers, via the United States government, bailed out the commercial savings and loan associations caught in this reversal of the interest curve. Among the pricetags paid by denominational agencies was a decrease in the trust level among the constituents.

2. Don't try to be an investment trust!

A parallel system called for a denominational agency to persuade church members, congregations, and church-related organizations to invest their money with them. In simple terms, they guaranteed a return of perhaps 7 percent annually and thanks to the booming stock market realized an annual return of perhaps 20 percent or more. They were able to pay the investors 10 percent, which brought in more investments, and could use the spread to fund various ministries. When the market "correction" (or "slowing of the economy" or "recession") came, their annual returns dropped to zero or below. The investors who were left holding an empty bag often did not raise their level of trust in the operation of their denomination.

The reaction to one of these ventures was summarized by the headline above a front page story in *The Wall Street Journal* for November 21, 2000: "When a Church Made Some Bad Bets, Donors Say They Were Fleeced: Parishioners Sue Over Losses From Risky Investments." The article described what happened when one denominational money-management agency was rocked by the financial waves of the new American economy.

3. The pasture is the same, but the cows are not!

A few of today's dairy farmers are able to make a living on the same farm that also produced a comfortable living for grandfather's family in the 1930s. One reason is today's dairy cows produce more than twice as much milk every day as did the average cow when grandfather farmed this land.

Back in 1965 it was not unusual for the five largest Protestant congregations in a community to report a combined average worship attendance of 2,500 to 3,500. All five of those very large churches carried a denominational label such as Methodist, Baptist, Presbyterian, Lutheran, Episcopal, Reformed, or United Church of Christ.

In that same community today the five largest Protestant congregations report a combined worship attendance of 8,000 to 12,000. One is a relatively new nondenominational congregation. Another is a Bible church. A third is an independent Christian or Church of Christ congregation. The fourth is affiliated with the Assemblies of God or one of the Baptist denominations. Only one is affiliated with a mainline Protestant body. Two other independent churches are larger than any of those five largest from the 1965 era are today.

The pasture is the same, the grass is different, and the cash cows are larger and more numerous, but most carry a different brand than was on the cows in this pasture four decades ago.

The moral of that story is make sure your denominational brand is on several of those new cash cows if you expect to rely on contributions from congregations to fund a large portion of your denominational budget! Many of those very old cows are more likely to be good for hamburger than for milk.

4. In the old ecclesiastical culture in America denominational loyalty often was reinforced by nationality and/or language.

This was most clearly visible in German Catholic, Irish Catholic, Italian Catholic, and other nationality Catholic parishes. A second reinforcement was the parish elementary school. The counterparts in American Protestantism were the Norwegian Lutheran, German Methodist, Italian Baptist, Scotch Presbyterian, and Swedish Covenant congregations and similar nationality churches. The reduction in immigration from Europe that began in the early 1920s gradually eroded that reinforcing tie.

By the 1960s it was apparent that the children, grandchildren, and great grandchildren of those earlier immigrants identified themselves as Americans. The Southern Baptist

Convention was largely immune to this change since it (a) was not an immigrant denomination and (b) had focused on evangelism and missions, not ancestry, as the central organizing principle. (During the past quarter century the Southern Baptist Convention has become increasingly polarized over whether regulation should become a major responsibility of denominational headquarters.)

The moral of this lesson is if the new system for financing denominational budgets will depend heavily on contributions from congregations, a high priority should be given to national denominational leaders, regional judicatories, and congregations walking side-by-side down the same path.

5. Obligations and loyalties no longer are powerful motiating forces.

Church members born before 1945 usually can be persuaded to support their denomination out of a sense of obligation and institutional loyalty.

As was pointed out earlier, institutional loyalties and a feeling of obligation tend not to be powerful motivating forces with the generations born after 1960.

If that new system for financing denominational budgets depends on contributions from congregations, it should include that redundant effort to reinforce denominational loyalty described earlier in this chapter.

6. Don't feed them all out of the same trough!

Dairy farmers in the 1930s often raised a few hogs, partly for meat, but largely to sell to have the money to pay the property taxes on that farm. The farmer could feed a half dozen hogs with one trough.

Today's hog farmer raises thousands of pigs that are fed out of scores of troughs.

Back in the old ecclesiastical economy of the 1950s a regional judicatory often boasted that at least one-half of all of the benevolence dollars received from congregations were forwarded to the national denomination. Today their successors complain if someone suggests that even one-third of the receipts of that regional judicatory should be forwarded to the national denominational treasury.

The moral to that story is the primary source of funds for the regional judicatory should not be the same as the primary source of funds for the national denominational budget. Every year the number of hungry hogs at that regional judicatory trough increases. A system designed to feed both budgets out of the same trough probably will result in severe financial malnourishment in one place or the other.

The BIG exception to that generalization is in those religious bodies that (a) operate with a clearly, precisely, and narrowly defined belief system, (b) project relatively high expectations of anyone seeking to become a full member, and (c) have a relatively short agenda of responsibilities for both regional and national denominational agencies. Their goal is to grow lean pigs that can run faster and change direction more quickly than slow, fat hogs.

What Are the Guidelines?

The first question, for those denominational policymakers who have read this far, is, Do we need to design a new financial plan?

One response is, "Of course not. The old plan is producing all the money we need."

A second is, "That's not the problem! Our problem is how do we persuade our congregations to support our present plan? What we need is for you to tell us how to recreate the conditions that made our present plan a success when we first adopted it back in 1925 or 1955."

That is the natural, normal, and predictable response by anyone in denial. That brings the discussion back to the central issue of this book. What worked in the old ecclesiastical culture of the old American economy probably is not the best strategy for this new ecclesiastical culture in this new American economy!

The sixteen questions raised earlier in this chapter may be helpful in preparing to design that new plan. In addition, these additional guidelines may be useful.

1. The more income streams, the less likely any one change will be severely disruptive. A regional judicatory should plan on at least four major income streams; a national denominational budget should include at least six. No one stream should account for more than one-half of the total annual expenditures.

2. Contributions from congregations should not be the number-one source of receipts for both the regional judicatories and the national denominational budget! (The one big exception was noted earlier.)

3. The plan should include both short term strategies and long term strategies.

Create a foundation to receive major gifts, bequests, legacies, and other receipts (such as the sale of real estate) with an understanding that the annual income from investments will be allocated only to implementing that long term strategy. The Presbyterian Church (U.S.A) has demonstrated that a national denominational foundation with a billion dollars in assets is a realistic goal. In this new American economy a denomination with 500,000 or more confirmed members should be able to create a foundation with assets in 2030 of one to five billion dollars.

A short term strategy is the one-year capital campaign spread over two calendar years for tax purposes.

4. Capital assets should not be used for operational expenditures!

One of the most effective tactics for destroying the trust of the constituency is to appropriate "idle" capital assets (income from the sale of property, capital reserves, depreciation funds, etc.) to meet operating expenses.

5. Feel free to borrow ideas from others. What is working for other denominations? Could that be incorporated into our new financial plan? It is rare to find all the creativity in one room at one time. A half dozen income streams already in use can be adapted to any denomination for funding either the regional or national budget.

Six Income Streams

What are the potential major income streams?

A. Fees for Services and for Memorable Experiences

This is the number-one income stream in the new American economy. The number-one income stream in the old, old American economy consisted of charges for commodities and goods.

Instead of offering heavily subsidized services to congregations, this means charging full cost including overhead. This not a new idea! For years congregations have been paying the full cost for both goods and services received from grocery stores, building contractors, architects, utility companies, itinerant evangelists, television stations, publishing houses, visiting preachers, money managers, fund raisers, parish consultants, custodial services, insurance companies, and the producers of continuing education experiences.

This does require that denominational agency to be able to compete in terms of quality, creativity, and costs in that increasingly competitive ecclesiastical market place. Fees for services and meaningful and memorable experiences could represent somewhere between 50 percent and 100 percent of the annual income for either a regional or national denominational agency.

The most dificult step in making fees for services and experiences the largest single item on the income side of the denominational budget is how to calculate the fee. One pattern has been to subsidize these services which means another source of income is required to cover the subsidy. A second alternative is to charge full costs including a share of the overhead.

In this new consumer-driven economy fees should reflect, not costs to the producer, but rather the value added for the consumer.

B. The Franchise Tax

While gentler language should be used to describe it, this can provide 50 percent to 90 percent of the administrative costs of operating the national headquarters.

One version is all organizations and institutions that carry that denomination's name on their articles of incorporation and/or public image (colleges, universities, publishing houses, seminaries, homes, camps, retreat centers, etc.) will allocate one penny for every ten dollars of operating expenses toward the administrative costs of the national denominational headquarters. That is a one-tenth of one percent "tax" on operating expenditures for permision to use that denomination's name.

A second facet could be a one percent "tax" on the operating expenditures of all congregations and regional judicatories affiliated with that denomination.

C. Foundation Income

This is an increasingly popular income stream for congregations, educational institutions, regional judicatories, and retreat centers as well as for national denominational budgets. The annual income from investments can account for 5 percent to 50 percent of total annual receipts.

D. The Executive's Friendship Circle

This is a widely used strategy by university presidents, political candidates, the chief executive officer of charitable organizations, and at least a few denominational executives. This was described earlier as item 5 in designing a strategy for a regional judicatory, but it also can be utilized by the chief executive officer of the denomination.

The number-one reason it is widely used is because of the sharp increase since 1980 in the number of wealthy Americans.

E. Go to the Well Every Year!

The old American economy was organized on the assumption there is a scarcity of money. That was an appropriate assumption in 1935. That generated the admonition, "Don't go to the well too often! Don't reinforce the image the church is always asking for money." The operational translation was a congregation should allow at least three years between capital fund campaigns, regional judicatories should not go to that money well more than once or twice in a decade, and national denominational agencies should be even more restrained.

For nearly all Americans the old economy functioned on the assumption that everybody is dependent on current income to pay their bills. Churches asked members to return a tenth of their income to the Lord by way of that congregation's treasury.

The new American economy includes tens of millions of people with substantial accumulated wealth. Most of the leaders who articulated those admonitions about not going to the well too often are dead, but their advice lives on long after their demise.

A reasonable design for a financial plan for at least 70 percent of American Protestant congregations is one low key annual campaign to request designated gifts for somewhere between a dozen and sixty special needs. These might include world missions, expanding the parking lot, adding a new ministry to reach a neglected constituency, helping to shelter the homeless, partial financing of a new church plant, scholarships, partial funding of the cost of sending nine volunteers to work for ten days with fellow Christians in a sister church in Africa, replacing the roof, funding a drama club for children, and helping to feed the hungry.

In even-numbered years the regional judicatory could run its capital funds campaign and in odd-numbered years the national church could run its campaign.

Congregational operating expenses usually are funded by contributions from the current income of the constituency. These annual capital campaigns can be designed so most of the receipts come from accumulated wealth.

A common alternative is for congregations and denominational agencies to limit their appeals to the current income of members and thus leave more money on the table for the more aggressive representatives of other charitable, religious, and educational causes. That money left on the table was one reason it was possible to raise over one billion dollars in six weeks after September 11, 2001, for aid to the victims of that disaster. This paragraph explains why the funding of parachurch and paradenominational agencies deserves a brief separate chapter.

F. What Are the Successors to Obligation and Institutional Loyalty?

In the old ecclesiastical economy denominational agencies could depend on obligation, duty, and loyalty to motivate church members and congregations to send money to fund the denominational budget.

In the new ecclesiastical economy those motivating forces have been replaced by relationships, trust, causes, and persuasive messages. Build relationships with potential donors and earn their trust! If you don't, the representatives of other attractive charitable causes will fill that vacuum.

What Is the Central Issue?

What is the most important question the New American economy has raised for denominational leaders?

Despite the length of this chapter, the answer is not the need to design a new system for financing denominational budgets! At least a few will argue the key fork-in-the-road policy question is, "Do we want to swap our historic denominational identity for membership in the American counterpart to the United Church of Canada?"

Others will contend the crucial fork-in-the-road question is, "Do we devote our resources to perpetuating the old or do we focus on giving birth to the new?"

Those who are convinced that one central distinction between the old economy and the new American economy is the decreased influence of the producers of goods and services and the increased power of the consumer may agree with business consultants Pine and Gilmore. As was pointed out earlier, they contend the new basis for calculating charges to customers is not the cost to provide that service or goods. The new American economy assumes charges reflect the value added.[12]

How many dollars will congregations and the people in the pews send to finance the budget of their denominational agencies? The response will be in proportion to the value added by denominational agencies to the life and ministries of that congregation. In other words congregations shop for resources and help from organizations on the basis of value added, not costs, not loyalty, and not precedents.

That may be the most useful guiding generalization in designing a new financial system for your denomination for the twenty-first century.

CHAPTER TWELVE

The Impact on Parachurch Organizations

A financial strategy for most parachurch and parade-nominational organizations can be condensed into one seven-sentence paragraph.

Focus on filling the vacuum by responding to needs not being addressed effectively by denominational agencies, theological schools, teaching churches, or for-profit corporations. Build on your strengths and concentrate on what you do best.[1] Specialize in those areas where you can at least match the very best competitors on both quality and price. Charge full cost for all services. Fees for services should be sufficient to cover a modest amount of pro bono work as well as allowing for uncollectable "bad debts." Do not hesitate to pick up the money others leave on the table (see the last paragraph of point e in the previous chapter). Be comfortable responding to requests for help on an issue outside your specialized competence with, "Sorry, we don't do that."

Five Advantages

The best of the contemporary parachurch organizations have five huge advantages over denominational agencies and the traditional interchurch organizations.

The first is that the pioneers were created to fill a vacuum. Typically that gave them somewhere between five and twenty years to sharpen their definition of their role or niche, to improve their level of competence, and to earn a positive reputation.

Second, most of today's parachurch organizations came into existence concurrently with the national trend to outsource functions once staffed by the in-house labor force. One example is many colleges and universities now outsource the operation of their bookstore, their dining halls, part or all of their financial administration, and, in many places, most or all of the residential housing for students. Muncipalities are outsourcing or privatizing many of their responsibilties. A growing number of denominationally affiliated congregations now turn to parachurch organizations and teaching churches for Christian education materials, for resources for their youth ministry, for leadership in a capital funds campaign, for parish consultations, for continuing education for their leaders, for architectural advice, for videotapes, and for dozens of other needs. At least two dozen have replaced the live preacher who personally delivers the sermon with a videotape from a teaching church.

Third, while a few depend on a generous benefactor or income from an endowment fund or annual grants from a denominational budget or a foundation or one or two giving circles for a substantial proportion of their income, most rely on user fees. This motivates them to be sensitive to the market. Instead of being producer-driven, they are forced to offer relevant and high qualilty services and experiences. For the very best, this means their reputation is based on relevance and quality, not on an institutional label shared with others.

Fourth, their primary constituency consists of tomorrow's customers, not people who are committed to perpetuating yesterday. This gives the parachurch organization both the incentive and the freedom to be driven by a strong future-orientation. Thus they are able to earn a reputation for helping to invent a new tomorrow.

Fifth, since most operate in a highly competitive, rather than a subsidized ecclesiastical marketplace, this forces them to learn how to be competitive on price. That reinforces the motivation used in the customer service business, not in "pushing our product" to a captive audience.

These are five of the reasons why the financial system for a parachurch organization bears only a modest resemblance to the financial system for a congregation or a denominational agency.

Those five advantages enjoyed by most parachurch organizations suggest the best analogy for a parachurch organization is not to begin by looking at the ecclesiastical marketplace, but rather at the deregulated commercial marketplace.

The Deregulated Marketplace

The deregulation of the commercial airlines was a major component in the creation of the new American economy. Deregulation in 1978 led to the creation of scores of new airlines. More than 130 failed. Several were absorbed into other airlines via mergers. Southwest Airlines is the big success story to come out of that bit of recent American economic history.

A second component of the new American economy came with the court ordered breakup of AT&T in the 1980s. That marked the deregulation of telecommunications. It opened the door to new players in what has become an increasingly competitive game. The majority of the new players in telecommunications also have been absorbed by competitors or have run out of money.

When several large denominational bodies in American Protestantism decided to cut back on planting new missions, that was the equivalent of deregulation of new church development. The resulting vacuum was filled by new independent churches, by new movements such as the Vineyard Christian Fellowship, by a variety of newer denominations, by the decision of the Southern Baptist Convention to change from a regional body into a North American denomination, and by hundreds of large congregations becoming multisite churches.

When congregations affiliated with the mainline Protestant denominations felt the need to call for help in the increasingly competitive ecclesiastical climate of the 1960s and 1970s, these denominations were faced with three choices. One was to sharply expand their capability to resource long established congregations. A second was to focus on creating the new rather than resourcing the old. That would have required tripling or quadrupling the number of new missions launched each year. A third was to expand an already long agenda of denominational concerns and thus enlarge the vacuum for resourcing congregations.

This was the equivalent of deregulation. Instead of continuing to depend on their denomination for relevant, high quality, and innovative resources to meet new needs, a growing number of congregations turned to parachurch organizations, entrepreneurial individuals, for-profit corporations, retreat centers, teaching churches, nondenominational publishing houses, and others for resources.

What Are the Consequences?

One normal and natural consequence of deregulation is an increase in competition. One product of increased competition is a large number of success stories and a much larger number of failures. The number-one example in the United States since 1948 is that the sharp increase in the competition among the producers of food and fiber has produced many more losers than winners.

Another example is the recent proliferation of organizations, individuals, books, periodicals, videotapes, conferences, web sites, teaching churches, theological schools, musicians, fundraisers, Bible colleges, consultants, workshops, website designers, and media specialists that are available to congregational leaders. The deregulated ecclesiastical marketplace is more competitive and also offers more choices. One parallel is television in the 1960s with three to six channels available to the typical viewer and television in the era of cable and the direct TV dish that offers scores of channels to viewers.

A third consequence of the deregulated marketplace is the disappearance of old brand names. A fourth is the appearance of new brand names. A fifth is the emergence of new partnerships. One example is the replacement of the campus-based approach to theological education by the new partnership between a teaching church and a seminary to create a congregation-based design for theological education.

A sixth consequence is creative, productive, and market sensitive entrepreneurs are rewarded in the ecclesiastical marketplace if they also make sure receipts exceed expenditures. Well over one-half of today's Protestant megachurches are primarily the creation of an entrepreneurial pastor.

Seventh, incompetence, unless supported by financial subsidies, in the deregulated ecclesiastical marketplace usually leads to failure. This can be seen most clearly in (a) new church development and (b) long established churches in communities currently experiencing substantial population growth.

Eighth, the deregulated commercial marketplace is an attractive option for venture capitalists. Likewise the deregulated ecclesiastical marketplace is attractive to philanthropists who are eager to contribute to new, innovative, well designed, competently managed, and promising ministries.

Ninth, today's Americans are willing to hire someone else to do what their parents did for themselves. That very long list inclues changing the oil in the car, transforming commodities into attractive meals, child care, cleaning the house, caring for one's aged parents, investing savings, tutoring children, and care of the lawn. One consequence is a growing market for the services, goods, and experiences offered by "outside" vendors. That means a competently managed parachurch organization can cover all expenditures by fees for services.

Finally, despite the occasional "economic slowdown" or "recession," the new American economy is populated by an unprecedented large number of Christians with discretionary income and/or accumulated wealth. This makes it relatively easy for a parachurch organization to raise the "start up" funds for new ministries or to finance certain types of ministries that cannot be expected to be financially self-supporting from user fees—such as a residential high school for teenagers from dysfunctional families or new missions in central Africa.

Good News or Bad News?

Finally, is the emergence of fee-based parachurch organizations and partnerships between parachurch organizations and congregations good or bad? The answer, of course, depends on one's perspective.

From a congregation's perspective, the availability of relevant, high quality, and customized goods, services, and experiences is a plus. The clearest example is described in the previous chapter. The congregation averaging sixty-five at worship would like to be served by a minister who combines the gifts and qualities of the loving shepherd, the wise administrator, the superb preacher, the inspiring spiritual mentor, and the visionary leader. Instead of settling for a series of three-year pastorates by itinerant ministers, they turn to the Stephen Ministry to train three or four volunteers to serve as shepherds, they rely on a retreat center to prepare a half dozen volunteers to be spiritual mentors, they use videotapes by a top quality preacher in worship, they ask a parish consultant to help them design a five-year ministry plan, they send another volunteer to a teaching church to learn how to fill that slot for a wise administrator, they utilize the services of another teaching church to equip three or four volunteers to serve as a worship team, and they turn to a retired pastor to officiate at weddings and memorial services.

From a denominational perspective, this raises at least four options. One is to resource congregations in this increasingly competitive marketplace. A second is to serve as a broker between congregations and vendors. A third is to define a new and different role and ask a group of generous benefactors to finance that role. A fourth is to take advantage of the times and create a denominational foundation with the income from the foundation used to finance that new role.

From the perspective of the competently managed and competitive parachurch organization or the teaching church, and despite the huge unknowns that fill the future in a war on terrorism, the deregulated ecclesiastical marketplace has produced the best of times!

CHAPTER THIRTEEN

What Are the Consequences?

One of the polarizing debates fostered by the new American economy can be summarized in a brief question. Which is the more meaningful criterion in evaluation—the inputs of resources or the outcomes?

The most highly visible example was how investors evaluated ecommerce. One group placed a high value on an input called customers. It was widely assumed in the 1995–99 era that building a huge customer base was the best road to profitabilty. By early 2000, however, more and more investors concluded the most meaningful yardstick for calculating the value of an ecommerce company was an outcome described by that old-fashioned word profits.

In the early 1990s denominational officials called for allocating more money to plant new missions. By the late 1990s the donors of those dollars were beginning to ask what happened to those new missions? How many are strong, vital, and growing churches? How many closed before their tenth birthday?

In the 1980s and early 1990s one criterion for evaluating a public school system was the annual dollar expenditures per student. A second was the salary schedule for the teachers. A third was the academic credentials earned by the teachers. Another was the quality of the buildings. A fifth was voter support in a referendum to raise school taxes.

By 1999 the emphasis had begun to shift from inputs to attempts to measure outcomes. What proportion of the high school graduates went on to college? What proportion of those who did were required to take remedial work in writing, reading, and mathematics? How do the eighth grade students compare with eighth graders in other schools in standardized achievement tests? What proportion of today's fourth graders read at or above grade level? Should teachers' salaries reflect what the students have learned?

The new American economy places a lower value on inputs and a higher value on outcomes. One consequence is a demand for valid criteria to measure outcomes. Another is charitable dollars tend to go to institutions and causes that have been producing the desired outcomes. A third is to redesign budgeting systems to focus on desired or anticipated outcomes. Performance is moving ahead of the sales pitch that focuses on the need for money as as a powerful motivating factor in the competition for the charitable dollar.

The big push for measuring outcomes came in early 2001, following the creation of the White House Office of Faith-Based and Community Initiatives nine days after George W. Bush was inaugurated as President of the United States. The first director of that new agency, John J. Dilulio, made it clear that he was committed to measuring outcomes. The big shock came with the discovery that was a new idea! The body of respected, scholarly, and peer reviewed research that measures the outcomes of religious efforts to solve social problems does not exist. Do faith-based organizations excel in delivering social services to the needy? No one really knows.

Thus far the evaluations have been highly subjecrive and most fall into the "feel good about it" category. The closest we have to a reliance on an objective data-based evaluation on the performance of congregations can be summarized in one question. Are the numbers going up or down? That immediately raises a subjective question. Which numbers are most important? Worship attendance? Dollar receipts? New converts to Christianity? Dollars sent to denominational headquarters? Baptisms? Sunday school attendance? Number of teenagers involved at least twice weekly? Proportion of receipts allocated to missions? How many lives were transformed last year?

It is possible that the greatest impact of the new American economy on the churches will be a demand for specific, objective, and measurable criteria for congregational self-evaluation. This is one more reason those who believe in accountability describe these the best of times.

A Transfer of Influence

Two of the distinctive characteristics of the new American economy consist of an unprecedented and growing array of choices offered Americans plus the increased level of competition among those supplying goods and services.

In Fort Myers, Florida; Rockford, Illinois; St. Paul, Minnesota; Seattle, Washington; and scores of other cities across America, parents have a tax-funded choice when the time comes to enroll their child in a public school.

One consequence is a very large number of bewildered parents. They have had zero experience in making such a decision. As a result many parents choose the route of least effort and pick the closest public school. Others shop. A growing number invest a huge amount of time and energy in an effort to become exceptionally well-informed consumers.

In the old American economy the producers of educational services, the officials of the local public school district, decided where each child would go to school.

Most economists agree that in a highly competitive and efficient free market, a relatively small number of well-informed shoppers spread the word. They feed the grapevine on what they have concluded are the best motor vehicles, the worse supermarkets, the best dentists, the worst restaurants, the best child care centers, the worst airlines, the best handyman for home repairs, the worst high schools, the best kindergartens, the worst hospitals, and the best churches. One consequence is that the well -informed, or the most self-assured, consumers are replacing the producers of goods and services as powerful influences in the marketplace.

Another consequence is this consumer-driven competition has transformed the marketing practices of public schools, churches, and hospitals as they seek to build a new constituency. One facet of that is the effort to make the producer-controlled web site more influential than the grapevine or the counsel of a small number of well-informed consumers.

The Bar Has Been Raised!

In April 2001, Catherine Ndereba of Kenya was the first woman to cross the finish line in the Boston Marathon. Her time was 2 hours, 23 minutes and 53 seconds. That compared to Lisa Weidenbach's time of 2:34:06 in 1985. Ms. Weidenbach's victory also was the last time an American finished first among the women in that historic race. Ms. Ndereba's time was better than that of Franjo Mihalu's 2:25:54 in 1958 when he finished first in that year's marathon. Back in the 1927–38 era, the winners of the Boston Marathon all required more than 2 ½ hours to complete the race. In recent years the winners beat those times by twenty minutes.

How much money is required to finance a competitive political campaign to be elected President of the United

States? To be elected to a seat in the House of Representatives? A whole lot more than was required in the 1980s!

What is the level of competence required of a teacher to hold the undivided attention of a class of twenty-eight high school seniors for fifty minutes? A far higher level of competence than was required in the pre-television world!

Who is the chief competitor for this Protestant congregation founded in 1897 to serve a farming community constituency? That white frame building is located in the open country six miles from a small town with 300 residents. As recently as 1950 that village included two grocery stores, a gasoline station, a bank, an elementary school, a high school, a lodge hall, two taverns, a hardware store, a blacksmith shop, the local telephone exchange , a postoffice, and three churches. Only one of those three village churches was seen as a potential competitor for the loyalty of the constituents of that open country church.

Today the list of competitors includes at least five other congregations, all at least ten miles away, but each within twenty minutes' driving time.

When the viable choices for churchgoers in that rural community increases from two to seven, what happens? The quality and the relevance of the ministry has to be raised a notch or two to be competitive.

The impact of this increased competition can be seen in the distribution of congregations by size. In the Presbyterian Church (U.S.A.), for example, 908 congregations reported an average worship attendance between 21 and 30 in 1999, up from 857 in 1990. By contrast, the number of larger PCUSA congregations reporting an average worship attendance of 101 to 500 decreased by nearly 8 percent, from 3,740 in 1990 to 3,457 in 1999. The number reporting an average worship attendance of more than 500 decreased slightly from 258 in 1990 to 252 in 1999.

Several other denominations, in which the vast majority of today's congregations trace their origins back to before 1960, report similar trends. This runs counter to the larger trend which finds an increasing proportion of younger Protestant churchgoers worshiping with large congregations. The bar has been raised in what is required to be competitive in professional sports, in retail trade, in the education of children born after 1980, in health care, in attracting new generations of churchgoers, in attracting viewers to a television newscast, in manufacturing and selling motor vehicles, in motels and hotels, in public restrooms, in library service, in selling books, and in competing for that growing quantity of charitable dollars.

One consequence of the new ecclesiastical culture is the competition from the thousands of new Protestant congregations launched during the 1990s and the emergence of hundreds of new nondenominational megachurches. This means younger generations of churchgoers have far more choices as they search for a church home than were available to older generations.

Disappointment + Affluence = Litigation

Perhaps the most predictable consequence of the new American economy is a product of two factors. One is the higher expectations consumers bring to the marketplace. The other is more deep pockets. The deeper the pockets, the greater the incentive to sue. (This is one reason why the United States leads the world in the number of lawyers per 1,000 residents!) The higher the level of expectations, the greater the disappointment when those expectations are not met. One natural, normal, and predictable consequence is an increase in litigation. The defendants include physicians who do not always produce miracle cures, realtors, Roman Catholic dioceses, therapists, public safety departments, hospitals, parents of teenagers guilty of serious crimes, financial institutions, public school districts, commercial airlines, and hundreds of others engaged in providing person-centered services.

One consequence is liability insurance has become a standard line item in congregational budgets. Another is the doctrine of ascending liability may be the greatest threat to the future of traditional denominational systems.

That Fourth Economy

If the contemporary debate over measuring inputs versus examining outcomes is the most polarizing debate in public education, the stock market, government, and the churches, a close second is the place of entertainment. Entertainment and memorable and meaningful participatory experiences have become integral components of the American culture. This is transforming the workplace, traditional approaches to education, retail trade, professional sports, the design of single family homes, journalism, military service, television, the design of resort hotels, air travel, vacations, the delivery of health care, family reunions, retirement villages, and "how we do church."

Federalism or Centralization?

In 1776 the American colonies united in a war for their independence from what at the time was the most powerful nation in the world. Twelve of the thirteen colonies ratified the Articles of Confederation shortly after the Congress had approved them, but another 42 months dragged by before the compromises necessary to win the approval of Maryland were made. The Articles of Confederation guaranteed each state "its sovereignty, freedom, and independence." The absence of the right of the Continental Congress to levy and collect taxes or to compel the states to obey the nation's laws led to the adoption of a stronger centralized government under the new Constitution adopted in 1787.

Another one hundred sixty years that included several crucial decisions by the United States Supreme Court, the Civil War, a half dozen amendments to the Constitution, and the New Deal of the Franklin D. Roosevelt era had to pass before the United States had a truly strong central government. Some readers will extend that period of time to include the civil rights movement of the 1960s.

For more than four decades following the end of World War II and the beginning of the cold war, France and Germany moved to an ever closer partnership. One of the motivations was a fear of the Soviet Union. More recently they were united by their common disagreements with the United States.

By 2001, however, the growth of support for the European Union began to drive a wedge between those two industrialized nations. The French clearly favored a relationship similar to the Articles of Confederation. The Germans wanted a strong centralized government with a parliament, a chief executive office, and a centralized bureaucracy. With each passing year those two partners have moved farther apart on this issue. The threat of terrorism, however, has narrowed the political gap between France and Germany while widening it between Great Britain and France.

Beginning with the Great Society programs of the administration of President Lyndon B. Johnson, the United States has moved in the direction of the decentralization of governmental responsibilities. Examples include the growing number of states relying on sales taxes and gambling for revenues, block financial grants by the federal government to states, counties, and municipalities, a variety of decisions by the United States Supreme Court, the welfare-to-work program, Medicaid, federal aid to public schools, and the allocation of federal tax dollars to nongovernmental organizations to implement programs formerly carried out by governmental agencies (see chap. 7).

Black Tuesday 2001 interrupted that trend. The response to that attack called for a shift back toward greater centralization. At this writing it is too early to predict whether that will be temporary or only a blip on the radar screen describing 2020.

Similar trends in decentralization can be seen in the restructuring of large for-profit corporations, the administration of state systems of higher education, and the use of the electronic information highway.

This is far from a settled issue, however! The differences in values and goals between those favoring greater centralization and those demanding more decentralization has generated a huge variety of adversarial relationships. One pits states and local governments against Washington. Another is the quarrel between the four big national television networks and their local affiliates. A third is between parents and the professional educators who administer the public schools. A fourth is between automobile manufacturers and new car dealers. Another is the Democrats versus the Republicans. Another is between health care providers and the third party payers.

One consequence of these adversarial relationships is a large number of litigators agree these truly are the best of times!

What will the next two decades bring to the American ecclesiastical landscape? Three trends are clear. One is the normal, natural, and predictable bureaucratic pressures for greater centralization. This can be seen in the Evangelical Lutheran Church in America, the United Methodist Church, the Presbyterian Church (U.S.A.), the Southern Baptist Convention, the Episcopal Church, and a dozen other American religious traditions.

A second pattern is the emergence of highly divisive adversarial relationships between congregations and/or regional judicatories and the officials of national denominational systems.

A third trend is attributed to the new information age. For decades change usually was initiated by large organizations, often with a centralized command and control system of governance. One example was the revolution in American agriculture in the middle third of the twentieth century. It was initiated by the United States Department of Agriculture. Another was the consolidation of public schools in the 1930-1960 era. A third was the revolution in the sale of meats and groceries also beginning in the 1930s.

In recent years the most innovative changes in the American economy have been initiated by individuals and fed by that increasingly competitive marketplace. On the ecclesiastical landscape the two most highly visible examples are the new nondenominational megachurches and the new religious movements.

One consequence of this new source of innovation is the increasing number of Christian churchgoers born after 1960 who can be found in disproportionately large numbers in congregations that are fully and completely autonomous and self-governing. These are frequently referred to as "independent" or nondenominational churches or as partners in a new religious movement.

Who will prevail in this contest between centralization and localism? The national denominational leaders born before 1950? Or the churchgoers born after 1960? Which age cohort will be casting the decisive votes in this contest in 2025?

What Will Tomorrow Bring?

During the late 1980s it was widely assumed the arrival of the personal computer would produce the paperless office. Paper, like quill pens, would become an artifact of the past. This signaled the coming of the worst of times for

Canada's paper industry. Canada was and is the world's largest exporter of office printing paper. In 1986 exports totaled slightly over 200,000 metric tons of cut office paper.

What was the impact of the computer? The technological revolution ushered in the best of times for the manufacturers of white office paper! In 2000 Canadian paper exports came to 520,000 metric tons! Those fax machines, computer-driven printers, and plain paper copy machines had to be fed. Books, sometimes described as "dead trees wrapped in cowhides," still have a market.

Most major changes produce unanticipated future consequences. All we know for certain today is the context for ministry in the year 2025 will have changed substantially from what it is now. What are the current trends that will shape the context for ministry in 2025? Here are seven guesses.

1. The war on terrorism may drag on for several years. The most rapidly increasing expenditures, and the least productive in terms of raising the standard of living, will be for security, both public and private. Instead of allocating more dollars for education, health care, housing for the poor, care of the national park system, raising the level of productivity in this nation's manufacturing facilities, or improving transportation, those dollars will be allocated to the protection of people and property and to the war effort.

What will be the impact on church finances?

2. It now appears the babies born in the 1970s and early 1980s represent a more heterogeneous and diverse collection of people than any previous age cohort. That obviously is true in the United States, but it also appears to be the pattern in Iran, Germany, Australia, Brazil, Russia, Japan, Mexico, Pakistan, Korea, China, and dozens of other countries. What will be the goals, values, lifestyles, and expectations of the forty- and fifty-year-olds of 2025? How will they differ from the forty- and fifty-year-olds of today?

What expectations will they have of government? Of the churches? Of employers? Of the economy?

3. On the American ecclesiastical scene the twentieth century was marked by dozens of denominational mergers. Will the contemporary intradenominational quarrels mean the early decades of the twenty-first century will be marked by schisms?

4. The past few decades brought a huge increase in the number of weeknight and weekday Bible study groups. Most of these are composed of adults who are members of the same congregation. Most meet either in homes or in church buildings.

Will a substantial proportion of the weekday Bible study groups meeting in 2025 bring together people from several different congregations plus individuals who are not regular churchgoers? Will public school buildings and commercial office buildings be among the most common meeting places for these groups?

5. Between those two Black Tuesdays the United States changed the world by exporting technology, food, entertainment, jobs, safe places to invest one's savings, education, military forces, hundreds of billions of dollars in financial aid, Peace Corps volunteers, Christian missionaries, tourists, construction crews, Bibles, medical assistance, and economic advice.

Will the most influential exports of the United States during the next few decades be representative democracy, human rights, a free enterprise economic system, the individual's right to self-determination, and the separation of religion and government?

6. Several demographers currently predict the United States is changing from the day when the vast majority of Americans traced their ancestry back to western Europe. The new scenario suggests the United States is well on the way to becoming a nation populated by a variety of population clusters including Asian Americans, African

Americans, Latin Americans, Euro-Americans, Arab Americans, Native Americans, and other hyphenated groups.

Will the hyphen be more common in 2025? Or will intercultural marriages, patriotism, education, economic assimilation, the Internet, and television decrease the use of that hyphen?

7. The past three decades have brought (a) a sharp increase in the number of American Protestant congregations averaging fewer than twenty-five at worship (including thousands of new lay-led house churches), (b) in percentage terms, an even greater increase in the number averaging more than 800 at worship, and (c) a decrease in the number averaging 100 to 200 at worship.

What will be the dominant trend during the next two or three decades? The one safe prediction is 2025 will not be a clone of 2002!

NOTES

Introduction

1. An interesting effort to recapture the culture of 1929 in the United States is Maury Klein, *Rainbow's End: The Crash of 1929* (New York: Oxford University Press, 2001).

2. Jim Collins, *Good to Great* (San Francisco: Harper, 2001), line one of page 1 of the first chapter.

3. This human need for a stability zone in a time of discontinuity was first impressed on me by Alvin Toffler, *Future Shock* (New York: Random House, 1970), 335-39. I am now convinced that most human-led institutions also need a stability zone when confronted with change. One example is the regional judicatory that is ideologically progressive and institutionally conservative.

1. From Black Tuesday to Black Tuesday

1. B. Joseph Pine II and James H. Gilmore, *The Experience Economy* (Boston: Harvard Business School Press, 1999).

2. Lyle E. Schaller, *What Have We Learned?* (Nashville: Abingdon Press, 2001), 119-23.

3. David Moss, *When All Else Fails* (Publisher yet to be identified.)

4. Hernando de Soto, *The Mystery of Capital: Why Capitalism Triumphs in the West and Fails Everywhere Else* (New York: Basic Books, 2001).

5. Peter Drucker, "The World Is Full of Options," Foreword in Bob Buford, *Stuck in Halftime* (Grand Rapids: Zondervan, 2001), 9.

6. Anthony Beevor, *Stanlingrad* (New York: Viking Penguin, 1998), 428.

7. This issue is discussed in Lyle E. Schaller, *The Evolution of the American Public High School* (Nashville: Abingdon Press, 2000).

8. Paul Johnson, "The Answer to Terrorism? Colonialism," *The Wall Street Journal*, October 9, 2000, A-22.

9. Charles W. Ferguson, *Organizing to Beat the Devil* (Garden City, N.Y.: Doubleday, 1971).

10. Lyle E. Schaller, *Community Organization: Conflict and Reconciliation* (Nashville: Abingdon Press, 1966).

11. William J. Bouwma, *John Calvin* (New York: Oxford University Press, 1988), 204-13.; Francois Wendel, *Calvin* (New York: Harper & Row, 1963), 69-107.

12. Peter S. Field, *The Crisis of the Standing Order* (Amherst, Mass.: University of Massachusetts Press, 1998). Leonard W. Levy, *Origins of the Bill of Rights* (New Haven: Yale University Press, 1999) and Cornelia Hughes Dayton, "Was There a Calvinist Type of Patriarchy?" in *The Many Legalities of Early America*, ed. Christopher L. Tomlins and Bruce H. Mann (Chapel Hill: University of North Carolina Press, 2001), 337-56.

13. Leonard W. Levy, *The Establishment Clause* (Chapel Hill: University of North Carolina Press, 1994), 17-18, 33.

14. Field, *The Crisis of the Standing Order*, 30.

15. Levy, *The Establishment Clause*, 106.

16. David Tyack and Elisabeth Hansot, *Managers of Virtue* (New York: Basic Books, 1982).

17. Among the hundreds of books that describe that long era of anti-Catholicism in American church history, two are especially relevant to this discussion. David Nasaw, *Schooled to Order* (New York: Oxford University Press, 1979), 68-79; and Curtis D. Johnson, *Redeeming America: Evangelicals and the Road to Civil War* (Chicago: Ivan R. Dee, 1993), 9-30, 153-61.

18. For a thoughtful and informed analysis of Islamic miltancy, see Charles A. Kimball, "Roots of Rancor," *The Christian Century*, October 24-31, 2001.

19. Akbor Ahmed and Lawrence Rosen, "Islam, Academe and Freedom of the Mind," *The Chronicle of Higher Education*, November 2, 2001, B11-12.

20. For my introduction to the writings of Sayyid Qutb, I am indebted to Judith Shulevitz, "At War with the World," *The New York Times Book Review*, October 21, 2001, 39.

21. For an explanation of why this should be perceived to be a modern religious war, see Andrew Sullivan, "This Is a Religious War," *The New York Times Magazine*, October 7, 2001, 44ff.

22. Mohammed Ali Jinnah, the founder of Pakistan, married to a wife who was a non-Muslin, was a strong supporter of human rights, women's rights, minority rights, and the rule of law. He hoped Pakistan would model the combination of Islam and human rights. Jinnah was overthrown by an Islamic military coup in 1977.

23. For a brief report on the erosion of the real presence as a line of

demarcation, see James D. Davidson, "Yes, Jesus Is Really There," *Commonwealth,* October 12, 2001, 14-16.

24. An excellent recent summary of the state of religion among middle class suburbanites is Alan Wolfe, *One Nation, After All* (New York: Penguin Books, 1999), 39-87.

3. The Great Debate

1. Quoted in David Nasaw, *Schooled to Order* (New York: Oxford University Press, 1979), 52.

2. Ibid., 53.

3. David Cay Johnson, "Ohio Chapter Head Named United Way President," *The New York Times,* November 6, 2001, A14.

4. In a brief but lucid essay, a college professor writing from a Reformed perspective predicts a continued valuable future role for denominational systems but suggests that will require downsizing and decentralization. Corwin Smidt, "The Future of Denominations," *The Banner,* April 23, 2000, 20-21.

5. Robert T. Carlson, "Where Do We Go from Here?" *The Congregationalist,* August/September 2000, 4-5.

4. Values, Rules and Denial

1. Lyle E. Schaller, *What Have We Learned?* (Nashville: Abingdon Press, 2001), 109-18.

2. See Michael S. Hamilton, "We're in the Majority: How Did Evangelicals Get So Wealthy and What Has It Done to Us?" *Christianity Today,* June 12, 2000, 36-43.

3. Quoted in Mark Schmitt, "Torments of Liberalism," *The American Prospect,* December 4, 2000, 42.

4. Daniel Yankelovich, *The Magic of Dialogue: Transforming Conflict into Cooperation* (New York: Simon & Schuster, 1999).

5. See Schaller, *What Have We Learned?* 119-30.

6. The Two New Economies

1. B. Joseph Pine II and James H. Gilmore, *The Experience Economy* (Boston: Harvard Business School Press 1999).

2. The pioneering research on the size of high schools is Roger G. Barker and Paul V. Gump, *Big School, Small School* (Stanford, Calif.: Stanford University Press, 1964).

3. Lyle E. Schaller, *The Evolution of the American Public High School: From Prep School to Prison to New Partnerships* (Nashville: Abingdon Press, 2000).

4. Kathleen Hall Jamieson, *Eloquence in an Electronic Age* (New York: Oxford University Press, 1986).

5. Nick Morgan, "The Kinesthetic Speaker: Putting Action into Words," *Harvard Business Review*, April 2001, 113-20.

7. The New Face of Philanthropy

1. David Barstow, "In Congress Harsh Words for Red Cross," *The New York Times*, November 7, 2001, B1 and 7.

2. An early reference report is Douglas W. Johnson, *North American Interchurch Study* (New York: National Council of the Churches of Christ in the U.S.A., 1971).

3. An early introduction to the spread of distrust of institutions and the rise of individualism is Herbert J. Gans, *Middle American Individualism* (New York: Oxford University Press, 1988), 107-15.

4. Conrad Cherry, *Hurrying Toward Zion* (Bloomington: Indiana University Press, 1995).

5. Theda Schocpol, *Protecting Soldiers and Mothers* (Cambridge, Mass.: Harvard University Press, 1992).

6. David Nasaw, *Schooled to Order: A Social History of Public Schooling in the United States* (New York: Oxford University Press, 1979).

7. Gustav Niebuhr, "A Church Sells Its Silver, and Finds a Silver Lining," *The New York Times*, February 3, 2000, A9.

8. How Many Income Streams?

1. The average salaries for pastors were derived from the Census of Religious Bodies: 1936 conducted by the United States Bureau of the Census (Washington, D.C.: Government Printing Office, 1941), Part 1, 117-45.

9. How Competitive Is This New Ecclesiastical Marketplace?

1. For a challenging essay on this subject by a veteran university professor, see Larry D. Spence, "The Case Against Teaching," *Change*, November/December 2001, 11-19.

2. For a brief introduction to one facet of this competition see David J. Wood, "Where Are the Younger Clergy?" *The Christian Century*, April 10, 2000, 18-19.

3. Lyle E. Schaller, *The Evolution of the American Public High School* (Nashville: Abingdon Press, 2000), 62-96, 173-93.

10. The Impact on Congregations

1. For a brief and lucid introduction to the use of tax dollars to finance Christian churches in the United States, see Leonard W. Levy, *Origins of the Bill of Rights* (New Haven: Yale University Press, 1999), 79-102

2. Robert Moats Miller, *Bishop G. Bromiley Oxnam: Paladin of Liberal Protestantism* (Nashville: Abingdon Press, 1990), 398-446.

3. Quoted from Edwin Scott Gaustad, *A Religious History of America* (New York: Harper & Row, 1966), 56.

4. J. Timothy Ahlen and J. V. Thomas, *One Church, Many Congregations.* (Nashville: Abingdon Press, 1999).

11. The Impact on Denominational Systems

1. Lyle E. Schaller, "The Multisite Option," in *Innovations in Ministry* (Nashville: Abingdon Press, 1994), 112-13.

2. Lyle E. Schaller, "Which Road to Multiculturalism?" in *What Have We Learned?* (Nashville: Abingdon Press, 2001), 197-214.

3. Lyle E. Schaller, "Inputs or Outcomes? Encouraging Creativity in New Church Development," *Net Results,* April 2001, 10-11.

4. Lyle E. Schaller, *The Very Large Church* (Nashville: Abingdon Press, 2000).

5. Two provocative examples of how a regional judicatory can be transformed into a resource ministry are described in Claude E. Payne and Hamilton Beasley, *Reclaiming the Great Commission* (San Francisco: Jossey-Bass, 2000), and B. Carlisle Driggers, *A Journey of Faith and Hope* (Columbia, S.C.: The R. L. Bryan Company, 2000).

6. For those seeking a brief historical introduction to the new American economy, a good place to begin is Robert Handy, "Tocqueville Revisited: The Meaning of American Prosperity," *Harvard Business Review,* January 2001, 3-19.

7. Lyle E. Schaller, *The Evolution of the American Public High School* (Nashville: Abingdon Press, 2000).

8. Ronald Dworkin, *Sovereign Virtue: The Theory and Practice of Equality* (Cambridge, Mass.: Harvard University Press, 2001).

9. The pioneering essay on this trend is Craig Dystra and James Hudnut Beumler, "The National Organizational Structures of Protestant Denominations," ed. Milton J. Coalter, et al., *The Organizational Revolution* (Louisville: Westminster/John Knox Press, 1992), 307-31.

10. Lyle E. Schaller, *Tattered Trust* (Nashville: Abingdon Press, 1996). The historical argument was offered years ago by Willis J. Ballinger, *By Vote of the People* (New York: Charles Scribners, 1946).

11. Schaller, "Which Road to Multiculturalism?"

12. B. Joseph Pine II and James Gilmore, *The Experience Economy* (Boston: Harvard Business School Press, 1999), 188.

12. What Are the Consequences?

1. For one critique of the dismal current state of affairs on evaluations of the performance of faith-based organizations, see Eyal Press, "Lead Us Not into Temptation," *The American Prospect*, April 9, 2001, 20-27. For an academic perspective see Brian Steensland, et al., "The Measure of American Religion: Toward Improving the State of the Art," *Social Forces*, September 2000, 291-318. This pilgrim's contributions include Lyle E. Schaller, *44 Questions for Congregational Self-Evaluation* (Nashville: Abingdon Press, 1998), and Lyle E. Schaller, *The Interventionist* (Nashville: Abingdon Press, 1997).